Sir Walter Scott's
Edinburgh Annual Register

SIR WALTER SCOTT'S
Edinburgh Annual Register

By KENNETH CURRY

The University of Tennessee Press ᑤ *Knoxville*

Library of Congress Cataloging in Publication Data
Curry, Kenneth.
   Sir Walter Scott's Edinburgh annual register.

   Part III, Reprints of uncollected essays of Scott
(p.   ): Prospectus.—Of the living poets of Great
Britain.—Cursory remarks upon the French order of battle,
particularly in the campaigns of Buonaparte.—The inferno
of Altisidora.—On the present state of periodical criticism.—View of the changes proposed and adopted in the
administration of justice in Scotland.
   Includes index.
   1. The Edinburgh annual register. 2. Europe—
History—1789–1900. I. Scott, Walter, Sir, bart., 1771–
1832. II. Title.
D299.C87   082   77-8136
ISBN 0-87049-208-X

To
my friends and colleagues
LeRoy P. Graf
and
Alvin H. Nielsen

Preface

SIR WALTER SCOTT is best known as a novelist and a poet
of wide popularity and influence, but he is no less interesting as
a man of letters whose far-ranging concerns span not only literature but also law (his profession), antiquities and antiquarian
lore, history, literary criticism, editing, and publishing. The
Edinburgh Annual Register admirably reflects these facets of
Scott: it is the purpose of this book to survey the volumes of
the *Register* during the nine years when Scott was active in its
direction, to show the importance and interest of much of its
contents, and to reprint for the first time the rare prospectus
and the five essays by Scott from the *Register* which have never
been reprinted. Scott's penchant for editing and publishing—and
promoting such a work as the *Register*—led directly to his ultimate financial failure and the bankruptcies of the Ballantyne
and Constable firms in 1826. No attempt has been made to
survey the *Register* after the ninth volume (1816, published in
1820) when it passed from Scott's supervision into the hands of
the geographer Hugh Murray, years for which virtually no information has come to light. Even for the years when Scott was
active as promoter and contributor there are still wide gaps in
our knowledge of the *Register* and its contributors. I hope that
students whose familiarity with the byways of Scottish literature
and history is greater than mine will be able to add further details to our record of this interesting—if financially unsuccessful—
adventure in publishing. The *Register* is by no means a rare
periodical. Almost every large library in the United States and
Britain contains a substantial run of its volumes. The *Union List
of Serials in Libraries of the United States* (1965) lists forty-
seven libraries which contain long runs of the *Register.*

I have referred to a few works so many times that a list of
short titles has seemed advisable. These are: *Letters of Scott* for
The Letters of Sir Walter Scott, ed. H. J. C. Grierson (London,
1932–1937), 12 vols.; *Memoir . . . Taylor* for J. W. Robberds,

*A Memoir of the Life and Writings of the Late William Taylor
of Norwich* (London, 1843), 2 vols.; and *Register* for the *Edinburgh Annual Register.*

I have many persons to thank for assistance. I am grateful to
the University of Tennessee and the Department of English for
released time from teaching and departmental chores to enable
me to finish this study begun several years ago. I am also grateful to the Graduate School of the University of Tennessee for a
grant during the summer of 1970. Mr. C. S. Minto, librarian of
the Central Public Library of Edinburgh, sent me a copy of the
rare prospectus to the *Register* missing from most files but
present in that library's copy. The Librarian of Corpus Christi
College, Oxford, sent me a reproduction of perhaps the only
copy of the *Journal of a Levant Pirate,* reprinted by Scott in the
Register (but not reproduced in this study). Professor Galen
Broeker of the Department of History of the University of
Tennessee has helped me with materials and advice for the
political background of the period. My former student, Professor Robert Dedmon of Lenoir-Rhyne College, carefully read the
manuscript and made many valuable suggestions.

The publication of this book has been assisted by a grant from
the John C. Hodges Better English Fund.

KENNETH CURRY

Knoxville, Tennessee
August, 1976

Contents

Part 1

Founding of the *Edinburgh Annual Register*:
Politics and Literature

*T*HE *Edinburgh Annual Register,* a title familiar to every reader acquainted with the works and biography of Sir Walter Scott, led a troubled and often precarious existence for the eighteen years (1810–1828) during which it recorded the history of each year from 1808 to 1826. A publication of the newly founded firm of John Ballantyne and Company, it was first conceived as a competitor and rival to the established and successful *Annual Register,* published in London since 1758, but it failed in this attempt to displace the older *Annual Register* as a standard work of reference, to make a special niche for itself, or to achieve either wide circulation or financial success. In fact, it contributed importantly to the financial difficulties and the eventual bankruptcy of the Ballantyne firm.

Whatever may have been the reasons for the commercial failure of the *Register,* its pages presented, especially during the early years of Scott's active interest, the work of many prominent authors. Robert Southey wrote the historical section for the first four years, amounting to four substantial volumes of several hundred pages each. After Southey retired from this post as annual historian, Scott and John G. Lockhart wrote the historical section for three years (VI–VIII, 1813–1815). In addition to the account of the year's history, the *Register* published —perhaps its most interesting feature—a section devoted to poetry, critical essays, travel notes, and antiquarian lore, usually with a Scottish orientation. For this miscellany Scott himself was chiefly responsible, acting both as prolific contributor and as assiduous collector of contributions from writers such as John Wilson, Joanna Baillie, James Hogg, Robert Surtees, Robert Southey, and John Leyden.

The *Edinburgh Annual Register* consisted of two parts—the first and most essential part was the history of the year. For the first year (1808, published in 1810) this section, called the "History of Europe," contained twenty-three chapters of 459

3

pages, most of it a description of the war against Napoleon with special emphasis upon the war on the Iberian peninsula. Domestic affairs received much less emphasis and were largely presented through quoting the debates in Parliament upon pertinent issues. Part I concluded with a reprint of 100 pages of official letters and documents chiefly concerned with the war. The second part (issued as a second volume) opened with a chronicle of events and statistical tables. The remainder (259 pages) of the second part contained essays and poetry, where Scott's hand is seen both in his own contributions and in the work he solicited from his literary circle. This format was retained for the first nine years until the control of the *Register* passed from Scott's hands to those of Hugh Murray, the geographer.

Despite the literary interest of much of the *Register* and its bibliographical importance for several authors, histories of literature and of literary periodicals (such as Walter Graham's) ignore the publication, while biographies of Scott and Southey mention it only as occasion strictly requires. One reason for the neglect is Scott's own somewhat offhand attitude toward the *Register*. With many more projects than he could ever hope to handle efficiently, Scott only mentioned the work to his correspondents when necessary, remained silent where we would like him to give details, and, with his characteristic love of mystification and anonymity for some (at least) of his works, even on occasion disclaimed knowledge of his own contributions. He may also have thought some so slight as not to be worth claiming. This reluctance of Scott to discuss the *Register*'s concerns is revealed in the confusion of such a simple fact as the identity of the editor. Both *The Cambridge Bibliography of English Literature* and *The Dictionary of National Biography* (s.v. Southey) list Southey as the editor, but Lowndes' *Bibliographer's Manual* and the catalog of the Library of Congress say Scott. Yet the letters of Scott and Southey clearly show that James Ballantyne was the editor, although it was quite evident that Scott frequently countermanded Ballantyne's orders and made many, perhaps most, of the editorial decisions. As Scott phrased it in a letter of December 30, 1808: "Mr. Ballantyne, the editor, only undertakes for the inferior departments of the work, and for keeping the whole matter in train" (*Letters of Scott* II, 144).

The purposes of this study are threefold: to tell the story of its origin and publication in order to rescue the *Register* from its almost complete oblivion; to identify some of the contributors; and to reprint several essays by Scott which have been neither collected nor reprinted hitherto. The materials for such a study are full, although not full enough to enable us to answer every question or clear up every mystery about authorship or provenance of every selection. Scott's letters, the correspondence of Archibald Constable, both published and in his letterbooks in the National Library of Scotland, Southey's letters, and the pages of the *Register* itself—these yield most of what is essential.

Beginning and History of the *Register*

The idea of a new annual register to be published in Edinburgh to challenge the supremacy of the long-established *Annual Register* published in London came not from Scott but from William Davies of the firm of Cadell and Davies, who first proposed it to A. G. Hunter, who passed on the suggestion to his partner, Archibald Constable, in a letter of March 18, 1807: "I have just come from Cadell and Davies, both of whom I have seen; and Mr. D. has been proposing to me that we should sound our friends to see whether a new Annual Register might not be started by them and us (or rather *us* and *them,* as he said), under the title of The Edinburgh Annual Register,—Messrs. Brougham, Horner, Allan, etc. to be the writers, *and their friends.*"[1] Constable replied promptly but cautiously on March 22: "The plan of an Edinburgh Annual Register, so far as I have yet considered it, I confess is not unpromising; but we need not think of getting either Horner or Brougham to engage in it. I shall however consult with Mr. Jeffrey and Mr. Thomson, and see what they think of the scheme. The great difficulty would be to get a proper editor, for I am convinced the success of such a work would depend entirely upon its execution."[2] Hunter answered on March 25, after having seen Scott and learned in turn of Scott's plan

---

1. Thomas Constable, *Archibald Constable and His Literary Correspondents* (Edinburgh, 1873), I, 111.
2. Ibid., I, 117.

for a literary and antiquarian miscellany—called either *Rhada-manthus* or the *British Librarian.*

> I am very happy you think so well of the scheme about the Annual Register. I saw Walter Scott yesterday, and mentioned it to him in strict confidence; and I am happy to say he approves most highly of our plan, and says that if a proper editor and conductor be got it will do most famously, and that it can be so well subdivided among all the proper and right folks. He has a scheme of an antiquarian repository along with young Rose, Ellis, Canning, etc. and he says that one of these works will assist the other and go hand in hand. I completely agree with you that it is out of the question to attempt getting Horner to do anything, except to give his advice and countenance to it; but I confess I do not see what should hinder Brougham from being the most active operator of the whole. He has nothing very material other-ways to prevent him, and he is, in short, the very man I should look for as editor.[3]

Hunter and Constable, unable to gain the support of those already actively engaged in the *Edinburgh Review,* abandoned the idea of a new annual register at this time. Scott, however, had not forgotten the project, and one year later revived the idea for himself and for the publishing firm of John Ballantyne and Company—excluding Constable from the project.

In 1808 Scott made drastic changes in many of his personal and business arrangements. His business transactions with the Constable firm had been growing more and more strained, especially his relationship with Constable's partner, A. G. Hunter, who was often tactless and insufficiently deferential. Scott's association with the *Edinburgh Review,* of which Constable was the publisher, also grew more difficult and culminated in Jeffrey's sharply worded review of *Marmion* in the issue of April 1808. In politics, under the influence of Jeffrey and Brougham, the *Review* was definitely allying itself with the Whig interest— some persons even thinking the Jacobin. The same issue that contained the depreciatory review of *Marmion* also contained an article on the Spanish situation, which threw doubts upon the fighting ability of the new allies in Spain, and asserted the futility of pursuing the struggle against Napoleon. The result of these twin irritations—personal and political—led Scott to break completely with the *Review* and its sponsors.

3. Ibid., I, 119.

At this point, John Murray, the enterprising young publisher of London, made a trip to Ashestiel in October 1808 to enlist Scott's aid in support of the newly projected *Quarterly Review,* designed to support the ministerial party and to counter the opposition influence of the *Edinburgh Review.* Scott declined the editorship, but promised his active support and contributed seven articles during the first year. At this same time Scott remembered the abandoned idea of an Edinburgh annual register, and during the same month wrote to George Ellis: "Another bomb is about to break on him [Constable] besides the Review. This is an Edinburgh Annual Register, to be conducted under the auspices of James Ballantyne, who is himself no despicable composer, and has secured excellent assistance. I cannot help him, of course, very far, but I will certainly lend him a lift as an adviser. I want all my friends to befriend this work, and will send you a *prospectus* when it is published. It will be *valde* anti-Foxite. This is a secret for the present."[4] Scott may have thought of himself only in a subsidiary or advisory role, but his disclaimer of active assistance and management is belied by the numerous and continual references to the *Register* both during its planning stages and its early years as he sought contributions and recommended the annual to his correspondents.

On December 13, 1808, Scott wrote again to Ellis in great enthusiasm for the new *Register* and of those who had been engaged. In the light of later developments it seems doubtful that the persons mentioned as having agreed to undertake departments in the new work had made firm commitments as there is no evidence that they ever contributed. He relates his plans for the new work to his personal and political dissatisfactions:

I have many reasons for favouring this work as much as I possibly can. In the first place, there is nothing even barely tolerable of this nature, though so obviously necessary to future history. Secondly, Constable was on the point of arranging one on the footing of the Edinburgh Review, and subsidiary thereunto,—a plan which has been totally disconcerted by our occupying the vantage-ground. Thirdly, this work will be very well managed. The two Mackenzies, William Erskine, *cum plurimis aliis,* are engaged in the literary department, and that of science is conducted by Professor Leslie, a great philosopher, and as abominable an animal as I ever saw. He writes, however, with great eloquence, and

4. *Letters of Scott* II, 129.

is an enthusiast in mathematical, chemical, and mineralogical pursuits. I hope to draw upon you in this matter, particularly in the historical department, to which your critical labours will naturally turn your attention. You will ask what I propose to do myself. In fact, though something will be expected, I cannot propose to be very active unless the Swift is abandoned. . . I have some reason to believe that Ballantyne . . . will commence publisher.[5]

The plans, bravely outlined in this letter, did not all come to pass. The firm of John Ballantyne and Company, however, did commence in 1809, and the *Register,* in an evil day for that firm's future solvency, appeared under its imprint. Constable would have had every right to feel aggrieved that the project he had mentioned to Scott one year earlier was to be published under rival sponsorship, and it may be this matter to which Ballantyne refers in a letter to Murray of March 1809: "Constable, I am told, has consulted Sir Samuel Romilly and means, after writing a book against me, to prosecute me for *stealing his plans*! Somebody has certainly stolen his brains! "[6] The prospectus appeared in December, but like all too much of the work for the *Register* it was hastily done and instead of promising what might reasonably be attained included a little of everything for everyone. Scott admitted to Ellis that it was in "too stately a tone."[7] The proposed work was to include in addition to the "History of Europe," the collection of state papers, and the chronicle of remarkable events, biographies, histories of literature, science, the fine arts, the useful arts (engineering and technology), meteorology, and various statistical tables. Since most of the features promised in the prospectus were not included in the first volume, the preface to that volume had to be written in a very excusatory style. Some of the features, however, did appear in subsequent volumes. This "Advertisement" to the first volume for 1808—the advertisement is dated July 21, 1810—explained the delay in the appearance of the first volume as "from

---

5. Ibid., II, 134–35.

6. Samuel Smiles, *A Publisher and His Friends* (London, 1891), I, 148. This suggestion comes from Oliver F. Emerson in his article, "The Early Literary Life of Sir Walter Scott," *Journal of English and Germanic Philology,* 22 (1924), 415–16. Emerson's excuse for Scott's action is: "Doubtless Scott, who had been told in confidence of Constable's plan, justified his somewhat unethical procedure by his intense and sincere patriotism."

7. *Letters of Scott* II, 140.

the unexpected necessity of looking round, at a late period, for contributions, which they had all reasonable grounds to believe they had secured from the commencement of their plan."[8] This apologetic tone was prophetic of the troubles and disappointments that were to plague the proprietors of the *Register.*

Scott was aware that it was of the greatest importance to have the history of the year done by a capable hand. The miscellaneous essays, the chronicle, and the various statistical tables and reprints of documents were only incidental to the main work. Scott first turned to Charles Kirkpatrick Sharpe, his antiquarian friend, and sent him this outline of what needed to be done:

> But the historical department is that in which I would chiefly wish to see you engaged. A lively luminous picture of the events of the last momentous year, is a task for the pen of a man of genius; as for materials, I could procure you access to many of a valuable kind. The appointments of our historian are £300 a year—no deaf nuts. Another person has been proposed, and written to, but I cannot any longer delay submitting the thing to your consideration. Of course, you are to rely on every assistance that can be afforded by your humble comdumble, as Swift says. I hope the great man will give us his answer shortly—and if his be negative, pray let yours be positive.[9]

Sharpe declined the post, and in August 1809 a historian was found in Robert Southey, who welcomed the £400 per volume for the financial security it would bring—"it will make me altogether at ease in my circumstances"[10] was the way he phrased it to his friend John Rickman, who was to provide him with abundant materials for the task and even to write a few pages of the second volume. Southey proved a willing and able coadjutor, promptly going to work collecting documents and writing assiduously until May 30, 1810, when he was able to report that the history for the first volume was complete and that he was then turning to the second.

Once the decision concerning the historian of the *Register* was made, Scott and the Ballantynes went their respective ways. Scott was busy writing poems—*Rokeby* and *The Lord of the Isles,* editing Swift, and suggesting publishing ventures, most of

---

8. I, i, i–ii.
9. *Letters of Scott* II, 143–44. Dec. 30, 1808.
10. C. C. Southey, *The Life and Correspondence of the Late Robert Southey* (London, 1849–50), II, 273.

them to be financial failures, for the publishing firm of John Ballantyne and Company of which he was a silent partner. For the rest of 1809 and most of 1810 Scott is silent in his letters about the *Register,* but when the work was published, he attempted to promote an awareness of the *Register's* existence by writing to his friends: "Have you read the Edinr. Register?. . . Have you seen a periodical work called the Edinr. Annual Register."[11]

The greatest difficulty in following with any chronological minuteness the fortunes of the *Register* lies in the fact that it was—and certainly significantly so—a relatively minor interest of both Scott and the Ballantynes. As the deadline for publication drew near, Scott and James Ballantyne must have worked together on the final copy, Scott supplying deficiencies by writing either an essay or by inserting bits of antiquarian lore and poems either solicited by him or submitted by their authors for publication in the *Register.* Several of these essays and poems are directly traceable to Scott. Every volume of the *Register* has a certain air, if not of desperation, at least of hurried, last-minute arrangements.

Scott continued, along with his other literary projects and his constant concern over the development of Abbotsford, to cater for the *Register,* contributing and putting in a good word for it wherever he could. But the work was not selling, and it proved to be a considerable loss, one that John Ballantyne and Company could ill afford. The other publishers associated with Ballantyne were growing disenchanted, and on December 5, 1812, John Murray withdrew, resigning his one-twelfth share with the forthright comment that "after making every effort to serve the book, I can be of no further use; and therefore you will not consider me as having any concern with the future publication of that work."[12]

From the beginning the *Edinburgh Annual Register* was doomed as a financial undertaking. The *Annual Register* published in London was an established and successful enterprise

11. *Letters of Scott* II, 382, 392. Oct. 3 and 15, 1810.

12. Smiles, I, 196. According to Southey the London booksellers were not interested in selling the *Register,* and he attributed its failure "to the London booksellers, who being almost all concerned with the other two, by every possible means impeded its sale; so that where ten copies sell in Scotland, scarcely one is sold in England." *Selections from the Letters of Robert Southey,* ed. J. W. Warter (London, 1856), II, 321. Apr. 24, 1813.

with an unbroken series of annual volumes since 1758, and its subscribers would have needed compelling reasons to change their allegiance. A new publication in order to undercut the old would have had to be distinctively better in all its departments: a comparison of the first issue of the *Edinburgh Annual Register* with its rival shows that it was not superior. Not only was the Ballantyne work in competition with the *Annual Register* but also with the *New Annual Register,* published in London by John Stockdale and a close imitation of the original. A comparison of these two *Registers* for 1807 with the first volume of the *Edinburgh Annual Register* shows that the older rivals contained much more material on natural history as well as many extracts from new books of travel, science, and personal memoirs.

We have already noted that the emphasis of the *Edinburgh Annual Register* was political with a major purpose that of counterbalancing the Whig influence of the *Edinburgh Review,* especially in lending support to the war against Napoleon. It was, however, the *Quarterly Review,* founded in the same year with ministerial backing and modeling its format upon that of the *Edinburgh Review,* that successfully challenged the supremacy of its rival with rewards for its backers, both popular and pecuniary. The *Edinburgh Annual Register* should be seen principally as a rival to the *Annual Register* and not to the *Edinburgh Review.* Conceivably, readers might subscribe to both the *Quarterly* and the *Edinburgh,* but who would care to have two annual registers? No one—which is to say the two Ballantynes and Scott—ever really thought out a competitive plan for the *Register* nor laid a strategy for its success. By way of contrast, the *Quarterly* had in William Gifford an editor who devoted his chief energies to this business and exercised his editorial blue pencil freely over every contribution to each issue. John Murray, the publisher of the *Quarterly,* was the most astute publisher of the era and took a day-to-day interest in the routine of the review's business. How differently were the affairs of the *Register* conducted! James Ballantyne, the editor, and Scott both looked upon it as a part-time affair, and John Ballantyne and Company, starting with inadequate capital and rapidly acquiring a large list of unsalable titles, could not promote the *Register* with vigor.

The business history of the *Register* is involved with the complicated affairs of Scott, the Ballantyne brothers, and Archibald

Constable. Scott was the silent partner in the two firms of James
Ballantyne and Company (the printers) and John Ballantyne and
Company (the publishers) and certainly made the important
decisions about the business. All three worked closely together
in all facets of their enterprises, and it is difficult to distinguish
their separate responsibilities. Scott's efforts as contributor,
part-time editor, and promoter are all part of the commercial
side of his life and especially the secrecy with which his involve-
ment as a silent partner with the Ballantyne firms was shrouded.
Eighteen thirteen was a difficult year financially for everyone,
and Scott and the Ballantynes were not exempt. Distress was
widespread, bankruptcies were frequent, and credit was difficult
to find. Such financially insecure a publishing firm as John Ballantyne and Company would have had great trouble riding out
the storm. The result was that Scott approached Constable for
assistance. Constable was delighted to have Scott back since he
was a best-selling author, and he agreed to take over the stock
of the publishing firm but on the condition that its affairs be
terminated. The *Register* appears to have been the single heaviest
loser on the Ballantyne list. The letters of Scott and Constable
contain numerous references to the *Register,* and the reason for
Scott's assumption of the role of historian for the two years of
1814 and 1815 was the feeling that his name, when known as
the writer of the "History of Europe," would not only sell the
current issues but also enable Constable to sell complete sets of
the work and recoup some of the losses he had assumed when he
agreed to help in selling off the Ballantyne stock. Looking back
upon the whole affair, one is surprised that Constable should
have continued the *Register,* but its final abandonment did not
come until 1826 when a more serious financial crisis than that
of 1813 involved not only the Ballantynes and Scott but also
Constable himself in bankruptcy.

Scattered references in the Scott and Constable correspondence
indicate that for the first eight years 3,000 copies of the *Register*
were printed annually, but that Constable reduced the number
to about 2,000 since its sale had not exceeded that number.[13]

13. The circulation of periodicals during the early nineteenth century was very
small compared to the large figures achieved later in the century. According to R. D.
Altick, *The English Common Reader* (Chicago, 1957), App. C (pp. 391–96), the
weekly *Examiner* had 2,200; the *Monthly Magazine* had between 3,000 and 4,000;
the *British Critic* and *Critical Review,* 3,500; the *Universal Magazine,* 1,750. The

The 1817 volume had only 1,750 copies printed, and later volumes may have had even smaller editions. After 1813 Constable devoted considerable effort to selling for almost any price the accumulated sets of the *Register* and usually attempted to tie in their sale with the more salable Scott titles. After the eighth volume three years elapsed between its publication and that of the ninth. In 1823 the three-year gap was filled by the publication of three volumes in one year, but by this time Scott had no further connection with the work and the volumes were much reduced in size.

One consequence of the financial crisis of 1813 was the loss of Southey as writer of the "History of Europe." The details as set forth in the correspondence of Southey are obscure, but Southey had been promised £400 per volume and was later given a share in the profits of the first volume as a bonus. The payment for the year 1811 (published in 1813) was not forthcoming, and the evidence indicates that he was never paid the full sum for his work for that year. Southey withdrew from the *Register* with the comment that he ceased to write for the *Register* because it ceased to pay him. In 1815 he reported that he was still not paid for this work, and in 1818 the business was settled after a fashion with a payment of about one half of what was due.[14]

After the two-year stint of James Russell[15] as the historian of the year, Scott himself undertook the task. In the absence of any but casual references to the *Register* in Scott's correspondence one can only conjecture concerning the reasons for his assump-

---

Register, however, made the mistake of printing more copies than could be sold. References to these problems will be found in *Letters of Scott* I, 417, 453, 473, 496; III, 267, 285; and in the published correspondence of Archibald Constable. Constable's Letter Book in the National Library of Scotland contains many references to selling the unsold sets of the *Register,* but there is no evidence that these efforts were marked with success.

14. Southey's letter of complaint to Scott (Aug. 31, 1813) is published in *New Letters of Robert Southey,* ed. Kenneth Curry (New York, 1965), II, 62–64, and Scott's reply in *Letters of Scott* III, 365. Further details concerning the final payments are in *Letters of Scott* V, 114, and C. C. Southey's *Life . . . Robert Southey* IV, 107.

15. James Russell (1790–1861), born at Stirling, received an M.A. from the University of Glasgow and was a barrister, the Inner Temple, 1822. A reporter in the courts of the lord chancellor and master of the rolls, he became a queen's counsel in 1841. He was later for a time an editor of the *Annual Register.* See W. I. Addison, *Roll of the Graduates of the University of Glasgow, 1727–1897* (Glasgow, 1898) and the *Dictionary of National Biography.*

tion of this considerable task. Despite the failure of the *Register* to sell in great numbers and to challenge the established London *Annual Registers*, there seemed to be a stubborn wish on Scott's part to continue the venture in the vain hope that its fortunes would take a turn for the better. Beginning with the sixth volume, the *Register* is noticeably thinner. Instead of two parts issued in two separate volumes, the two are compressed into one, and the miscellaneous prose essays that had graced the first five volumes are missing. Only the section "Original Poetry" continued to give a literary flavor to current history. The sixth volume is the last to bear the imprint of John Ballantyne and Company, and the seventh has that of Archibald Constable and Company. Even Scott's best and noblest efforts were insufficient to give life to the *Register*. After the publication of the eighth volume (1815) in August, 1817, a span of three years passed before the ninth volume (1816) appeared in 1820. For the post of historian the *Register* looked to the youthful John Gibson Lockhart, who had first met Scott in 1818 and in 1820 married Scott's daughter Sophia. This volume, it must be confessed, shows a distinct falling off in quality and quantity. The history is written in a perfunctory style with little evidence of Lockhart's caustic and biting wit and exhibits little of the considerable and conscientious effort that the three earlier historians had taken to produce a revealing and complete illumination of the events of the year. In number of pages the *Register* was also declining. The history of the year 1816 consisted of only 152 pages as opposed to the 373 pages of the eighth volume and to the 879 pages (the highest number) of the second volume.

The history of the *Register* after 1820 is obscure. Lockhart received £400 for his work on the ninth volume. He may have done the tenth, but there is no sure evidence that he did. Lockhart's biographer, Marion Lochhead, does not even mention Lockhart's work on the *Register*.

Scott's last reference to the business affairs of the *Register* occurred in his letter to Constable of August 20, 1820, regarding the editorship of the annual: "I think if Mr. [Hugh] Murray will exert himself on the Register, the arrangement will do very well. He is, I know, a most respectable person and his literary efforts of various kinds have been highly creditable. I should wish it be considered, however, that the editorship should be considered as a temporary engagement from year to year. . .

Respecting the plan, Mr. Murray's letter is as candid and sensible as possible."[16]

Hugh Murray (1779–1846) was best known as a geographer, editor for a time of the *Scots Magazine,* and producer in 1834 of the *Encyclopaedia of Geography.* The usual biographical and bibliographical sources do not indicate anything about his connection with the *Register,* but the character of the work changes noticeably at this time with a reduced emphasis upon literature and an increased emphasis upon science. The tenth volume has an essay on geographical discoveries, a new feature and a regular one for the remaining volumes (except for the thirteenth volume, when all special articles were omitted). Scott's last contribution to the *Register* was a short poem, "Farewell Address, Spoken by Mr. Kemble," in the tenth volume. After that date it is safe to assume that Scott's connection with the *Register* ceased completely, the work going into other hands and losing the distinct literary and antiquarian flavor it had shown during the nine active years when Scott was, if not editor, certainly its guiding spirit and chief adviser.

🙜 The *Register* and the Contemporary Political Scene

The lengthiest and most important feature of each issue of the *Edinburgh Annual Register* was the "History of Europe," where its political views are most apparent.[17] An annual register, by its very nature, is a work of reference, a record of the events of the

16. *Letters of Scott* VI, 261.

17. In writing the present chapter the following books have been helpful: Michael Roberts, *The Whig Party: 1807–1812* (London: Macmillan, 1939; reprint by Gass, 1965) is especially useful in ordering the extremely complex currents and crosscurrents of political parties and issues for these years; Keith J. Feiling, *The Second Tory Party, 1714–1832* (London, Macmillan, 1938, later reprinted); John Clive, *Scotch Reviewers: The Edinburgh Reviewers, 1802–1815* (London: Faber, 1957); Arthur Aspinall, *Lord Brougham and the Whig Party* (Manchester Univ. Press, 1927); Denis Grey, *Spencer Perceval, the Evangelical Prime Minister, 1762–1812* (Manchester Univ. Press, 1963); Roger Fulford, *Samuel Whitbread, 1764–1815: A Study in Opposition* (London: Macmillan, 1967); Austin Mitchell, *The Whigs in Opposition, 1815–1830* (Oxford: Clarendon Press, 1967); Geoffrey Carnall, *Robert Southey and His Age* (Oxford: Clarendon Press, 1960); H. J. C. Grierson, ed., *The Letters of Scott.* 12 vols. (London: Constable, 1932).

past year, not only for contemporaries but also for future readers; although much of each volume is nonpartisan, it should
always be remembered that one of the reasons for the founding
of the *Register* was a desire to support the government in its
policy of active pursuit of the war in Spain against Napoleon
and to counteract the spirit of defeatism expressed in Parliament and in the pages of the *Edinburgh Review*. The *Register*,
however, was not an official voice of the government, and except for its consistency in supporting the ministerial party in its
active prosecution of the war its attitude toward other issues of
the day is less predictable. The views of Scott in the seventh and
eighth volumes are not necessarily those of Southey in the first
four, but the ministerial party (the Pittites) was usually supported.

Britain's military situation at the end of 1808 and the beginning of 1809 was both discouraging and frustrating despite the
opportunity the events in Spain and Portugal afforded for a new
front against Napoleon. Nelson's victory at Trafalgar in 1805 had
given Britain control of the seas and the chance to seize many of
France's distant island possessions, but Napoleon's land forces
did not cease to achieve success after success on the continent.
Eighteen seven saw the defeat of Russia and Prussia and the
occupation of Lisbon with the forced departure of the Portuguese royal family for Brazil. In 1808 Joseph Bonaparte became
King of Spain after Ferdinand's abdication, a Spanish delegation
visited London to seek British assistance, and Arthur Wellesley,
the future duke of Wellington, led an expedition to Portugal
where he won a victory; but Junot's army was permitted to sail
for France by the terms of the Convention of Cintra (thought
by Wordsworth and Southey to be most infamous terms). January of 1809 witnessed the evacuation of the British army sent
to assist the Spaniards and the death of the much-respected
commander, Sir John Moore. Elsewhere Napoleon continued
his victories: the Papal States and Austria suffered defeat, and
the British attempt in that year to aid the Austrians by a military diversion toward Antwerp—the disastrous and ill-executed
Walcheren Expedition—ended in defeat and a parliamentary investigation. It was not a situation from which to extract much
confidence or hope.

Discouraging as military affairs might be, the country supported the policy of continued resistance to Napoleon, as well

as the Pittite ministries of Portland, Perceval, and Liverpool. Even if the peace policy of the opposition was not, during the years following the collapse of the Ministry of All the Talents in 1807, a popular issue, the Whig party was nonetheless able to voice its opposition and to needle the ministerial party through the *Morning Chronicle* and the *Edinburgh Review.* By 1809, under the influence of Henry Brougham, the *Review* was being transformed into an organ for promulgating the views of the younger and more radical members of the Whig party. This aggressive new policy[18] became evident in Brougham's and Jeffrey's review-article of Don Cevallos' pamphlet on the subjugation of Spain. This article (October 1808) stressed the futility of expecting to defeat Napoleon by sending forces to Spain and Portugal in support of the Spanish insurgents, whose fighting spirit and abilities were depreciated. The tone of the article was aggressive, unconciliatory, satiric, and defeatist, the authors maintaining that to believe Spain could put down such a power as Napoleon's was to live in a fool's paradise. The article also pointed out that the Spanish insurgents represented the mob: "the mob itself—alone, uncalled, or unaided by the higher classes." Thus the old fears of Jacobinism and the French Revolution were revived with their threat to the established order in Britain and elsewhere. "We can once more utter the words *liberty* and *people* without starting at the echo of our own voices, or looking round the chamber for some spy or officer of the government," the reviewers exulted. It was this expression of radical Jacobinism that frightened so many of the *Edinburgh's* readers, including the earl of Buchan, who, according to an oft-quoted anecdote, kicked the offending number of the review into the street.[19] For Southey and Scott, however, it was not so much Jacobinical fears as the lack of faith in the Spanish people and the righteousness of their cause that led to their disenchantment with the *Review* and their subsequent actions in support

18. Arthur Aspinall (*Lord Brougham and the Whig Party,* pp. 47–48), points out how thoroughly reactionary the *Edinburgh Review* and Brougham were on such subjects as slavery and prison reform in the early issues.

19. A good account of the Don Cevallos article is in Clive, pp. 110–14. Brougham's later statement on the article was: "In 1808, Cevallos on Spain and the war generally first made us conspicuous as Liberals, and called the *Quarterly* into existence in three months, an event sure to happen as soon as we took a bold line. But that very article, I can assure you, offended Lord Grey and Holland House as much as it did the Tories." Quoted by Clive, p. 112.

of the *Quarterly Review* and the *Edinburgh Annual Register*.
Not to pursue this new military front against Napoleon was perhaps to lose the last chance to defeat his forces.

To Southey the war in Spain was a struggle between good and
evil, "a Holy War," he called it in writing John Rickman.[20] The
first volume of the *Register* countered the cynical despair of the
writers in the *Edinburgh* and the Whitbreads in Parliament by
such eloquent words as these: "from the moment that the
Spaniards called upon us for aid, we felt that we had obtained
allies worthy of our own good cause, and the war assumed a
higher and holier character. It now became . . . a war for all
good principles; and we looked on to the end with faith as well
as hope. Never since the glorious morning of the French Revolution, before one bloody cloud had risen to overcast its beauty,
had the heart of England been affected with so generous and
universal a joy . . . the people universally longed to assist a
nation who had risen in defence of their country" (I, i, 261).
The first chapter of the *Register* also gives the reader an excellent idea of the condition of Britain and Europe after the fall
of the Ministry of All the Talents and the start of the campaigns
in the Peninsula at the beginning of 1808. The war had reached
a stalemate with the British in control of the sea and the French
of the land so that "we were carrying on the war, equally without fear and without hope."

The yearly volumes of the *Register* provide an important
source of information upon all public business, but the sheer
bulk of each volume is a formidable barrier to any reader. The
chapters on domestic affairs are largely narrated by means of
the debates in Parliament, which are quoted *in extenso,* para-
phrased, or summarized, but accompanied with comments
which left the reader in no doubt about the stand of the author
and the *Register*. Military affairs are largely told in the author's
own words, and since the war in Spain was the first concern of

20. John Rickman (1771–1840) prepared the first census in 1800 and was responsible for the three succeeding censuses of 1811, 1821, and 1831. He was also responsible for many important governmental reports such as the annual abstracts of
poor-law returns, 1816–36. Rickman was secretary to Charles Abbot, speaker of the
House of Commons. He assisted Southey with materials on economic matters and
even contributed passages which Southey used in the *Register* and *Quarterly*. Rickman was also a friend of Charles Lamb. His biography by Orlo Williams is entitled:
Lamb's Friend the Census Taker: Life and Letters of John Rickman (1912).

the first few years, it is not surprising to find that this account
occupies about half of the "History of Europe."

The selection of Southey as the historian for the *Register* was
fortunate because he was personally familiar with the terrain of
some of the scenes of the war—the route of Moore's retreat to
Corunna was one—from his travels in Portugal and Spain one
decade earlier. Less fortunate perhaps was his lack of firsthand
knowledge of military tactics and strategy; but for this deficiency he substituted a firm belief in the spirit of the Spanish people
and a firm conviction in the rightness of the British policy in
supporting the Spanish insurgents against Napoleon. Such an
attitude for political polemical writing during the days when
these issues were paramount was most important, especially
given the policy of the *Register*. Scott's comment in a letter to
J. B. S. Morritt praised the parts dealing with the war: "the
history is written by Southey and though with some tinge of
opinions which neither you nor I approve yet there is much
eloquence and a great deal of what every body must admire.
The principles respecting France are particularly excellent the
general tone of political impartiality gives them great weight
and to my knowledge they are beginning to *tell* among those
who would have called them *party clamour* through any
medium."[21]

Since Samuel Whitbread was the most effective speaker of the
opposition in his support of Napoleon—he often praised him—
and because of his contention that the struggle in Spain was a
hopeless one, much of the righteous indignation of the *Register*
was directed at him. After summarizing Whitbread's speech of
February 29, 1808, in which peaceful overtures of negotiation
toward Napoleon were moved, the *Register* commented: "He
seemed as if he were utterly ignorant of those crimes which
Napoleon Buonaparte has committed, . . . against the law of
nations, in which all nations are interested; the rights of neutral
and of friendly states; the security of peaceable individuals; the
faith of treaties, and those common principles of honour,
courtesy, and humanity, which, till his baleful ascendancy,
distinguished the warfare of Europeans from that of barbarians
and savages" (I, i, 54).

On the issue of reform the *Register* was generally sympathetic

21. *Letters of Scott* II, 382.

except upon that of parliamentary reform. The long struggle for
the abolition of offices in reversion in which the measure passed
by the House was several times rejected in the Lords was sponsored by the *Register:* "it gives a check to the shamelessness of
political rapacity, and acknowledges a principle which it will not
be easy to set aside" (I, i, 169). One reason for seeking an end
to corruption in departments is that it deprives the demagogues
of an issue in which "the haranguers of the day never fail to find
topics for invective; and the difficulties which interested individuals oppose to every attempt at reform, are so great, and oftentimes so successful, as to bring Government itself into discredit"
(I, i, 175). To the various legal reforms sponsored by Sir Samuel
Romilly, the *Register* gave wholehearted support. In the first
volume Romilly's speech in favor of his bill on privately stealing
received approval.

> These proceedings have been thus noticed at length, because it is to be
> hoped that they will lead to changes not less extensive than beneficial
> in the whole system of our criminal laws. A society, of which Sir
> Samuel Romilly is a member, has been formed for procuring the aboli-
> tion of the punishment of death in all cases. How far the principle
> upon which they proceed may be right to this extent, may more proper-
> ly be examined hereafter, when the subject is introduced into parlia-
> ment. Some good must undoubtedly be produced by the society. We
> have lived to see the slave trade abolished, and limited service intro-
> duced into our army,—measures which have cleared the character of
> England from its two foulest stains. Let us hope and trust that we
> shall see also a thorough reformation of our penal laws (I, i, 156).

Romilly's advocacy the following year of legislation to do
away with imprisonment for debt also received Southey's en-
dorsement (II, i, 354). Several investigations were being made of
conditions prevailing in prisons, and Southey's rather remarkable
recommendation was: "Place our prisons under the superinten-
dence of the Quakers, and they will be made schools of reform
and industry which will do honour, not only to our age and
country, but even to our nature. Invite the Methodists to labour
there;—these are the hospitals in which such soul-practitioners
would indeed be useful!" (II, i, 358).

The attitudes of the *Edinburgh Annual Register* to the great
and moving issues of the day are less easily discerned and less
dramatically represented than those of the *Edinburgh Review*

and *Quarterly Review.* The *Register* was obligated to record all
the events of the preceding year; the editors of the two quarter-
lies were at liberty to choose significant or entertaining books
and pamphlets for review and thus appeal more directly to the
political, social, and literary interests of their readers. The *Register,* however, does reveal a rather consistent pattern toward the
problems of its age. It never wavered in its conviction that the
war against Napoleon should be waged with all vigor. On all
matters of humanitarian reform, of necessary changes in the
armed forces, of the administration of justice in the courts, the
Register spoke out for the individual in the lower or middle
ranks of society who often suffered undeservedly at the hands
of those in authority. Its opposition to Catholic emancipation
and to concessions to the Roman Catholics in Ireland softened
somewhat as the national temper changed, but Scott, no less
than Southey, remained opposed to many aspects of the Roman
church, objecting to the revival of monasticism and of the Jesuits
at the end of the war. Although the *Register* sympathized with
administrative reforms involving inefficiencies in office, it
staunchly opposed parliamentary reform. To Burdett's plan in
1809 the response was: "the direct road to anarchy is by way of
Parliamentary Reform," ending in military despotism, "the consummation of all evils" (II, i, 289).

It must be confessed that for the most part reading the "History of Europe" is a dull business, many chapters consisting solely
of uncondensed parliamentary speeches, but there are still parts
of chapters—and even entire chapters—that deserve a good word
as examples of lively narrative. From the second volume (1809)
the entire investigation of the duke of York–Mrs. Clarke affair
cannot fail to interest. From the third volume (1810) Burdett's
arrest and transfer to the Tower (chap. 3), the account of the
sailor Jeffrey set ashore on deserted Sombrero Island by the
tyrannous Captain Lake (chap. 4), the gruesome accounts of
slavery (chap. 9), and the narrative of naval actions at Guada-
loupe and St. Martins (chap. 7)—all these are accounts that the
reader of today can read easily and enjoyably. In the fourth
volume (1811) the account of the unbelievable intrigue of the
court of Naples and the struggle for the control of Sicily is a
skillful chapter in history that can be read as a story in itself.
Surely in Scott's two volumes of the *Register* it is not too fanciful to see the hand of the novelist: in chapter 18 of the eighth

volume (1815) the account of General La Bédoyère, who had led
a rebellion against Louis XVIII, suggests a comparison with the
similar fate of Fergus MacIvor in *Waverley;* the entire eleventh
chapter of the same volume detailing the ill-fated and dangerous
attempt of Joachim Murat to seize control of all Italy is narrated
with all the verve of an accomplished storyteller. The ninth volume (1816)—from the pen of Lockhart—contains a readable
chapter (5) based upon the reports of committees investigating
mendicity, vagrancy, and the London police, describing the lives
of the beggars and their schools that seems anticipatory of
Oliver Twist. It is not at all surprising that there are chapters
and stories of great human interest because the years of the
Register were years in which great and stirring heroic events
were of daily occurrence, and it was the business of that *Register* to record them.

⳼ Antiquarian and Literary Aspects

The most readable section of the *Register,* especially to anyone
who feels himself remote from the political disputes and issues
of one and one-half centuries ago with which the "History of
Europe" concerns itself, is certainly the second part. The mixture is varied: a potpourri of poetry, surveys of the arts and
sciences, letters, and documents of literary, historical, and antiquarian interests. This miscellaneous fare was not unlike that
purveyed to the public by the venerable *Gentleman's Magazine*
and the newer *Monthly Magazine.* This section, however, owes
much to an abandoned project of Scott's—abandoned during
the time when plans for the *Register* were taking shape. Southey
had suggested to Scott a review of old, rather than contemporary books, to be entitled the *British Librarian* or *Rhadamanthus.* Scott in turn, had sent John Ballantyne to Southey
with a note of introduction, suggesting that Southey be the editor of this magazine which the new publishing firm of John
Ballantyne would publish. Ballantyne's proposal was liberal and
would have enabled Southey to earn £250 a year. Southey explained the project and the terms to William Taylor, whose support he solicited: "The terms proposed are, £100 a year for the

editor, ten guineas a sheet for the writers; the place of printing, Edinburgh; the mode, quarterly five shilling numbers. Definitively settled it is not: . . Scott proposed to bear a part, and will be a very useful assistant."[22] Taylor's reply was discouraging: "I do not think the project you are forming will answer. Rhadamanthus may pay Charon and his subferrymen, but poor Ballantyne will repent of this bargain. Only the literary world cares about old books."[23]

Scott, however, had thought of the new periodical not only as a review of old books but also as a means of reprinting "smaller tracts which have an interest independent of their scarcity or antiquity . . . so that the miscellany might in some respects be a continuation of the Harleian, on a better plan."[24] Neither the Ballantynes nor Scott pursued this plan of the *Rhadamanthus,* and in a few months they had found another task for Southey, one that was far more lucrative for him, as the historian of the *Register* at £400 a year. The *Rhadamanthus* may be said to survive, without the reviews of old books, in the second part of the *Register,* where it became the repository for a variety of documents and miscellanea that came to Scott and that he could not forbear to share with his readers.

The best way to view the literary-antiquarian aspects of the *Register* is to inspect the tables of contents for the first few years. Poetry occupies an honored place in the first volume— twenty-eight poems including Southey's "King Ramiro," "Queen Orraca," and two excerpts from *The Curse of Kehama,* just published in 1809. Many of the poems in this first volume were reprinted from the *English Minstrelsy,* another project of Scott and Ballantyne and published in 1810, the same year as the publication of the *Register* for 1808. Scott's essay, "Of the Living Poets of Great Britain," began a series of articles by various hands on poetry, criticism, drama, the theater in Edinburgh, together with biographical tributes to such deceased writers as James Grahame and John Leyden. All sorts of odd bits of topographical, antiquarian lore—often with a Scottish bearing—turn up from sources that can often be traced to Scott and his circle: such items as an account of the Bell Rock Light

22. *Memoir . . . Taylor* II, 274. *Letters of Scott* II, 195, contains Scott's response to Southey's proposal.
23. *Memoir . . . Taylor* II, 277.
24. *Letters of Scott* II, 195.

House, a wooden coffin, the journal of a Levant pirate (the Scotsman William Davidson) in the Mediterranean, fragments of Scott's journal of his trip in 1814 to the Western Islands, old letters from William Shenstone, David Hume, Joseph Spence, the earl of Eglintoune, the earl of Perth—all find a place in these early volumes. Poetry is, however, the most constant literary feature of the *Register* as long as Scott had a hand in the publication. If no poems of the very first rank appeared, nonetheless names of such well-known poets as Southey, Scott, John Wilson, and James Hogg appear along with many names recognizable by readers acquainted with Scott's circle and the lesser poetical lights of the day, English and Scottish.

If much of the poetry had been published elsewhere, many of the prose essays were published in the *Register* for the first and only time. Scott reprinted his biography of Dr. John Leyden in his *Miscellaneous Prose Works,* and from his "History of Europe" for 1814 and 1815 he extracted large sections for his *Life of Napoleon Buonaparte.* Southey, for his part, reprinted "The History of Lope de Aguirre" in book form in 1821, and used many chapters from his "History of Europe" in his *Peninsular War.* Scott, however, did not reprint most of his essays, but their high quality and general interest make the decision hard to understand especially since at the end of his life he republished so many of his earlier works. These articles reveal his wide interests from literary criticism and the law to the familiar essay.

ﾨﾟ Audience and Influence

Did the *Register* have a wide audience and did it influence the public in any way during its lifetime? The answer is not clear. It seems probable that the sale of each year was between fifteen hundred and two thousand copies, which was by no means a small number by the standards of the day. The *Register* was the center of no controversy—as were the *Edinburgh* and the *Quarterly*—and a search of indexes to other periodicals, to memoirs, diaries, and letters of the period yields very few references. The largest number of references are in the letters of Scott and Southey, whose friends were made aware of the publication and who seem to have read the work, or at least a part of it.

The nearest thing to a public controversy occurred when Henry Brougham cited the attack upon Samuel Whitbread's "peace-mongering" in the "History of Europe" for 1808 as an infringement upon the privileges of the House of Commons. Jeffrey pursued the topic and recommended that the *Register* be prosecuted for this breach of privilege.[25] A study of the context in which these remarks was made suggests that both outbreaks were only bursts of rhetoric against the ministerial party by the minority party. The recommendation for prosecution was in reference to the trial and imprisonment of John Gale Jones, who had been prosecuted for his libel upon Lord Castlereagh in 1810; it was simply a means by which the Whigs might point out that it was quite safe for ministerial supporters to attack one of their opponents, but it was quite another matter for a member of the radical press to attack a member of the government.

The most lavish praise of the *Register* came from Coleridge on Southey's writing in the third volume:

> You would oblige and serve me if you could . . . entrust to my Care for two or three days only that Sheet of the unpublished Ed. Ann. Register, which contains the Remarks on the parliamentary Schemes and Labors of Mr. Banks, and his Co-adjutors of the Finance Committee, on Sinecures, Audit office &c &c. . . . I dare challenge the malignity of party Spirit itself to deny, that the Historical Portion (two thirds of the whole) of this and the former Volumes forms beyond all comparison the noblest specimen of recent and progressive History in the annals of Literature. In all rival works I have found little or nothing which I had not or might not have previously learnt from the Newspapers; but in this independent of the dignity, perspicuity, and vivacity of the Style, more than half of the most interesting and important Facts, both domestic and foreign are in the strictest sense new to the English reader.[26]

Southey's friends John Rickman and William Taylor read the work and offered comments but did not always agree with Southey's position. Rickman, although he helped Southey to

---

25. The attack on the *Register* in the *Edinburgh Review* was in the article, "Campaigns of 1809," XVIII (1811), 392–425.

26. To John Murray, May 16, 1812. *Collected Letters of Samuel Taylor Coleridge*, ed. E. L. Griggs (Oxford, 1959), III, 411.

obtain materials and even wrote some long passages, objected to Southey's insistence on calling the struggle in Spain against Napoleon a holy war. Taylor, an erudite Unitarian and contributor to the *Monthly Magazine,* the *Annual Review,* and the *Monthly Review,* was basically unsympathetic to a publication which so wholeheartedly supported the ministerial party. He praised the narrative of Spanish affairs in the first volume but disagreed concerning the opposition in the *Register* to Catholic emancipation, a cause with which Taylor sympathized.[27]

Shelley, who was a visitor in Keswick during the winter of 1811 and 1812, read Southey's history in the *Register* for 1809 and quoted with great disgust a passage critical of Sir Francis Burdett in a letter of January 20, 1812, to Elizabeth Hitchener. Shelley was by this time disappointed in Southey, and this attitude toward Burdett was one of the final bits which led to his disillusionment with the poet whose work he had formerly so much admired.

Byron had certainly read at least a part of the first volume, for in a long note (an attack on Southey) to line 557 of *Hints from Horace* he cited the passage praising Southey in Scott's essay on the living poets with this caustic remark: "it is a good deal beneath Scott and Campbell, and not much above Southey, to allow the booby Ballantyne to entitle them, in the *Edinburgh Annual Register* (of which, by the bye, Southey is editor) 'the grand poetical triumvirate of the day.'"

References to the *Register* in the correspondence and journals of the day are quite few. Thomas Moore in his journal entry for September 19, 1818, records that Miss Edgeworth had asked him if he "had seen a poem in the 'Edinburgh Annual Register,' called Solyman (I think): the hero's fate depends upon getting a happy man to give him the shirt from his back, but finds he has none." The poem is Scott's "The Search After Happiness; or the Quest of Sultaun Soliman" in the *Register* for 1815 (published in 1817).

Mrs. Anne Grant of Laggan had high praise for Scott's history of the year 1814, which "does as much honour to his sound judgment and discrimination as some of his past writing have done to his genius and creative power of fancy. One could

---

27. *Memoir . . . Taylor* II, 296.

scarcely imagine a poet to have so much common sense as to write prose with such elegant simplicity."[28]

Writers and historians are quite aware of the existence of the *Edinburgh Annual Register*. Complete or partial sets of the *Register* are available in almost all large libraries, and the work is sometimes cited in scholarly works. Edward Dowden in his *Life of Shelley* (1886) used the essay on Oxford education to describe the course of Oxford studies in Shelley's day. The editors of the letters of Shenstone and Hume note the fact that certain letters first appeared in the *Register*, but although the biographers of Scott and Southey mention the work, they do not seem to have studied the *Register* intensively. Of all the writers on Southey only Geoffrey Carnall in his *Robert Southey and His Age: The Development of a Conservative Mind* (Oxford, 1960) makes an extensive and thorough use of Southey's writings to illustrate the views of Southey on political and social issues: his quotations are apt and illuminating.

It is not unusual for a writer to cite the historical department of the *Register* without knowing the identity of the author. The most striking and curious—as well as the most extensive—example of this use of the *Register* is in S. Maccoby's *English Radicalism, 1786–1832* (London, 1955). Maccoby's fourteenth chapter entitled "The Agitations of 1808–10" is largely derived from the "History of Europe" in the *Register* for 1808 and 1809. This is, rather oddly, the only chapter in which Maccoby uses the *Edinburgh Annual Register,* for in his other chapters he relies upon the *Annual Register* and the *New Annual Register*. Maccoby, ignorant of Southey's authorship, quoted the work with approval, introducing a long quotation with this sentence: "Here are extracts from an account of the Convention of Cintra in the *Edinburgh Annual Register,* a very well-written record, composed partly, it would seem by Walter Scott" (p. 242). Another long quotation on page 245 includes an entire page from the *Register* (II, 229–230) with a compliment as to "its able writing." The conclusion to be drawn is that Maccoby's research for his fourteenth chapter was almost exclusively derived from the first two volumes of the *Register!*

28. Grant, J. P., ed. *Memoir and Correspondence of Mrs. Grant of Laggan* (London, 1845), 2d ed., II, 133.

Part 2

Scott and His Collaborators:

Problems of an Editor-Proprietor

Scott as Editor and Contributor

If James Ballantyne may be said to have been the nominal editor of the *Register,* it is always well to remember Scott's remark that Ballantyne would look after the inferior parts of the work—Scott presumably looking after the literary parts and having nothing to do with the drudging details of editing a work of over one thousand pages. Since Ballantyne was no editorial tyrant holding absolute control over the contents and destinies of the work, as did Gifford and Jeffrey over the affairs of the *Quarterly* and *Edinburgh Reviews,* a great deal was simply left undone, and Scott, when the deadline approached for getting the *Register* to the printer, stepped in, wrote an essay or two, looked in the drawers of his desk for whatever a correspondent had sent him, and dispatched some sort of copy. His correspondence indicates that he was active in soliciting contributions for the *Register.* When the passages in Scott's correspondence referring to the *Register* are read consecutively, the reader quickly recognizes an air of desperation, disappointment, and on occasion shortness of temper. It is all easy to understand. The *Register* was the biggest undertaking of John Ballantyne and Company, and the success of the enterprise depended upon the sale of the *Register.* Scott thus emerges in the many-sided role of business manager, editor, contributor, and promoter-speculator, and it is a tribute to his energy and genius that he was able to do so many things so well.

In the dealings of the *Register* with Southey, who as the writer of the "History of Europe" for the first four years was the key figure, James Ballantyne was the correspondent, making the arrangements and sending the proofs. But Scott was always in the background, encouraging, counseling, and seeing that when Southey requested materials and documents for his writing they were dispatched to him. And when Southey was disappointed about the arrangements for the fourth volume, it was to Scott that he complained about the treatment—specifically the lack of payment—he received from John Ballantyne. Scott corresponded with many friends requesting that they send him something for the *Register*. The original letters of Shenstone, Hume, and Spence came in as the result of soliciting his old friends Patrick Murray and Charles Kirkpatrick Sharpe. His friend, J. B. S. Morritt, sent him his poem "The Curse of Moy." Many other poems Scott simply appropriated from published works, many of the poems in the first volume coming from the *English Minstrelsy,* another Scott project published in 1810. Scott's phenomenal memory enabled him to remember a poem after hearing it recited, and he was fond of reciting Southey's "Queen Orraca" and "The Inchcape Rock." Southey was mystified about how the *Register* had secured "The Inchcape Rock" since it had appeared only in the newspaper the *Morning Post* about ten years earlier.[1]

A quick glance at the table of contents of the second part of the *Register* for the years when Scott was active in its direction will give a rough idea of Scott's important participation in the literary-antiquarian section. For the first volume he wrote two lengthy essays: "View of the Changes Proposed and Adopted in the Administration of Justice in Scotland" and "Of the Living Poets of Great Britain." In addition were five of his poems from the *English Minstrelsy* as well as miscellaneous items from his correspondents. For the second volume he wrote a special essay entitled "The Inferno of Altisidora" as a preface to three of his poems; a military essay, "Cursory Remarks upon the French Order of Battle"; a critical essay, "The Present State of Periodical Criticism"; he reprinted his long poem, *The Vision of Don Roderick,* and a short epitaph on the father of Anna Seward. He had also secured original letters of Shenstone, Hume, and Spence. One can speculate about other essays in this second volume—perhaps the richest in literary interest of any of the set—in regard to their provenance and authorship, but Scott's contribution is impressive in bulk and quality.

Scott's contributions to the third volume are less numerous, but most noteworthy is his "Account of the Poems of Patrick Carey." He had procured, however, a copy of the *Journal of a*

1. Scott admitted that he supplied "The Inchcape Rock" from memory. "I have transcribed Sir Ralph the Rover from memory very imperfectly and inaccurately I do believe." *Letters of Scott* II, 227.

Levant Pirate which the *Register* reprinted. This journal was by
a Scotsman named William Davidson who had served on a pirate
ship. Scott had thought that the journal might serve as material
for a tale, but the journal was so gruesome and bloody that he
concluded that it was unsuitable. The work is extremely rare;
perhaps the only copy surviving is in the library of Corpus Christi
College, Oxford.[2]

The fourth volume of the *Register* contained only Scott's biography of Dr. John Leyden. The fifth volume contained extracts
from his journal kept on his trip to the Western Islands in the
summer of 1814, and the reprint from the Red Book of the
campaigns of Montrose was from the book in his possession at
that time. Volume six—the first to compress the two parts into
one bound volume—contains only two poems by Scott. For volumes seven and eight Scott performed the herculean task of
writing the "History of Europe" (367 and 373 pages, respectively). After this year Scott had very little to do with the management of the *Register*. A three-year interval elapsed between
the publication of volume eight and volume nine, the history of
1816, being written by John Lockhart, a bit of business arranged
by Scott. Constable consulted Scott about turning over the
management of the *Register* to Hugh Murray in 1820, and after
that event Scott had no further interest in the work. Certainly
all his work as contributor and solicitor of material was at an
end.

The *Register* contained, in addition to the "History of
Europe" and miscellaneous literary-antiquarian contributions, a
considerable amount of statistical information, public records,
reprints of public documents, and a chronicle (a record of notable events of the year arranged by month and day). This valuable reference feature of the *Register*—still valuable today—had
to be done by someone, and we do know that Robert Lundie
and William Laidlaw did this work for several numbers. Robert
Lundie (1774–1832) was a clergyman of Kelso, the home town
of the Ballantynes, and he undertook the chronicle for the second volume, consulting Southey about the arrangement of the
material. Southey's reply of October 14, 1810, suggested that
the chronicle be confined mostly to domestic events and that

---

2. The article on Davidson in the *Dictionary of National Biography* appears to be
derived from the material in the *Register*.

duplication between the chronicle and the history be avoided, but his letter was for the most part one of reassuring Lundie and urging him to use his own best judgment in arranging the materials for the chronicle, gazette, and state documents.[3] How long Lundie continued in this employment is uncertain. William Laidlaw (1790–1845), a man of business who assisted Scott in many affairs, did service similar to Lundie's for several volumes as the obituary notice in the *Gentleman's Magazine* said: "He wrote and strung things together for the 'Edinburgh Annual Register.' "

An interesting aspect of the contributions in the *Register* is the influence of Scott, who was an indefatigable collector of things curious and historical. The first out-of-the-way book to be used in toto was the *Journal of a Levant Pirate* in the third volume. The book, privately printed in 1812, has the following title page:

> THE / BLOODY JOURNAL, / KEPT BY / WILLIAM DAVIDSON, / ON BOARD / A RUSSIAN PIRATE, / IN THE YEAR / 1789. / [rule] / MEDITERRANEAN: / PRINTED ON BOARD HIS MAJESTY'S SHIP CALEDONIA, / [rule] / 1812.

A collation of the text printed in the *Edinburgh Annual Register* with the copy in the library of Corpus Christi College reveals only minor changes in capitalization, spelling, and punctuation. The Corpus Christi copy bears the following inscriptions: "Presented to the Library of Corpus Christi College, Oxford by John Brickenden Frowd, B. D. Fellow, February 27th 1818.": and "J. B. Frowd H.M.S. Caledonia May 14th 18 [*sic*] From Sir Edward Pellew." A much later hand has recorded: "This book is of extreme rarity. There is no copy either in the Bodleian or in the British Museum. C.P." Frowd (1786–1865) was a student and fellow of Corpus during all his long life; Sir Edward Pellew (1757–1833), later Lord Exmouth, was commander-in-chief of the Mediterranean fleet after 1811, and was married to Susan Frowd. Scott's connection with these persons seems to have been through Edward Hawke Locker, civil secretary to Sir Edward from 1804 to 1814. Locker was on the *Caledonia* and could easily have procured the copy for Scott, but whether this is the copy in the Corpus Christi Library cannot be established.

3. This unpublished letter of Southey is in the National Library of Scotland.

Perhaps the most interesting of the various reprints Scott used in the *Register* was the "Account of the Campaigns of Montrose, Translated from the Gaelic Language," which appeared in the fifth volume published in 1815. Scott did not admit any responsibility for the insertion of this selection, but it is possible to trace his steps and to observe the way in which he thriftily utilized the material not only for the *Register* but for the poem *The Lord of the Isles*. The prefatory note in the *Register* is as follows:

> The curious manuscript from which these historical memoirs are extracted, contains several Gaelic poems and genealogies, written by the MacVuirichs, hereditary bards or seannachies of a distinguished western chieftain. The following literal version contains many particulars respecting the wars of Montrose, totally unnoticed by our historians, and may be considered, at the same time, as affording an authentic historical document, and a curious specimen of the manners and habits of the Gaelic tribes, recorded by one of their own historians. No attempt has been made to correct the language of the translator, who seems to have been better skilled in the Gaelic language, than capable of transfusing its spirit into the English version.

The "curious manuscript" is the Book of Clanranald, the famous Red Book of the Ossianic controversy, written by the Mac Vurichs, hereditary bards and historians of the family of Clanranald. According to Alexander Cameron the history of the Montrose wars is "clearly the work of Niall Mac Vurich, who lived till a great age, his youthful recollections being, as he himself says, of the reign of Charles I." The translator to whom Scott refers was the Reverend Donald Mackintosh, whose translation was later corrected and amplified by William Forbes Skene. Scott did not own the Red Book, but at one time he had its use, and he quoted extensively from it in note 7 to *The Lord of the Isles*, published on January 8, 1815, a few months before the publication of the fifth volume of the *Register*. The portion of the Mackintosh translation printed in the *Register* is paralleled by the Gaelic text and the revised translation in Alexander Cameron's *Reliquae Celticae* (Inverness, 1892–1894) II, 177–209; note 7 of *The Lord of the Isles* summarizes and quotes the materials not used in the *Register*: paragraphs 2–7 are direct quotation and are paralleled by Cameron, II, 159–67, while paragraph 8 summarizes much of what follows and the note concludes with a direct quotation corresponding to Cameron, II, 211, paragraph 6. It is curious to observe the way in which the long extract in the *Register* is surrounded by the shorter extract in the note to *The Lord of the Isles;* Scott appears not only reluctant to cast aside any material in hand but also to be arranging the selection for the *Register* and composing the note for the poem at the same time.

A third example of Scott's use of the *Register* for publishing the work of a neglected and forgotten author is his publication of six poems of Patrick Cary (1624–1656), a seventeenth-century author whose poems may be said to have been added to the corpus of English literature through Scott's efforts. The publisher, John Murray, had given him the manuscript of the poems, and from this manuscript Scott published six poems in the *Register* for 1810. In 1819 Scott assembled the complete manuscript of thirty-five poems (twenty-four secular and eleven sacred) in a seventy-page volume which Murray published. A few years later Scott remembered Cary and quoted some of his stanzas in *Woodstock,* where he had the disguised King Charles sing a stanza from one of the songs.[4]

Scott contributed to the fifth volume (1812, published 1814) slightly less than one fourth of the journal he had kept during his summer tour to the northern and western islands of Scotland in the summer of 1814. Lockhart gave the complete diary in chapters twenty-eight through thirty-two of the *Memoirs.* In the *Register* Scott printed five extracts, but not in consecutive order. These sections, their dates, and the corresponding passages in Lockhart are as follows:

Register	Lockhart's *Life*[5]
"Introduction," August 6, 1814, Lerwick, Zetland, V, 431–34	II, 412–16

4. George Saintsbury in his *Minor Poets of the Caroline Period* (Oxford, 1906), II, 445–82, reprinted Scott's volume with a full introduction and annotation. The knowledge of Cary increased slowly after Scott's discovery of the poet. Both the *Dictionary of National Biography* and the *Cambridge Bibliography of English Literature* (1940) fail to give the dates of his birth and death. Cary is mentioned in passing in the *Cambridge History of English Literature,* is the subject of a footnote in *A Literary History of England,* ed. by Albert Baugh, and Douglas Bush lists him in his bibliography to *English Literature of the Earlier Seventeenth Century.* The best account of Cary is in an appendix to Kurt Weber's study of Cary's older brother, *Lucius Cary, Second Viscount Falkland* (New York, 1940).

5. The Cambridge edition of Lockhart's *Memoirs of the Life of Sir Walter Scott*

"The Superstitions of the Zetlanders," last paragraph, V, 434–35	A summary of the paragraph, II, 410
"The Fair Isle," August 10, 1814, V, 435–38	II, 429–34
"The Cave of Smowe," August 19, 1814, V, 438–42	II, 458–64
"The Orkneys," August 14–15, 1814, V, 442–46	II, 443–49

A detailed comparison of the two texts reveals that Lockhart's text is fuller and more accurate.[6] Most of Scott's omissions in the *Register* are of minor detail such as the names of some of the people he met at the various stops. The *Register* contains only two passages of any length that are not in Lockhart, and these are as follows: "passing two Swedish vessels, and a large one, say 600 tons, we speak them, but got no news from Norway. Getting out of the Sound of Holm, we see on the right the harbour, or roadstead, of the Long Hope, now protected by a small fort. A sloop of war, and some other shipping, seem to be lying there. On the left-hand we see and land into the harbour, or roadstead of Widenwall" (*Register,* V, 443: col. 1:15; Lockhart, II, 443:29). The second passage is somewhat longer:

> for, before this light-house was established, vessels were obliged to go round the whole Orcadian archipelago, or to involve themselves on the hazardous and complicated passages of the firths of Westra, or North Ronaldsha, rather than attempt the Pentland firth, where those un-happy Skerries lie, forming the salient angle of a triangle between the islands of Swona and Stroma, to catch any ship that might pass be-tween them. But now the lighthouse renders the Pentland firth quite accessible at the proper hours of the tide. (*Register* V, col. 1:46 to col. 2:14; Lockhart, II, 446:35)

(Boston, 1901) in five volumes. The diary (II, 401–512) was begun on July 29, 1814, and concluded on Sept. 8.

6. Mr. Davidson Cook reported in the *London Times Literary Supplement,* Aug. 1936, p. 680, that the manuscript of the diary was in the Honresfeld Collection of Sir Alfred J. Law, and that Lockhart's text was inaccurate. The plan there announced to publish the journal from the manuscript was not realized. Scott included in the notes (No. 39) to *The Lord of the Isles* another long extract from this diary: this pas-sage was dated Aug. 26, 1814. F. A. Pottle, "The Power of Memory in Boswell and Scott," *Essays on the Eighteenth Century Presented to David Nichol Smith* (Oxford, 1945), p. 172, is aware of the differences between the text in the note to *The Lord of the Isles* and Lockhart's *Memoirs*.

58 Scott's *Edinburgh Annual Register*

Scott's greatest contribution to the *Register* in sheer bulk was, of course, his "History of Europe" for the two years 1814 and 1815. It was an arduous task, competently done by his skilled hand, and when in later years he was striving in every way to earn money to pay off the debts incurred by his bankruptcy, he found the passages on Napoleon—the escape from Elba and the great events of the Hundred Days with Napoleon's subsequent misfortunes—all ready to be inserted with little change into his *Life of Napoleon Buonaparte*.

To summarize briefly, Scott published many of his own poems and was apparently responsible for the insertion of most of the other poems in the first seven or eight numbers of the *Register;* he is the author (quite certainly) of six prose essays, of which five are reprinted in this book for the first time. His hand can be traced in the insertion of many of the miscellaneous antiquarian-historical documents and may be suspected in many others. His two volumes of the "History of Europe" amount to the amazing total of 740 pages. In addition, Scott was constantly prodding the Ballantynes about publishing details, urging speed in the printing of the work that it might be out in time to encourage sales; he made the arrangements with William Laidlaw to put together much of the miscellaneous factual and statistical features of the *Register;* and when all these matters were tended to he acted as a sort of press agent to promote a knowledge of the *Edinburgh Annual Register*. All in all, it is an impressive amount of work, but it must be regretfully concluded that all the labor was still insufficient to make the *Register* popular and thus keep the Ballantyne firm solvent.

๑ Books Derived from the Pages of the *Register*

An important indicator of the value of the *Edinburgh Annual Register* is the number of books and essays which were published by their authors from material which had first appeared in the *Register*. The two most important works to incorporate large segments of the *Register* were Southey's *History of the Peninsular War* (1823–1832) and Scott's *Life of Napoleon Buonaparte* (1827). Southey's *The Expedition of Orsua; and the Crimes of Aguirre*

(1821) was reprinted from an essay in the third volume of the *Register*. Scott's edition of the poems of Patrick Cary (1819) was an expansion of his work on Cary for the *Register*. Other items of less importance will be mentioned at the end of this chapter.

Southey's *History of the Peninsular War* is the book most heavily obligated to the *Edinburgh Annual Register*. Southey quite frankly stated that he used his work in the *Register* for his history, but the considerable extent of this transfer has never been detailed. The indebtedness is enormous, whole chapters and paragraphs being transferred without alteration or with only the change required by a transitional sentence or paragraph. Several hundred pages from the *War* are reprinted or very slightly revised from the *Register*. The four years from 1808 to 1811 covered the exciting years of the war, and Southey had actually recorded these events as they occurred within one or two years afterward. Hence the writing of his *History of the Peninsular War* could be largely a work in revision, albeit a very considerable revision. A comparison of the texts of the *Peninsular War* and the *Register* in the table below shows that chapters and sections of chapters have been taken over completely or with slight revision. It is not feasible—unless this were a complete study of Southey's *Peninsular War*—to indicate any more exactly these parallels since a complete and accurate collation would easily extend to one hundred pages of figures.

The first volume of the *Register* (1808) contained in its "History of Europe" 459 double-column pages, and of these one half are devoted to the war. Save for chapter 17 Southey reprinted all these war chapters in the first volume of his *History* (1823). In fairness to Southey, however, it should be said that he also included much additional material in this volume. The second, third, and fourth volumes of the *Register* devoted proportionally less space to the war, approximately one third, but Southey was able to use most of this one third. Of these four volumes containing the "History of Europe" we may say that the *History of the Peninsular War* used about 30 percent of the space.

The table below indicates the corresponding chapters between the *Register* and the *War*. Very close parallels are indicated by citation of page numbers, and a dagger designates a chapter taken over completely and almost verbatim into the book. It will be noted that very few chapters on the war were completely discarded from the *Register* but were used as the basis. There was considerable rearrangement of paragraphs and sections so that a collation is often tricky. Occasionally, isolated sentences will be picked up and salvaged, for example, the sentence on the death of the Princess Amelia. For any one interested in studies in revision, a thorough investigation of Southey's methods would provide a study in detection and historical revision.

Register		*Peninsular War*	
I (1808)		I (1823)	
Chapter 12	225–27	Chapter 2	62–64
12	228–38	3	149–73 with additions
†13	239–65	4	174–236
14	266–76	5	237–61
15	291–97	8	345–52
†16	307–21	9	399–424
18	355–56	11	526–27
19	357–61	11	530–34; 538–40
20	386–90; 393–94; 395–98; 401–403	12	616–30; 633–38; 668–70
†21	404–17	13	671–94
22	430–41	14	
		15	756–77
†23		15	777–806
II (1809)		II (1827)	
Chapter 3	56–85	Chapter 21	246–78 speeches rephrased
19		16	
20	515–28	18	139–58
21	539–47	17	83–95
22		20	
23		19	
29		22	
30		24	
31	745–67	25	451–70
32	768–87	26	
III (1810)			
Chapter 1		Chapter 21	
1		27 at 571	
†12	381–401	28	594–630
13	407–13	30	683–92
†14		29	
†15	438–50	31	701–24
16		32	

Register		*Peninsular War*	
		III (1832)	
17		33	
18		34	
IV (1811)			
9	247–48; 249–64	35	121–22; 129–56
10	264–86	37	214–40
†11	287–99	36	156–80
12	300–13	38[7]	250–310
13	314–27	39	328–38; 346–61
14	328–35	39	314–28
	336–43	40	365–78
15	344–54	38[7]	259–77

The second most voluminous use of material from the *Register* is in Scott's *Life of Napoleon Buonaparte* (nine vols., 1827), where a great deal of what needed to be said of the last two momentous years of Napoleon's military career had already been included in the two volumes for 1814 and 1815, which Scott had written for the *Register*. The biography of Napoleon was a money-making project undertaken at the time when Scott was trying feverishly to earn as much as possible to pay off the debts of his bankrupt publishing and printing ventures. In his letters Scott mentioned that he was consulting or using the old volumes of the *Register* but did not state the extent to which he was transferring, rewriting, or rejecting his earlier composition. As with Southey's *Peninsular War,* there was no particular attempt at secrecy, but the exact nature and extent of the indebtedness has never been shown. Again, a table seems to be the best way to show the chapters and pages borrowed.

Life of Napoleon	*Register*
Chapter 73, 67–68[8]	VII (1814), Chapter 9, 204–205
74	10
76, 144–157	12, 258–63
84	VIII (1815), Chapter 8
85	10
86	12
87	13
88	13
90	16 to p. 275

7. Chapter 38 is composed from the *Register* IV, 300–303, ch. 12; 344–54, ch. 15; 303–308, 309–12, ch. 12.

8. The page numbers in this tabulation are to the *Miscellaneous Prose Works of*

Space does not permit the presentation of an elaborate collation between the *Napoleon* and the *Register,* but the comparison of the two texts shows that Scott was not unconscientious in his preparation of the copy for *Napoleon* from the old pages of the history, for he quite often rewrote, condensed, added new material, and, because information had become available in the intervening decade, discarded what he had written.

From the third volume of the *Register,* Southey published in 1821 *The Expedition of Orsua; and the Crimes of Aguirre,* which reprinted his fifty-page essay in a slender duodecimo of 215 pages. The account was actually a discarded chapter from the *History of Brazil,* on which Southey had been working at the time he published the story in the *Register.* "The History of Lope de Aguirre," its title in the *Register,* is the story of an expedition in 1560 in quest of a fabled kingdom in the interior of South America led by Pedro of Orsua and consisting of several hundred soldiers, adventurers, and mestizos. Its control was soon taken over by a bloodthirsty madman, Lope de Aguirre, who, after murdering Orsua, committed crime after crime on an expedition by riverboat through parts of Peru, Brazil, and Venezuela and terrorized for forty days the Caribbean island of Margarita, until the king's forces in Venezuela finally caught up with the adventurer. Straightforwardly narrated, the work is an account of incredible murder, treachery, intrigue, and hardship during the first century of Spanish settlement and conquest in America. The fifty double-columned pages of the article in the *Register* made up a volume of 215 pages. There is almost no revision of the pages from the *Register,* but the material is broken up into six chapters, a preface is supplied, a concluding paragraph, a few insertions concerning the previous life of Orsua and of Aguirre, and additional information at the opening of chapters five and six. Footnotes are sometimes expanded. Substantially, the book is a reprint of the essay in the *Register.* One topic is worth mentioning: the essay precedes an equally horrifying story of murder, bloodshed, and disregard for human life in the reprint of Davidson's *Journal of a Levant Pirate,* so that the reader of the *Register* for 1810 was served an unusual fare of violence and sudden death.

Sir Walter Scott, Bart. (Edinburgh: Adam and Charles Black, 1861), vols. XV and XVI.

Three of the essays Southey reprinted in 1832 (*Essays, Moral and Political*) were derived from the *Register*, about one half of the first essay and the second and third completely.

Essays		*Register*
Essay I.	"On Sir Francis Burdett's Motion for Parliamentary Reform." I, 3–19.[9]	II (1809), 285–93.
Essay II.	"Army and Navy Reforms. 1810."	III (1810), 155–62.
Essay III.	"On the Economical Reformers." 1811."	III (1810), 211–20.

The interesting point about the second and third of these essays is that although they were published under Southey's name they were actually the work of John Rickman. This fact is made clear by the Southey-Rickman correspondence at the time Southey was selecting some of his early work for republication. On August 15, 1827, Southey wrote Rickman: "I am about to reprint in a separate form such of my stray papers as are worth collecting from the *Q. R.* etc. . . . Shall I print with these your remarks upon the Economical Reformers—in the *Ed. Ann. Register* of 1810—and your paper upon the poor laws? . . . I will take care to notice that the credit of these papers is not due to me, either specifying whose they are, or leaving that unexplained as you think best."[10] Rickman seemed not to wish any public acknowledgment of his authorship, and on the republication of the essays from the *Register,* Southey was silent about Rickman's share.

Scott's "Account of the Poems of Patrick Carey" was so much expanded when it appeared as a book in 1819 that it can scarcely be called a book largely derived from the pages of the *Register:* only the first tentative draft was published there. Many poems and essays appeared in the *Register* for the first and only time, but others were later republished by their authors. The *Register* made no particular point of publishing only original material, and the practice is nowhere more clear than in the poetry section, often incorrectly titled "Original Poetry." The longest

9. The second part of this essay is derived from the latter part of Southey's review of Pasley in the *Quarterly Review* for May 1811.

10. Orlo Williams, *Lamb's Friend the Census Taker: the Life and Letters of John Rickman* (Boston, 1912), p. 234.

poem to be reprinted was Scott's *The Vision of Don Roderick,* published in book form in 1811 and then reprinted in the *Register* for 1809 (published in 1811). Four extracts from James Hogg's *The Poetic Mirror* were reprinted in the seventh volume of the *Register,* and John Wilson's *The Magic Mirror* (1812) was reprinted in the *Register* for 1810 (published in 1812).

✑ The Contributors to the *Register,* 1808–1816

I have attempted to ascertain the authorship of the essays, poems, and miscellaneous contributions to the *Register,* but a great many still remain unidentified. For essays to which I have not been able to assign an author, I can offer some possibilities. James Ballantyne is known to have written dramatic criticism and to have been a regular playgoer; it seems quite possible, therefore, that as the nominal editor of the *Register* he wrote the essays on the drama in the first three numbers and on the Scottish drama in the second and third volumes. The articles on science may be from Sir John Leslie, whose aid in such subjects was anticipated when the *Register* was first planned, but there is no later evidence that he had any hand in the *Register.* After Scott had no further interest or influence in the *Register* the scientific and geographical sections are certainly by the new editor, Hugh Murray. Murray might possibly have helped out in these departments before 1820, but there is no evidence that he did.

Able short biographies on Grahame and Windham are unassigned and could be by almost any writer. Dr. Robert Gooch admitted his authorship of the biography of Dr. Thomas Beddoes (*Memoir . . . William Taylor,* II, 383), and Gooch was certainly not a member of Scott's circle or even a Scot. The *Register* took part in the pamphlet warfare over Oxford education, entering the field in opposition to the *Edinburgh Review.* The eighteen-page article, "On the State of the University of Oxford," in the second volume (published in 1811), and followed by a note in the third volume, contains no clue about its author. The author's method is largely descriptive of the system of educational organization of Oxford and of the course of study and examinations. Edward Dowden pronounced it "a well-informed and seemingly not unfair account of education at the university." The author, although moderate, recognizes the need for some change. A possible author is Charles Kirkpatrick Sharpe, whom Scott had asked for assistance in the *Register* and who was then resident at Christ Church, Oxford, but letters of Sharpe acknowledging his few contributions to the *Register* fail to mention this essay. The author appears to be a Scot who had carefully read the pamphlets and prepared his essay from published materials. The essay need not have been written by anyone who was personally familiar with Oxford. Another well-written article, that on the Bell Rock Light House, could have come from many persons in Edinburgh, of whom there were many well versed in science and engineering.

The poems in the *Register* can usually be assigned to their authors since most of them are signed, while others are from the pens of authors who collected their poems in their later published works. Many ephemera, translations, and short lyrics must remain as anonymous as they were upon publication. Scott, whose hand is clearly evident in this department, made no effort to publish new unpublished poems. Many poems, including several of his own, in the first volume were reprinted from his own *English Minstrelsy.* For the second volume he reprinted his *Vision of Don Roderick,* and in the third volume John Wilson's *The Magic Mirror.* James Hogg's *The Poetic Mirror* appeared in the seventh volume.

A glance at the contents of any volume of the *Edinburgh Annual Register* shows that many of the poems are unsigned, as are virtually all of the prose essays. Although much, if not most, of the authorship of the *Register* remains unknown, many of the essays and a few of the unsigned poems can be assigned to their proper authors. It is known, of course, that the "History of Europe" for the first four volumes was written by Southey, the fifth and sixth by James Russell, the seventh and eighth by Scott, and the ninth by J. G. Lockhart. From the first volume the two essays by Scott—reprinted for the first time in this book—on the judicial system of Scotland and on the contemporary British poets—have long been known to be his. The unsigned poem, "How D'Ye Do and Good-Bye," was by W. R. Spencer, who contributed two other signed poems to the volume. In his book *Memoirs of a Literary Veteran* ([London, 1851], II, 12), R. P.

Gillies later acknowledged that he was the author of two un-signed poems, "Elegy" and "To the River N*******." "The Enchantress," although unsigned, is easily recognized as an ex-tract from *The Curse of Kehama* by Southey.

From the second volume three essays can be assigned to Scott either on his own admission or by internal evidence. These three essays are printed in this book. Scott also included his own *Vision of Don Roderick,* without his signature, and was respon-sible for the insertion of original letters by Shenstone, Hume, and Spence. Of the unsigned poems "Fragment Written in Glen-finlas" can also be assigned to R. P. Gillies on his own admission.

From the third volume the memoir of Dr. Thomas Beddoes is by his fellow physician, Dr. Robert Gooch; Southey wrote the "History of Lope de Aguirre"; and Scott was responsible for the "Account of the Poems of Patrick Carey." Scott was also re-sponsible for the insertion of the *Journal of a Levant Pirate* and original letters of the earl of Eglintoune. Of the unsigned poems, Southey's "Inchcape Rock" (in Scott's own version) is instantly recognizable, and "Polydore: A Ballad" and "Fragment, Com-posed by Moonlight" can be assigned to William Howison and C. K. Sharpe, respectively, on the authority of Scott's and Sharpe's letters.[11]

From the fourth volume the memoir of Dr. John Leyden is by Scott, the only essay from the *Register* which he chose to repub-lish. The unsigned poem, "Verses to the Memory of Dr. John Leyden," is by Sir John Malcolm and was published under Mal-colm's signature in Leyden's *Poetical Remains* (1819). From the fifth volume the source of only two items can be ascertained: the extracts from Scott's journal of his trip to the Western Is-lands; the account of Montrose's Campaign was devised by Scott from a book in his possession.

The sixth volume contained no essays, and of the unsigned poems, "The Lifting of the Banner" and "To the Ancient Ban-ner of the House of Buccleuch" are attributable to Scott and Hogg, respectively, since they later reprinted these poems. The seventh and eighth volumes likewise have no prose essays, and the three unsigned sonnets in volume 7 must remain as anony-mous contributions. The poem, "The Vision of Belshazzar" is

---

11. *Letters of Scott* VII, 57n; VIII, 54; and *Letters From and To Charles Kirk-patrick Sharpe,* ed. A. Allardyce (Edinburgh, 1888), I, 51.

by W. B. Villiers according to Scott (*Letters of Scott* IV, 516), but in 1824 W. K. Westly wrote Scott (*Letters of Scott* VIII, 469) and claimed the poem for himself. "The Dirge of a Highland Chief" in volume 8 was sent to the *Register* by "a literary friend of ours," with the hope that it might be inserted in some future edition of *Waverley.*

The ninth volume resumed the publication of essays and extracts from books, but the authorship of these essays has not been established. The two translations of old Spanish ballads are by Lockhart and were subsequently published by him in 1823.

Part 3

Reprints of Uncollected Essays by Scott

ᨦ Prospectus

The authorship of the Prospectus is not known. Scott presumably had a
hand in its composition, but it is more likely a work of composite authorship in which James Ballantyne may be suspected as a collaborator. Scott
once apologized for its "too stately" tone (*Letters of Scott* II, 140). The
Register failed to live up to the ambitious scheme of providing essays and
information under the nine headings promised in the Prospectus, but in
the nine very full and well-written volumes of contemporary history by
Southey, Scott, Russell, and Lockhart, it may be said to have fulfilled its
primary purpose of providing a detailed account of the great military and
political actions that occurred throughout Europe. During the nine years
during which Scott's influence was paramount, the *Register* was far more
literary and antiquarian than scientific (although it included frequently, if
not consistently, accounts of scientific and technical news). The Prospectus
is noticeably silent about the inclusion of poetry, original essays, and reprints
of recondite journals and documents of antiquarian-historical interest: inclu-
sions that give the modern reader the *Register's* most distinctive character.

The flourishing state of the literature of Britain and its widely-
extended influence among her inhabitants, are blessings only
inferior to those of civil peace and personal liberty, with which
they are so closely entwined. On the Continent, the voice of
historic truth has been silenced, and her researches interdicted.
The progress of despotism has been as universal as rapid. From
the shores of Holland to the Cimmerian regions of Tartary, light
after light has been quenched, and nation after nation consigned
to the darkness and apathy of ignorance. The states of Switzer-
land and of Holland, the smaller principalities and civic repub-
lics of Germany and Italy, have been forced to resign that independence, which had been spared by former conquerors, even
when defended only by an ancient and venerable name. Those
free cities, which cherished the earliest sparks of religious reformation, and the hardly less sacred embers of classical learning, have, one by one, beheld their press broken or fettered,

their academies new-modelled or dispersed, their authors awed into silence by proscription and military execution, or more shamefully bribed to plead the cause of foreign tyranny, by orders, ribbands, and pensions. Not only has the main current of history been intercepted, but the lesser channels of information, those journals, newspapers, and other periodical publications, whose supplies, though individually scanty, are as essential as those of brooks to a river, have been altogether cut off, or polluted at their very source. There is no voice left upon the Continent to tell the tale of universal subjugation, or bequeath to posterity the legacy of retribution.

In such emergency, it is fortunate, not for England only, but for the world, that there never was a period of our history, when knowledge was so widely diffused, learning so highly honoured, and literary merit so much fostered and caressed. We would willingly, in circumstances so honourable to Britain, trace an omen of the future political regeneration of Europe. If the love of knowledge, elsewhere damped or extinguished, glows among us with a brilliance more dazzling as more condensed, let us trust that it is preserved by the wisdom of Providence for the future exigencies of the universe. The Greeks, after the Persian invasion, decreed, that their household fires, polluted by the Barbarians, should be rekindled by a brand from the altar of Apollo. It may not be too proud, or too presumptuous a hope, that our island is destined one day to be the Delphos, where nations whose colleges and shrines have been contaminated by a yet more cruel, because a more systematic tyranny, shall repair to obtain a spark of re-illumination. Where, indeed, unless in the annals of Britain, can future historians derive materials for the history of this eventful period? It must not then be wondered at, that at such a time, and with such a prospect, each, even the feeblest among us, should proffer the exercise of his talents, where likely to be attended with the slightest advantage to the cause of British history: and it is under these impressions, that the Editors of this work offer to the Public the present plan, conscious, that while their task is humble and unostentatious, the execution cannot be considered as useless or unimportant.

In assuming, for their proposed Work, the Title of THE EDINBURGH ANNUAL REGISTER, the Editors are sensible that they load themselves with additional responsibility. The metropolis of Scotland has been long a mighty name in the annals of

literature, though, perhaps, never more universally honoured
than in the present day. The editors dare not hope that their efforts can add to its fame; yet, should they be able to carry into
effect the plan now submitted to the public, they trust THE
EDINBURGH ANNUAL REGISTER will be no discredit to the
city where it is published, and whence it derives its name.

I. THE HISTORY OF EUROPE, for the year 1808, will occupy the first general division of the proposed REGISTER. The
Editors are aware of the peculiar difficulties attending the composition of such annals; the enumeration of which may shew,
that they have carefully considered the subject, and are prepared to combat, if not to overcome them.

The requisites demanded for the composition of general and
of periodical history, do not, perhaps, greatly differ. A sacred
veneration for truth; a patient research through dubious and
contradictory authorities; a lucid arrangement of the materials
so painfully collected; a judicious selection, generalising details,
yet retaining every circumstance characteristic of the actors and
of the age; a style, emphatic and dignified in the narration of
important events, concise in the less interesting passages, but
natural, clear, and unaffected through the whole; these requisites
are as peremptorily demanded from him who compiles the annals of a year, as from the historian of a hundred centuries. Or,
if some abatement be made in favour of the humbler labourer,
it will hardly be found to counterbalance his disadvantages. The
materials of the Historian may indeed be of difficult access, of
dubious authority, meagre in amount, obscure in purport, and
irreconcileable with each other. But there are substitutes for
these deficiencies. Time to collect, to systematize, to collate,
and to arrange his materials, is at the writer's command; and,
where industry is totally unsuccessful, he possesses, or at least
often claims, the right of exercising ingenuity and conjecture.
The scantiness of facts may be lawfully supplied by hypotheses,
provided the author can make those which he possesses hang together, and depend upon each other. If one volume supply him
with the commencement of a war, and another authority with
its termination, the space between may be safely filled with conjectures, which cannot be easily refuted, if accommodated to
the admitted events. The historian may thus throw an arch over
a gap in his authorities, for he has facts on which to found the
abutments at each extremity. But the annalist has no such

licence. His conjectures rather resemble the bridge in the Vision of Mirza; one end, indeed, fixed and visible, but the other lost in the clouds and darkness of futurity. Even while he writes, the passing hour may give the lie to his theory ere it is dry upon the paper; and, should he venture at prophecy, he will do well previously to insure the gift of inspiration. Of the quantity of his materials, the Annalist has indeed little reason to complain; but, in value, they are far inferior to those of the Historian. Authentic documents and original state papers, can only be recovered after the lapse of generations, and their place is but poorly supplied by contemporaneous reports, founded so frequently on wilful falsehood, or popular exaggeration. The superabundance of such ephemeral and apocryphal materials encreases the difficulties arising from contradictory authorities, and doubles those peculiar to the Annalist, from the shortness of time permitted for selection, collation, and arrangement. It were to be wished that the evil stopped here. But, although the Historian himself ought to beware how he yields to the seduction of theory, or of prejudice, the danger from such prepossessions is enhanced in a more formidable degree to him, whose narrative comprehends only the passing events of his own times. The prejudices of the former are those of a solitary student, peculiar to himself, and which either the counsel of friends, or the voice of candid criticism, may enable him to correct. But the contagion of party feeling is not confined to the Annalist's own mind; it is above, about, and around him; he breathes in an infected atmosphere; and is strengthened in his errors, scarcely more by the factious applause of his friends, than by the no less factious opposition of his adversaries.

Yet these various disadvantages, though formidable, are not insuperable; they may be lessened, if not totally overcome. Sedulous attention, and the assistance of judicious and well-informed friends, may enable the Annalist to sift his materials, and to digest them in an order, which, though it can hardly be expected to exhibit the philosophy of history, may present, in a connected and systematized narrative, those facts, which have been given to the public in insulated and individual irregularity. The advantage of such contemporaneous history will be readily appreciated, when we attempt, without its assistance, to recall to memory the events of our own time. Such and so rapid has been their transition, and so frequently have the important news of yesterday been lost and merged in the yet more momentous intelligence of to-day, that the confused, dark, and indistinct impression is as shapeless as the cloud that has drifted to leeward after discharging its thunders. To this may be added, that, from the abrupt mode in which intelligence is communicated through the channels of gazettes and newspapers, it is often difficult, or impossible, to trace events to their operating causes. The Historical part of THE REGISTER will at once have the advantage of recalling the events of the past year to the memory, and of tracing their progress, bearings, and dependencies. No efforts shall be spared to procure the most enlightened and authentic intelligence concerning occurrences of importance, both Foreign and Domestic; nor would the Editors intrude themselves upon such a task, were they not confident of possessing sources of information not generally accessible to the Public. In narrating public struggles, and particularly those of a domestic nature, they feel equally the delicacy and the importance of their duty. To assert that they are capable of reviewing and relating the debates of two contending parties, each claiming the praise of unbiassed rectitude of intention, and boasting the distinction of the most splendid mental endowments, with minds uninfluenced by the arguments of either, would be the extremity of presumption; since it would be assuming to themselves the power of observing a golden mean, while the ablest and most enlightened of the kingdom were swerving into extremes. But, if to ground their political creed, not upon party, but upon principle; if to be absolutely and utterly unconnected with any political persons, in power or in opposition; if to be alike without hope and without fear, beneath flattery, and far above threats;—if these can give a claim to independence, the Editors may assert it with confidence and with truth. They therefore trust, that the annals which they essay to compile, may be found useful materials for future history, if themselves shall not be thought worthy of aspiring to that distinguished name. And if, as must happen after their best efforts, they shall be occasionally misled, future writers may learn from their errors the "form and pressure" of the time in which they lived, and observe, with advantage, how differently the same events affect the contemporary writer, and those who are removed from the misrepresentations and prejudices of the period in which they have passed.

II. As an APPENDIX to the History will be offered an ample

COLLECTION OF THE STATE PAPERS of the year. The use
of these is sufficiently obvious; and care will be taken, by com-
paring the translations with the originals, to give Foreign Documents in a more correct state than that in which they are usually
offered to the British Public.

III. CHRONICLE OF REMARKABLE EVENTS. This is intended to comprehend such incidents, as either form no part of
the general history of the year, or are only slightly touched upon.
It will naturally contain—

1. Proceedings of the Courts of Justice in remarkable cases in
England, Scotland, and Ireland.

2. Casualties, and Remarkable Occurrences, Foreign and
Domestic.

3. Promotions, Marriages, Births, and Deaths.

4. BIOGRAPHY of Remarkable and Eminent Persons. If the
Editors are able to render their publication valuable in other
respects, they have little fear that this Branch will be enlarged
at least, if not altogether supplied, by the voluntary contributions of those who seek a respectable place of deposit for the
commemoration of departed genius and worth.

IV. HISTORY OF LITERATURE, foreign and domestic. It
has been common for works of this kind to contain a Review of
new publications. But it appears to the Editors, that, from the
limited space which could be assigned to such a Review in their
volume, it would be in every point unsatisfactory, even if that
high department of literature were not already in the hands of
others, whose acknowledged abilities stand pledged to its fulfil-
ment. But a historical account of the state of learning, which,
without pretending to analyze popular works, or make extracts
from them, only professes to point out the extent and the causes
of their popularity; to trace how far they have been dictated by
the taste of the public, or have given it a new impulse; and, to
give a general and systematic view of contemporary literature;—
this is still a *desideratum,* yet cannot be alleged to interfere with
the labours of periodical criticism. In this view of the publications of the period, the usual rule of criticism is indeed in some
degree reversed; because, instead of enquiring how far they deserve success, it is intended to ascertain, how far popularity,
actually obtained, is grounded upon real merit, or upon adventitious circumstances. In short, it is designed to present a view
rather of the state of public taste, than of the individual works

by which it has been influenced, or attracted. General, however, as such a report proposes to be, it must necessarily include some account of those works which have gained a more than common share of popularity, as well as of the periodical criticism which has for its professed object the just direction of public taste.

V. HISTORY OF SCIENCE. A difficult but most important object in the plan, is to trace the annual advances of Science. Philosophical discovery is by its nature progressive; new objects rise in endless succession; the circle of the horizon swells on the view; and that perfection which admits continual approach is the term of all human attainments. Science presents two grand divisions—the Mathematical, and the Physical. Mathematics, after so many ages of successful culture, may be presumed to have, at length, reached their maturity. They still continue, indeed, to advance; but their progress is not marked by those corruscations [*sic*] which dazzle the incurious spectator. Much, however, is yet wanting in the beauty and adaptation of the materials, to complete the symmetry of that vast creation of genius.—The scattered acquisitions, whether calculated to enlarge the structure, or to improve its simplicity and elegance, shall be noticed with peculiar satisfaction.

The science of Physics forms the peculiar boast of modern times. Guided by the light of experiment, it has made the most astonishing advances, and continues to move forward with accumulated force. Wherever it has received the aid of Geometry, its progress has been solid and complete. Astronomy, founded on observation, combined with mathematical research, is justly regarded as the most perfect and sublime of all the sciences. It has acquired essential improvements, even in our own times; and the more recondite laws of the universe, which the revolution of ages will confirm, have been disclosed, by the skilful application of the higher analysis. These abstruse deductions will, no doubt, be gradually simplified and extended. But the kindred sciences of Navigation and Geography promise more rapid improvement. Discoveries must keep pace with that spirit of activity and enterprise which distinguishes the present period,—when intelligent travellers penetrate the remotest countries,—and ships, in the pursuit of schemes, either of war or commerce, cover the face of the ocean.

Natural philosophy, in all its branches, acquires successive improvements. Mechanics and Hydrostatics have already attained a

certain degree of stability. But Hydraulics, notwithstanding the
partial assistance it has derived from Geometry, is yet in a very
imperfect state. Within these few years, however, the investigations have been resumed with better effect; and the improvements which this useful branch of science is destined to receive,
may be anticipated with confidence.

Those parts of Physics which have not yet formed an union
with mathematical science, are to be considered as still in their
infancy, and therefore promising a plentiful harvest of discovery.
Magnetism affords curious and interesting results; but Electricity
exhibits the most brilliant and surprising combinations: And
these popular sciences, inviting a greater number of inquirers,
and as yet demanding no severe study, and little reach of
thought, are proportionally enriched with new facts. Galvanism,
which so closely allies with Electricity, has very recently given
occasion to some discoveries of the most unexpected and striking kind. Chemistry, for the came [*sic*] reason, is in a state of
rapid advancement. Natural History continues to be cultivated
with ardour and success. Mineralogy, in particular, has, within
these few years, acquired consistency, and received prodigious
improvements. Even Geology, which pretends, from such slender
data, to explain the formation of our globe, if it should not
withdraw the attention from more serious occupations, may at
least amuse its zealous votaries.

The details respecting the progress of science, are dispersed
through a multitude of works in various languages,—in Literary
Journals,—in the Memoirs of Academies,—and in the Transactions of Learned Societies. It shall be the sedulous endeavour of
the Editors to collect those scattered materials; to arrange, dis-
pose, and condense them into one connected view; and to in-
fuse interest and spirit into the historical deduction; to trace out
the various bearings which the new objects present, and to offer
such reflections and anticipations as the review of them may
suggest. In the execution of this arduous task, the Editors are
assured of powerful assistance, from some, who, having trod the
paths of discovery, feel intensely the passion for philosophical
inquiry, and will, with alacrity, contribute their unwearied efforts to forward a plan, which holds forth the prospect of such
important benefits to the general interests of science.

VI. HISTORY OF THE FINE ARTS; comprehending Painting,
Architecture, Music, and the Drama; in each of which depart-

ments, it is proposed annually to report new improvements and discoveries; the merits of new professors; the impression which they have made on the public, and its causes, to whatever sources they are to be ascribed.

VII. HISTORY OF THE USEFUL ARTS. In giving an account of the application of science to the Arts of Life, the Editors are sufficiently conscious of the importance and difficulty of their task. The various machines and processes, perpetually obtruded on our notice, are not unfrequently the copies of useless and forgotten inventions; and, even when distinguished by novelty or genius, they are seldom intelligible to the general reader. The studied obscurity and conciseness of the patentee, and the inability of illiterate mechanics to communicate their sentiments and plans, otherwise than in the dark and technical phraseology of their profession, have rendered uninteresting a branch of science, which has the most immediate influence on the happiness and advancement of our species. In detailing, therefore, the annual progress of the Useful Arts, the Editors will select from the shapeless mass which has accumulated during the year, and will describe only those machines which are ingenious and useful, and those processes in Agriculture and Manufactures which have received the sanction of observation and experiment. By thus concentrating the loose materials which are dispersed through the pages of periodical works, and by endeavouring to obtain Original Communications from the Inventors themselves, many valuable discoveries may be rescued from oblivion, while the ingenious and unfriended artist is honoured with the reward of national gratitude.

VIII. HISTORY OF THE ATMOSPHERE, or Progress of Meteorology. The present imperfect state of Meteorological Science will render this department of our Work peculiarly interesting and useful. A judicious collection of atmospherical phenomena, is the sole foundation for a sober and lasting theory, and can only be obtained from the enthusiasm and diligence of ingenious observers. By marking, therefore, the density, temperature, and humidity of our atmosphere;—by noting the variations of the tides, the temperature of springs, and the force and direction of the winds;—by recording the more brilliant and terrific changes among the elements, which issue in the thunderbolt and the meteor;—by recording these and other aerial phenomena, we may expect a rich harvest of

discovery, and contribute to give form and stability to an infant
science.

IX. COMMERCIAL, FINANCIAL, AND STATISTICAL
TABLES; comprehending Prices of Stocks, Grain, and general
Merchandise. Concerning these articles, the Editors can only
promise their utmost endeavours to render them at once accurate and comprehensive.

↶ Of the Living Poets of Great Britain

This essay has always been attributed to Scott and is so listed in the *New
Cambridge Bibliography of English Literature.* Scott also commented on
the essay in a letter (*Letters of Scott* II, 283 and note).

"Of the Living Poets of Great Britain" (*Register* I, 417–43) says something about over thirty poets who were active in 1810 with comments
ranging from a sentence to several paragraphs. Every reader today will be
struck with the great change that has occurred in critical judgments since
Scott wrote his essay. Scott judged Thomas Campbell, Robert Southey,
and Walter Scott to be the three leading poets and in that order. Those
who judge a poet by his adherence to the rules prefer Campbell, those who
"feel poetry most enthusiastically" prefer Southey, but the great mass of
readers have given their suffrage to Scott. Scott regrets, however, that
political party affiliation influences the judgments about poets and their
poetry. The followers of Pitt's policies admire Scott, the Foxites like
Campbell; and then Scott makes the interesting point that Southey has no
following among a political faction. This statement can be explained by
the fact that in 1810 Southey was not yet known for his association with
the *Quarterly* and the *Register,* and his appointment to the laureateship—
three years in the future—had not made him the special target of the
ministerial opposition. Scott, who placed Campbell at the top of the living poets, commends *Gertrude of Wyoming.* Scott's praise of Southey is
qualified because he "is sometimes too much wrapt in his own aerial
world to consider whether the general mass of readers can accompany his
flight." Scott also deplores Southey's departures from the "ordinary and
received" rules of poetry and for his use of the "language of base and rude
simplicity." Scott finds fault with his own poems because of their loose
structure and unindividualized characters but praises the descriptions
where he "frequently stands alone unrivalled." His success in such description he attributes to his "tenacious memory" and his antiquarian
reading.

Scott does not believe that Southey, Coleridge, and Wordsworth (sometimes grouped together as the Lake Poets) are in a conspiracy "combined to overthrow the ancient land marks of our poetry." Scott, however, is sceptical about the truth of Wordsworth's belief in the "language of low and rustic life" and denies that the lower classes have the feelings Wordsworth has attributed to them. Scott is nonetheless laudatory of Wordsworth's poetry and admires his dedication to poetry. His discussion shows a thorough familiarity with Wordsworth's poems, and he regrets that the public has not given Wordsworth his just due. Toward Coleridge, however, Scott is lukewarm and cites only two poems by title: "The Memory of a Deceased Friend" and "An Introduction to the Tale of the Dark Ladie." Although Scott had heard, remembered, and imitated *Christabel* in his *Lay of the Last Minstrel,* that poem was not published until 1816.

Most of the other poets Scott mentions are little more than names today. His long discussion of the poetic plays of Joanna Baillie serves only to reveal the shortness of a contemporary fame. Scott's letters of January 1810 are filled with minute details of the several performances of Baillie's *The Family Legend* in Edinburgh with Mrs. Siddons in the leading role. Not all Scott's judgments, however, seem out of place. His praise of Crabbe which he qualified by his inability to accept Crabbe's valuation of the middle and lower classes would be in line with critical judgment today. Scott's strong objection to the lasciviousness of the poems of Thomas Moore and Lord Strangford is symptomatic of the changing taste of the day, one that anticipates the Victorian era. The penultimate sentence of the essay is in keeping with this moral tone: "Nor is it our smallest boast, that the muses have been, of late, generally engaged in the cause of virtue and morality, and that the character of the libertine and spendthrift are no longer the frequent accompaniment of the sacred name of Poet."

Other bits from the essay can be briefly mentioned. Scott's aristocratic predilections show in his comments about the poetry of the Honorable William R. Spencer and Reginald Heber. Scott, who recognizes Spencer's agreeable talent for *vers de société,* wishes that the pleasures and diversions of a fashionable life had not taken him from the cultivation of poetry. Reginald Heber, known today only for his hymns, is praised for his long poems *Palestine* and *Europe,* but Scott concludes that Heber's wealth was a deterrent to his exerting himself to the extent necessary to achieve distinction as a poet. Conversely, his brief description of various peasant poets concludes with a prediction that the interest in them was a passing vogue as he spoke of the "meanness and poverty" of Robert Bloomfield.

The poet whom Scott could have mentioned as active in 1810—but did not—was Byron. Byron's *English Bards and Scotch Reviewers* (1809) had attracted considerable notice, and Scott's private comment on the poem's reference to him was one of amused irritation: "I can assure the noble imp of fame it is not my fault that I was not born to a park and £5000 a-year (*Letters of Scott* II, 214, August 7, 1809).

Despite the judgments so out of keeping with today's ranking of these

poets the essay still gives a fair view of the way a leading man of letters
looked at his poetic contemporaries in 1810. Of the poets discussed in the
essay Scott, Southey, Campbell, Leyden, Baillie, Spencer, Mrs. Hunter,
Hogg, and Montgomery contributed to the *Register.*

The importance and extent of our Historical Department has
necessarily encroached upon the other branches of our Register:
nor would it be either easy or desirable to comprise our literary
observations into such a size as might accommodate them to
the space to which we are in this volume unavoidably limited. It
appears to us a better arrangement, to divide the extensive subject before us into departments, and lay our report upon one of
these yearly before the public. This partial execution of our plan
not only gives us leisure and room to treat at becoming length
the subjects under our consideration, but promises the advantage
of supplying, by its regular rotation, important matter for the
same articles, as they revolve in the course of a few years. Proposing to ourselves, for example, in the following essay, to
characterize generally the Poets who at present engage the attention of the public, we could hardly hope to repeat such a disquisition in our next volume, with any prospect of exciting similar
interest. But poetical laurels are not perennial, although they
may not wither annually; nor dare we venture to conjecture the
change which a few years may make in our own respect for
those whom we consider at present as the most distinguished
followers of the Muses. Ere we return again to view the state of
British poetry, some of the masters of the lyre may have paid
the debt of nature; some, alive to the world, may yet have suffered poetical death, or literary bankruptcy; some may have
fallen innocent martyrs to the envy or malignancy of criticism;
and others, by a fate yet more deplorable, may have committed
suicide on their own reputation. These reflections, while they
reconcile us to our plan of subdividing our Review of Literature,
have no small influence on the feelings with which we advance
to discharge the first part of our task. We may take credit, with
the same courage as other unknown authors, for the justice of
our own praise and censure; we may be willing to risk the dishonour of false prophecy, and may be totally indifferent whether our judgment shall be confirmed by the public, or whether,
when resuming our speculations, after the interval proposed, we
may find ourselves obliged to make the *amende honorable,* and

confess the imprudence and injustice of a sentence reversed by the universal voice of the public. But, if we shall have gained on our own account this happy degree of apathy concerning the ultimate issue of our predictions, is it in human nature to consider with indifference the changes which must shortly take place among those who furnish the subject of our inquiries? Literary fame, so eagerly, so anxiously pursued, becomes the portion of so few, and is so unequally and unfairly distributed among those who possess it, is so short-lived when obtained, and so lamented when lost, that it is scarcely possible to view the crowds who faint in the ineffectual pursuit, the few whom transient success renders objects rather of envy and detraction than of admiration, the "grey discrowned heads"[1] upon whom its laurels have faded, without keen recollection of the *vanita[s] vanitatum*[2] of the Preacher; and some wonder that the people should, from generation to generation, continue to pursue a shadow, and to "imagine a vain thing."[3] Of all the restless impulses, indeed, with which the human heart is goaded, few surprise us more than this same longing after literary immortality. In no other race would the impotent propose themselves for the prize held forth for feats of vigour; in no other contest would the victor be rewarded, not only by the ill-suppressed execrations of his less fortunate competitors, but by an inward feeling of malevolence, even among those who never thought of rivalling him; and surely in no other profession was it ever dreamed that the repetition of honourable and successful efforts did, of itself, disqualify him who made them from again claiming his share of public favour. Yet so it is in Poetry. Those with whose music, however delightful, the public ear has once been satiated, can only again hope to attract attention by changing the nature of their subject, their style of composition, at every risk of incurring the ridicule due to versatility.

A moral poet, like Pope, may indeed continue to engross the public with undiminished interest, provided he will be contented

---

1. From "Majesty in Misery" attributed to Charles I and published in Gilbert Burnet's *The Memoires of the Lives and Actions of James and William Dukes of Hamilton and Castleherald* (London, 1677). I am indebted to Dr. Anthony J. Shipps for this identification.
2. Scott uses this phrase from Ecclesiastes in a letter of Oct. 3, 1810 (*Letters of Scott* II, 380).
3. Psalms 2:1.

to owe the permanence of his popularity to the least moral part of his writings,—the personality of their satire. But the follower of the Tragic, of the Epic, of the Pastoral, or of the Didactic muse, must be contented frequently to change livery, if he would remain a favourite servant of the public. We have heard of an excellent comedian, who, finding his usual attractions become a little hackneyed, drew a large benefit by performing the part of Richard the Third, for one night only. But, alas! these are experiments not to be tried, even once, without danger, and never to be repeated. If the successful poet remains silent, he loses his pre-eminence by the tacit operation of forgetfulness; if he renews his efforts from time to time, it runs every risk of being forfeited, by the actual condemnation of the public, instead of imperceptibly diminishing under their prescriptive neglect. If the situation of these poets who are still tottering on the top of the wheel of Fortune's favour, or who have toppled down headlong from the envied situation, be sufficiently melancholy, what shall we say of those who labour to gain the uncertain eminence, with the same labour, and the same success, as the turn-spit cur, who plies in the interior department of a similar machine! But in this, as in all his works, Providence has mercifully provided the means of reconciling his creatures to their whimsical and most infructuous labour. The best Christian does not believe more faithfully in the resurrection of the body, than these neglected minstrels confide in the arrival of a future period, when that justice shall be done to their writings by posterity, of which they have, in their own day, been deprived, by the ignorance of the public, the prejudices of fashion, the malicious arts of their contemporary rivals, the blunders of their printers, and the unparalleled sloth and partiality of their booksellers, who load with trash their counters and advertisements, while the works destined to delight future ages slumber neglected in their cellars and warehouses. This self-delusion may make these gentlemen happy, but can scarcely cloud the optics of their critics:—

> ——We've lived too long,
> And seen the end of much immortal song.[4]

Such expectants of immortality are in the same situation with

4. Untraced.

the dethroned monarch of Rabelais, who plied as a porter at Lyons, while waiting for the arrival of the *cocquecigrues,* upon whose approach he was to be reinstated in his kingdom.

With the feelings therefore of tenderness, which the nature of poetical reputation peculiarly demands, we proceed to examine the pretensions of those to whom the public discernment or caprice has most largely assigned it.

We do not hesitate to distinguish, as the three most successful candidates for poetical fame, Scott, Southey, and Campbell.[5] We are aware that there are many, and those too of good taste, who prefer Wordsworth, Crabbe, Rogers, Sotheby, and other names less generally known, to any of the triumvirate we have mentioned: but these are, in point of taste, sectaries and dissenters from the general faith and belief of the public at large, which, however divided upon the comparative merits of these three poets, give them, generally speaking, the precedence over their competitors. Were we set to classify their respective admirers, we should be apt to say, that those who feel poetry most enthusiastically prefer Southey; those who try it by the most severe rules admire Campbell; while the general mass of readers prefer to either the Border Poet. In this arrangement we should do Mr. Scott no injustice, because we assign to him in the number of suffrages what we deny him in their value. There is another principle which, ridiculous as it may appear, has certainly had some share in ranking the partizans of at least two of these candidates for fame. It is the fashion, and a pretty obstinate one, for the followers of political party to admire the poetry of Scott or Campbell, exactly as they happen to be attached to the parties headed by our late distinguished statesmen, Pitt and Fox. We must necessarily suppose that the political principles of the two bards are, in private life, agreeable to those of the persons who seem to follow them from that cause. Yet, as we can trace very little allusion to politics in the writings of either, and know enough of both to be certain that they do not intermeddle in state matters, this criterion seems about as absurd as it would be to judge of their poetry by the street in which they bought their neckcloths and their stockings. The fact,

5. Byron in his journal for Nov. 24, 1813, gave a ranking to the living poets, placing Scott at the top of the triangle, next Rogers, then Moore and Campbell, with Southey, Coleridge, and Wordsworth forming the base of the triangle. This estimate represented his belief as to what popular opinion would hold.

however, is certain, and only furnishes an additional example, that party must lend her seasoning to "Lays" and to "Gertrudes," as well as to Protestant muffins, or Liberty *petits pates.* Mr. Southey does not appear to number among his admirers any particular class of politicians; and if the circumstance deprives him of the support of a steady body of factious *proneurs,* it entitles his merits the more to candid attention from that part of his readers who choose to judge of poetry from poetry alone. Were we, on the other hand, to compare these three poets by their poetical attributes, we would incline, with some hesitation, to say, that Campbell excelled in taste, and correct elegance of expression; that Southey had a more rich and inexhaustible fund of poetical ideas and imagery; and that Walter Scott, if not superior to the others in fancy, possessed more forcibly the power of exciting that of his readers, by a freer and bolder style of description, embracing only the striking outlines of his picture, but giving these with full freedom, character, and effect. In point of learning, Campbell possesses classical knowledge, and Scott a large portion of that which a tenacious memory gathers from a miscellaneous course of antiquarian studies. The learning of Southey not only embraces both branches of knowledge, but in both surpasses, and, we believe, very far surpasses, that of his rivals. But this mode of balancing our triads will by no means answer our purpose of attaining a short view of the poetical character of each, with some notices of the extent and causes of their popularity.

Mr. THOMAS CAMPBELL met with early popularity. The Pleasures of Hope, a work written in youth, was justly hailed as one of the brightest dawnings which had ever attended the rise of a literary character. The faults, too, were evidently those of a young man, such as it might be hoped time and study would do away. A want of compactness in its parts, here and there a tinselly expression, intimated a fancy not yet tamed; the occurrence of passages, which necessarily reminded us of Goldsmith, of Johnson, or of Rogers;—these were his faults, and they were light in the balance, weighed against the beauty of his moral precept, the unaffected dignity of his sentiment, the flowing ease of his versification, and an expression which swelled, softened, or sunk like the murmurs of an Æolian harp, as the subject rose or fell.—His reputation, therefore, rose high, and with justice, while it was rather increased than diminished by the

various minor pieces which appeared in periodical or detached
publications, previous to a quarto edition of the Pleasures of
Hope, in 1803, to which were subjoined, the sublime poems of
Lochiel and Hohenlinden. These productions carried to the
height Mr. Campbell's fame, for they evinced that he possessed
power and spirit for the *paullo majora* of poetry, and that the
Epic Muse might, with confidence, claim him as her own. It was,
perhaps, partly owing to the over-stretched state of public expectation, that "Gertrude of Wyoming" has not hitherto met a
reception from the public worthy of the poet's name, or of the
merits of the poem. It was ingeniously urged by a friendly critic,
that the interest was of that elegant, unobtrusive, and refined
nature which was not adapted to attract general admiration. But,
alas! when we say a poem is too grand, or too refined, to be
popular, we only weigh the solitary opinion of the critic against
that of the world at large. The truth seems to be, that a story,
in itself extremely imperfect, was rendered less intelligible by
the manner in which it was told, and by a structure of versification, which, unless managed with uncommon address, is liable
to lead to the alternate extremes of obscurity and redundance.
We are satisfied it is to this cause, chiefly, that the failure of
Gertrude, so far as its not instantly attaining extensive popularity is a failure, must be attributed. The readers of poetry, generally speaking, are not very nice about the subject, and like
just as well to be melted with a tale of private distress, as to be
roused with a lay of war. But then the impression must be made
at the first perusal: they will not consent to wait till the bellows
are employed to blow the flame. Like the public at every former
period, they are complete egotists: it is amusement which they
demand, and if they do not instantly find what they seek, they
will not think it worth winning at the labour of a re-perusal. In
this view, the inverted and complicated construction of the
stanzas in Gertrude of Wyoming has been a great impediment
to its popularity, which neither the pathos of some passages,
nor the exquisite elegance, and poetical spirit which pervades
the whole, have been able to counterbalance. It is whispered Mr.
Campbell is at present labouring upon a large poem of an epic
nature. We heartily rejoice to hear it. He is in the prime of life,—
in that state of literary retirement most favourable to composition,—enjoying ready access to the best judges, and, at the same
time, the power of securing the command of his own time. Much

may be hoped from such talents and such opportunities. There
is much to be maintained, perhaps something to be recovered.
Yet a numerous class, comprehending many of the critics of
more strict and severe tone, place Mr. Campbell first among our
living poets; with what justice we do not attempt to say, but an
opinion so supported wears a face at least of probability.

Mr. ROBERT SOUTHEY, one of the highest names in English
literature, stands second of the triumvirate in our casual arrangement. His life was early dedicated to poetry and learning, in
preference to "preferment's pleasing paths."[6] It can be as little
doubted that he has found his own happiness in the exchange,
as that his choice has given him opportunity to add to that of
thousands. His most ardent admirers are of a class with whom it
is difficult to argue: They are the enthusiasts—almost the methodists of poetry. There is perhaps no species of applause so congenial to the spirit, or so flattering to the author, as that which
resigns the reins so totally into his hands, and allows itself to be
hurried along with his rapid movements, however bold, devious,
and even capricious. We dare not say, however, that the possession of this absolute monarchy over his admirers is altogether
favourable to the general character of the poet. Despotic power
leads, in almost every instance, to fantastic exercise of it on the
part of the possessor; and he who, within the circle of his partizans, feels himself exempted from the controul of criticism, is
too naturally led to neglect what is transmitted from more
remote quarters. Censure is always an unpalatable draught, even
when mixed and offered by a friendly hand; but when the cup
is presented by one that is cold, suspicious, or unfriendly, we
are afraid the salutary bitter stands little chance of being swal-
lowed. Yet we cannot quarrel with the wild and arbitrary exercise of genius to which we owe the wondrous tale of Thalaba,
and which has given rise to some anomalous luxuriancies in the
more regular poem of Madoc. It seems to us that the author,
giving way to an imagination naturally prolific of the fairest
visions, is sometimes too much wrapt in his own aërial world to
consider whether the general mass of readers can accompany
his flight. The beauties of such composition are calculated for
those who have the keenest and most exquisite feeling of poetic
excellence, and whose pleasure is too engrossing not to purchase

6. Southey, "On My Own Miniature Picture" (*Poems*, 1797).

pardon for a thousand errors. But the aristarch reverses this rule, because it is his profession to find fault; and the common herd of readers also reverse it, for the beauties of such a tale as Thalaba are beyond their comprehension; while its want of rhyme, irregularity of stanza, and extravagance of story, are circumstances at once strange, stumbling, and obvious. The judicious critic will, we think, steer a middle path, although we acknowledge the difficulty of keeping its tenour. We conceive that such, while he felt and acknowledged the warmth of Mr. Southey's feeling, while he admired the inexhaustible riches of his imagination, while he applauded with enthusiasm that generous sentiment which has ever tuned his harp to the celebration of moral and intellectual excellence, might, at the same time, be allowed to deplore the circumstances which have often hidden the light under the bushel, and limited to the comparatively small circle of a few enthusiastic admirers, that fame, which, in common justice to Mr. Southey's genius, ought to have been echoed and re-echoed from all the four seas which gird in Britain. Were we asked what those circumstances are, we should not hesitate to name a resolute contempt of the ordinary and received rules of poetry, and a departure from their precepts, too shocking to all our pre-conceived opinions and expectations. We cannot stop to enquire whether Mr. Southey may not, in many instances, be able to make a rational and reasonable apology for neglecting the prescriptive rules of art. It is sufficient to our present purpose, that no author, however undoubted his genius, can hope to stem the public opinion by swimming directly contrary to its current. But, besides the impolicy of this departure from the usual and generally sanctioned practice of his predecessors, we hold that there is a gross want of taste in many of the novelties thus fixed upon. Thus, the language of bare and rude simplicity, with which this beautiful poet sometimes chooses to veil the innate elegance of his conceptions, appears to us not only contradictory to our prejudices, which have been accustomed to ascribe a particular strain of exalted diction to their development, but in itself a great deformity. In assuming a quaker-like, and, of course, an unusual, and sometimes even a vulgar form of expression, Mr. Southey powerfully reminds us of the precept of Boileau: —

> Sans la langue en un mot, l'auteur le plus
> divin,

Est toujours, quoi qu'il fasse, un mechant
ecrivain.[7]

This is the more provoking, because it is obvious these aberra-
tions are not the consequences of ignorance, which might be il-
luminated, but of a determined purpose and system, which we
cannot hope our feeble exhortations will have any effect in
subverting. Yet we wish Mr. Southey would at least make the
experiment of shooting one shaft with the wind; and we venture
to pledge ourselves, that, without injuring himself with his most
enthusiastic admirers, he will add to them thousands who are
now startled at some obvious eccentricities, and care not to look
deeper, and judge more ripely. If a traveller should choose to
pursue his journey in a common labourer's jacket and trowsers,
we are afraid that his engaging qualities for conversation, and
even an innate dignity of manner, would be completely shrouded
from the common eye by the coarseness of his outward raiment;
and that even those who could discover his excellence through
the clouds which overshadowed it, would grant their applause
with a mixture of regret, that an unnecessary and rude disguise
should exclude the person by whom it had been incautiously
adopted, from the society in which he was fitted by nature to
occupy the highest place. We have only to add, that if any one
be disposed to question the rank which we think it our duty to
ascribe to Mr. Southey amongst his contemporaries, we beg
them, before condemning our judgement, to read attentively
the meeting of the Bards, in the eleventh section of the first
part of Madoc, or the procession in honour of the River Goddess
in the twelfth section of the second part. It is in such passages
that the felicity and richness of the author's imagination display
themselves, and at once obliterate all recollection of his errors.
If, on the other hand, we are accused of having judged harshly
of an author for whose genius we have so much reverence, we
will rather submit to the censure than gratify vulgar malignity,
by pointing the occasions on which he has flown with a low and
a flagging wing:—were it indeed in our power, and were we as
well convinced of the justice of our own criticism, as we are
conscious of its sincerity and good faith, we would willingly
communicate to the public only our motives for admiration,

7. Boileau, *L'Art Poétique*, Book I.

and to the authors themselves our grounds of censure; that the former might learn what they ought to applaud, while the latter might be taught to merit that applause more amply.

The author of the Lay of the Last Minstrel and Marmion may be considered as the minion of modern popularity; for the works of no living, and of few dead authors, have been so widely and so rapidly diffused.—We are, we believe, correct in stating, that upwards of 25,000 copies of the Lay have been printed in the space of six years, and 17,000 copies of Marmion since its first appearance in spring 1808. The effect of this extensive popularity has been almost ludicrous. Upon the annunciation of an expected poem, we are well assured that at least four musicians have prepared notes for unwritten songs;—two artists have been retained to illustrate scenes which were yet to be born of the author;—and as many satirists, having blessed God and the founder, have set them down to parody a work yet in embryo. These pleasing and painful marks of notoriety go in the main to prove the same issue; for even the master of a dung-barge knows enough of navigation to discover which vessel is likely to get soonest under weigh, and to obtain her assistance, if possible, to tow him out of harbour. We have been at some pains to discover the talisman upon which this popular enthusiasm depends, but we find it more easy to express ourselves on the subject by negatives than by positive assertion. Mr. Scott's fame certainly does not rest on the art of his story, for of that he has hitherto given no example; on the contrary, the incidents, both in the Lay and Marmion, are of themselves slightly interesting, and loosely put together. Neither can we consider his characters, though drawn with a bold and determined pencil, as entitling him, on their account, to occupy the distinguished rank which he holds in the poetical calendar. They are, properly speaking, the portraits of *genera* rather than of individuals. William of Deloraine, Marmion, Clara, and Constance, are just such persons as might represent any one predatory freebooter, ambitious noble, sentimental damsel, and reprobate nun, that ever dignified the pages of romance.

The features (perhaps with exception of Marmion's forgery) must be allowed to bear a striking general resemblance to the characters of these ranks in the middle ages; but there is a want of individuality. The knights and freebooters of Mr. Scott are, like Sir Fopling Flutter, knights of the shire, and represent each a whole class;—and, although the poet may have been more anxious to give a general view of the period in which he laid his scene, than a picture of individual manners; and in this he has assuredly succeeded; we must still deny the praise of excellence to him who has halted in full career, and stopped short in finishing his picture, even at the most interesting point; and so thinking, we cannot give unqualified approbation to Mr. Scott's skill in drawing portraits. To moral sentiment he has made little pretence: the few specimens which occur in his poetry are true, but they are obvious; and their best recommendation is, that they have uniformly a virtuous or honourable tendency, and are expressed with the unaffected simplicity and lofty feeling of one who is in earnest in recommending the truth which he delivers. The descriptive passages claim more unequivocal praise; and in this department of poetry Mr. Scott frequently stands alone, and unrivalled. Instances are so numerous, that their quotation seems unnecessary: but still, even of those passages, which have been most highly praised, many do not boast the luxuriance conspicuous in the descriptions of Southey, or the elegance which is frequently displayed by the bard of Hope. To what, then, are we to attribute a charm which has interested the old and the grave, as well as gay youth and frolic boyhood? It must, we apprehend, be ascribed to that secret art which will be found to pervade the popular writings of almost every country, despite of their sins against common sense or classical criticism; that, in short, of rendering interesting the story which they have to tell, not by its own proper merit, but by the mode of telling it. It is thus that De Foe has contrived to identify the feelings of every reader with those of Robinson Crusoe, to render his slightest wants and inconveniencies subjects of our anxious solicitude, and protract a tale, in itself the most unique and simple possible, with unabated interest, through so many pages of minute and trivial incident. In the same manner we lose the author in the admired passages of the Lay and Marmion, because he never seems to think of himself, but appears wholly engrossed with the desire of impressing on the auditor the outlines of a description which is vividly sketched in his own mind. In describing a battle, a siege, or a striking incident of any kind, he seldom brings forward objects unless by that general outline by which a spectator would be actually affected. He enters into no minute detail; it is the general effect, the hurry, the bustle of the scene,—

those concomitant sounds of tumult and sights of terror which
stun the ear and dazzle the eye, which he details to his readers,
and which have often the effect of converting them into spectators. In like manner, in scenes of repose, he seems more anxious
to enjoy than to describe them; his ideas crowd upon him, but
he dispatches each of them in a line, and leaves the imagination
of his reader, if it be capable of excitation, to follow forth and
fill up the outline which he has sketched. To an active fancy this
is a pleasant task, for which it returns to the author as much
gratitude at least as is his due. A slow comprehension, on the
contrary, catches the general proposition, and is pleased to
escape from that more minute detail, which, however pleasing
to true admirers of poetry, seems only embarrassing tautology
to those who, with inert imagination, and an indifference to the
beauties of protracted description, feel nevertheless a natural
interest in the incidents of the tale, and in the animation with
which they succeed to each other. Mr. Scott, we have remarked,
seems to be fully sensible of his strength in thus embodying and
presenting his scene to the imagination of his readers, and has
studiously avoided sliding into distinct narration. Every incident
is usually conveyed by the means of indirect description; and,
so remarkably is this the case, that, even when a narrative is
placed in the mouth of a personage in the poem, the scene is
instantly shifted, and the incidents of that very tale held up in
motion and action to the reader, something a-kin to the phenomena observed in dreams, where every thing is presented to the
eye, and little or nothing to the ear; and where, if our fancy is
crossed by the supposed report of another course of action, that
secondary train of ideas is immediately substituted for the original vision, and we imagine ourselves spectators of it instead of
being only auditors. It is indisputable, that the art of thus rivet-
ting the attention of the audience forms one great source of this
author's popularity.

We must not omit to mention Mr. Scott's learning, by which
we mean his knowledge of the manners of the time in which his
scenes are laid. The display of this knowledge has, perhaps, here
and there, degenerated into antiquarian pedantry, but the possession of it was essential to the purpose of the author. *Sapere
est principium et fons.*[8] It is the true touch of manners which

8. "Scribendi recte sapere est principium et fons." Horace, *Art of Poetry,* 309.

gives justice to a narrative poem, and discriminates it from those
which are either founded upon the vague imagination of an author, or tamely copied from the model of some more original
writer. The difference can be discovered by the least enlightened,
just as an individual portrait can be distinguished from a fancy
sketch even by those who are unacquainted with the original.
With these remarks upon the truth and spirit of his poetry, we
leave Mr. Scott, no unworthy member of the triumvirate with
whom he has divided the public applause.

According to modern custom we should now consider the
imitators, or, as the modish phrase is, the school of these respective poets; if that can be called a school where no pupil will
heartily yield pre-eminence even to his pedagogue, and where
each preceptor would willingly turn his scholars out of doors.
Upon professed imitators we shall bestow very short consideration, as the very circumstance of palpable imitation may be
considered as decisive against an author's claim to be noticed in
such a sketch as we are now drawing of national poetry.

The followers and imitators of Campbell would probably rejoice more in being termed of the school of Goldsmith or Johnson: yet when we read the Pleasures of Friendship, the Pleasures
of Solitude, the Pleasures of Love, and so forth,—or even when
we see such titles in an advertisement,—we are naturally led to
think the subjects could only have been chosen from the popularity of the Pleasures of Hope, or of the Pleasures of Memory.
The latter beautiful poem probably gave Mr. Campbell the original hint of his plan, though it expanded into a more copious
and bolder field of composition than had been attempted by
Mr. ROGERS, and contains beauties of a kind so different, that
the resemblance of title is almost the only circumstance which
connects them. The Pleasures of Memory is a gem in which the
exquisite polish makes up for the inferiority of the water. There
is not a line in it which has not been earnestly and successfully
refined to melody, nor is there a description left unfinished, or
broken off harshly. The sentiments are easy and elegant, and of
that natural and pleasing tendency which always insures a
favourable reception, even when destitute of novelty. We have
in Mr. Rogers' poetry none of Campbell's sublime bursts of
moral eloquence, which exalt us above the ordinary feelings of
our nature; but we are gently and placidly led into a current of
sentiment most congenial to all the charities and domestic

attachments of life. Yet those who have by heart the Deserted
Village of Goldsmith, will hardly allow Mr. Rogers' title to
originality. Something he has gained over his model by an intimate acquaintance with the fine arts, and the capacity of ap-
pretiating their most capital productions. The delicacy and accuracy of discrimination inseparable from such attainments,
diffuses, through his poetry, a certain shade of classical and
chastened taste, which may serve, perhaps, more than any of the
circumstances we have mentioned, to discriminate his productions from those of his contemporaries.

With the name of Southey those of Coleridge and of Wordsworth are naturally and habitually associated. We do not hold,
with the vulgar, that these ingenious and accomplished men are
combined to overthrow the ancient land marks of our poetry,
and bring back the days of Withers [*sic*] and of Quarles; on the
contrary, to those who give themselves the trouble of considering their works attentively, there will appear such points of
distinction as argue a radical difference in their taste, and the
rules they have adopted in composition. Still, however, connected as they are by habits of friendship, vicinity of residence,
and community of studies, some general principles may be
pointed out common to all three, and entitling them, more than
any other living authors, to the appellation of a school of productions. We regret to say, that the peculiarities which they
have in common do not by any means seem to us the most
valuable properties of their productions. They are all, more or
less, favourers of that doctrine which considers poetry as the
mere imitation of natural feeling, and holds that its language
ought in consequence to be simplified as much as possible to
the expressions of passion in ordinary life. To this proposition
Mr. Wordsworth adds another yet more doubtful,—that the language of low and rustic life ought to be preferred, because, in
his opinion, the essential passions of the heart find a better soil
in which they can attain their maturity, and because in that condition of life our elementary feelings co-exist in a state of greater
simplicity. Now this appears to us a radical error. Those who
have studied the lower orders of society, especially in a mercantile country, must be sensible how much the feelings and talents
of that class are degraded, imbruted, and debased by the limited
exercise to which they are confined, and the gross temptations
to which they hourly give way. Even among the more fortunate

inhabitants of a pastoral country, the necessity of toiling for daily bread burthens the mind and quells the powers of imagination: The few passions by which they are strongly actuated are those which are the most simple, the most coarse, and the worst regulated; nor can the expressions which they dictate be considered as proper for poetry, any more than the company of the swains themselves for the society of persons of cultivated taste, manners, and talents. The opposite opinion has led to that affectation of a simple nakedness of style, which has, in some instances, debased even the gold of Southey, and forms a far larger alloy to the coinage of his two friends, which we are about to consider.

We are, in some degree, uncertain whether we ought to view COLERIDGE as subject to our critical jurisdiction, at least under this department. He seems to have totally abandoned poetry for the mists of political metaphysics,—mists which, we fear, the copious eloquence showered from his cloudy tabernacle will rather increase than dispel. With extensive learning, an unbounded vigour of imagination, and the most ready command of expression both in verse and prose,—advantages which none of his predecessors enjoy in a greater, if any possess them in an equal degree; this author has been uniformly deficient in the perseverance and the sound sense which were necessary to turn his exquisite talents to their proper use. He has only produced in a complete state one or two small pieces, and every thing else, begun on a larger scale, has been flung aside and left unfinished. This is not all: Although commanding the most beautiful poetical language, he has every now and then thought fit to exchange it for the gratuitous pleasure of introducing whole stanzas of quaint and vulgar doggrel. These are the passages which render learning useless, and eloquence absurd; which make fools laugh, and malignant critics "dance and leap," but which excite, in readers of taste, grief and astonishment, as evidence of talents misapplied, and genius furnishing arms against itself to low-minded envy. To Mr. Coleridge we owe some fragments of the most sublime blank verse, and some lyric passages of a soft and tender nature, we believe unequalled. The verses addressed to "The Memory of a Deceased Friend," and those called "An Introduction to the Tale of the Dark Ladie," are sufficient proofs of our assertion. But these are short or unfinished performances, and others which we could quote from the same

author are of a nature so wild, so unrestrained by any rules
either in the conception or in the composition; forming such a
mixture of the terrible with the disgusting, of the tender with
the ludicrous, and of moral feeling with metaphysical sophistry,
that we can hardly suppose the author who threw forth such
crude effusions is serious in obtaining a rank among the poets of
his country, nor do we feel at liberty to press upon him a seat of
honour, which, from his conduct, he would seem to hold in no
esteem.

The feelings of Mr. WORDSWORTH appear to be very different. Although hitherto an unsuccessful competitor for poetical fame, as far as it depends upon the general voice of the public, no man has ever considered the character of the poet as more
honourable, or his pursuits as more important. We are afraid he
will be found rather to err on the opposite side, and, with an
amiable Quixotry, to ascribe to those pursuits, and to that character, a power of stemming the tide of luxury, egotism, and corruption of manners, and thus of reforming an age, which we
devoutly believe can be reformed by nothing short of a miracle.
But in this, as in other particulars, the poetry of Mr. Wordsworth
accords strikingly with his character and habits. We have made it
a rule not to draw the character of the man while we reviewed
the works of the author, and our sketch has suffered by this
forbearance, for we could have shown, in many instances, how
curiously they differed or coincided. But if we durst now raise
the veil of private life, it would be to exhibit a picture of manly
worth and unaffected modesty; of one who retired early from
all that sullies or hardens the heart, from the pursuit of wealth
and honours, from the bustle of the world, and from the parade
of philosophical pursuits; and who, sitting down contented in a
cottage, realized whatever the poets have feigned of content and
happiness in retirement. It might have been supposed, that, surrounded by romantic scenery, and giving his attention only to
poetical imagery, and to the objects by which they were best
suggested, the situation he had chosen was the most favourable
for his studies; and that such a happy coincidence of leisure,
talents, and situation, ought to have produced poetry more generally captivating than that of Mr. Wordsworth has hitherto
proved. But we have constant reason to admire the caprices of
human intellect. This very state of secluded study seems to have
produced effects upon Mr. Wordsworth's genius unfavourable to

its popularity. In the first place, he who is constantly surrounded
by the most magnificent natural subjects of description, becomes
so intimately acquainted with them, that he is apt to dwell less
upon the broad general and leading traits of character which
strike the occasional visitor, and which are really their most
poetical attributes, than upon the more detailed and specific
particulars in which one mountain or valley differs from another,
and which, being less obvious to the general eye, are less interesting to the common ear. But the solitude in which Mr. Wordsworth resides has led to a second and more important consequence in his writings, and has affected his mode of expressing
moral truth and feeling, as well as his turn of natural description.
He has himself beautifully described the truths which he teaches
us, as being

> ——The harvest of a quiet eye
> That broods and rests on his own heart.[9]

A better heart, a purer and more manly source of honourable
and virtuous sentiment beats not, we will say it boldly, within
Britain. But the observation of a single subject will not make a
skilful anatomist, nor will the copying one model, however
beautiful, render a painter acquainted with his art. To attain that
knowledge of the human bosom necessary to moral poetry, the
poet must compare his own feelings with those of others; he must
reduce his hypothesis to theory by actual experiment, stoop to
sober and regulated truth from the poetic height of his own
imagination, and observe what impulse the mass of humanity
receive from those motives and subjects to which he is himself
acutely alive. It is the want of this observation and knowledge
of the world which leads Wordsworth into the perpetual and
leading error of supposing, that trivial and petty incidents can
supply to mankind in general that train of reflection which, in
his speculative solitude, he himself naturally attaches to them. A
reflecting mind and a quick fancy find food for meditation in
the most trifling occurrences, and can found a connected and
delightful train of deductions upon an original cause as flimsy as
the web of a gossamer. The cleaving of a block of wood, the
dancing of a bush of wild flowers, the question or answer of a

9. "A Poet's Epitaph."

child, naturally suggest matter of reflection to an amiable and reflecting mind, retired from the influence of incidents of a nature more generally interesting. And such are Wordsworth's studies, or, as he himself expresses it,

> The outward shews of sky and earth,
> Of hill and valley he has viewed;
> And impulses of deeper birth
> Have come to him in solitude.[10]

In this situation, the poet's feelings somewhat resemble those of a person accustomed to navigate a small boat upon a narrow lake, to whom, if he possess an active imagination, the indentures of the shore, which hardly strike the passing stranger, acquire the importance of creeks, bays, and promontories. Even so the impressions made upon the susceptible mind of the solitary poet by common and unimportant incidents; and the train of "sweet and bitter fancies" to which they give rise are, in the eye of the public, altogether extravagant and disproportioned to their cause. We mark this with sincere regret; for though Mr. Wordsworth, to the affectation of rude and bald simplicity, which we have censured in Southey and Coleridge, adds that of harsh and rugged versification, often reduced in harmony several steps below well-written prose, yet his power of interesting the feelings is exquisite, and we do not envy the self-possession of those who can read his beautiful pastorals, "The Brothers" and "Michael," without shedding tears; for it may be said of such, that they have no interest in humanity, "no part in Jacob, and no inheritance in Israel."[11] It is therefore to be lamented, that Wordsworth should be, upon system, rude in diction and trivial in narrative; and that he should continue to exhibit traits of feeling bordering upon extravagance, and so metaphysically subtle that they are a stumbling block to the ignorant, and foolishness to the learned. But his muse is, we fear, irreclaimable, and pleads the freedom of a Cumbrian mountaineer:—

> O'er rough and smooth she trips along,
> And never looks behind;

10. Ibid.
11. "We have no part in David, neither have we inheritance in the son of Jesse." 2 Samuel 20:1.

And sings a solitary song
That whistles in the wind.[12]

Somewhat akin to Wordsworth in the train of his poetry, but beneath him in originality of genius, is JAMES GRAHAME, author of the "Sabbath" and the "Birds of Scotland." The most remarkable feature of his poetical character is his talent for describing Scottish scenery in a manner so true and lively as at once to bring the picture to the recollection of his countrymen. The ardent love of nature in which this power of description has its source, is uniformly combined with virtuous and amiable feeling. Accordingly, Mr. Grahame's poetry exhibits much of these qualities; but his religion has sometimes a tinge of fanaticism, and his views of society are more gloomy than the truth warrants. In his moral poetry he occasionally unites, with the nakedness of Wordsworth's diction, a flatness which is all his own. In his landscapes, on the other hand, he is always at home, and more fortunate than most of his contemporaries. He has the art of being minute without being confused, and circumstantial without being tedious. His Sabbath Walks are admirable specimens of this his principal excellence. But this is a vein capable of being exhausted, and it will be for the serious consideration of the Lord of the Manor, whether it has not been already sufficiently wrought out.

Those who may be considered as belonging to Walter Scott's school of poetry, or, to speak with more propriety, those who, like him, have dealt in imitations of the ancient minstrel compositions, or have laid their scene in the days of chivalry, form a list comprehending some respectable names. Among the imitators of the old ballad, a species of composition with which Mr. Scott begun his prosperous career, we might reckon JOHN LEYDEN, did not his removal to India withdraw him from our consideration. It may, however, be briefly said of him, that no man wrote better when the subject was dictated by his own feelings, and few have overwhelmed the public with an equal quantity of tinsel and *verbiage* where he substituted the resolution to write instead of the impulse which ought to have preceded his determination. An affectation of abstruse science, and a confusion of the various hoards of knowledge, ill-arranged

12. "Lucy Gray."

even by the retentive memory and powerful intellect to which
they were entrusted, have a farther influence in defacing Dr.
Leyden's poetry. But these faults are often redeemed by beautiful and expressive language, an acquaintance with ancient manners equal to that of his friend Mr. Scott, and an enthusiasm in
the pursuit of such knowledge, which, while circumstances permitted, was inferior to that of none who ever entered upon the
career of national antiquities. Among more professed imitators
of Mr. Scott, we have been able to distinguish few who merit
notice in a treatise limited, properly speaking, to the year 1808.
The Minstrels of Acre and the Fight of Falkirk, which have appeared about or since that period, are the only compositions of
the kind which are worth mentioning; and even these are chiefly
praise-worthy when they least remind us of their original. Imitation is in fact a miserable road to fame;—in those poets with
whom it has succeeded, the first who treads the path carries off
the merit of his followers, and a failure is attended with general
ridicule.

There is a species of legendary poetry of which Dryden set the
English an example in his Fables, and which has been cultivated
by the authors of Italy, France, and Germany. This department
comprehends modern imitations of such romantic tales as have
become obsolete through change of language and manners, skilfully adapted to the modern taste, yet retaining enough of their
antique guise to give them a venerable and interesting shade of
simplicity. This was a study which was successfully pursued by
the late Gregory Way, and in which Mr. WILLIAM ROSE has
more recently given us favourable specimens of his poetical
talents. But although we cannot well assign a reason, this
rifaciamento of the old romance has never been such a favourite
with us as on the Continent. Perhaps the changes which have
taken place in England, and the rapid increase of commercial
wealth, may have early banished all remembrance of the old
romances which amused our forefathers. We question much if
the popularity of any one of them survived the time of the great
civil war. The names of the old English romances, therefore, or
of the heroes and the incidents which they celebrate, do not
bespeak any favourable interest; we listen to the revival of
their history as to something which has no previous claim for
favour or sympathy; and, independent of such partiality, it
requires little argument to show, that the tales of a rude age

are rarely so ingeniously contrived as to interest the present.

There are, however, distinguished exceptions to the above general rule. It sometimes happens, that an ancient legend is so happily conducted as to unite interesting incident with simplicity of action, and supply to a modern poet the outline of a story which he cannot improve, otherwise than by shading and colouring it according to the taste of his own times. Such was the classical fable of Psyche, and such, in Gothic times, was the beautiful legend of Huon of Bourdeaux, the ground-work of Weiland's [*sic*] romance of Oberon. The German poet has happily found a congenial spirit in Mr. SOTHEBY, whose version of this fanciful and elegant romance is one of the best translations in our language. Sotheby has also distinguished himself by original composition; and his poem, entitled Saul, ranks him among the successful imitators of Milton. The tone, however, of this biblical history is indifferently suited to the taste of the age. The simple dignity of the scripture narrative is lost without any thing very valuable being substituted in its room; and saint and sinner see with regret talents and fancy wasted upon a subject, which both agree in considering as alien to decoration. That decoration, notwithstanding, evinces taste and genius in the artist, and Saul, though neglected by the multitude, will long continue a favourite study with those who love English blank verse when skilfully varied and modulated. This class of admirers is now diminished, as well as the number of those who put their faith, and rest their pleasure, upon the heroic couplet to which Dryden gave dignity, and Pope sweetness. The intrusion of a variety of rythms [*sic*], some borrowed from the German, some from the Italian, some from the middle ages, some from the loose and unregulated Pindarics of the seventeenth century;—and still more, the general misuse of the older and more classical structure of verse, by the shoal of unskilful pretenders to the lyre, have in some measure rendered them unfashionable, if not obsolete. They are, however, natural to our language, and will resume their native superiority when they shall be employed by those who can imitate the numbers which first exhibited English blank verse, and the heroic couplet, with vigour and success. Mr. Sotheby is not altogether adequate to effect this revolution, yet his efforts are not unserviceable, but resemble those of the swimmer who supports the head of a drowning person, although unable to insure his safety by dragging him to the shore.

We are now to consider a department of poetry, which, but for
one luminous and splendid exception, we should regard as a huge
waste, a wilderness traversed only by caitiff and ignorant barbarians, undeserving of notice, and incapable of profiting by
criticism. We mean Tragedy; which Dryden considered as the
most noble occupation of the muse. We mean not to call up
from Limbo Lake the damned ghosts of the wretched productions which have strutted and fretted their hour upon the stage
under the facetious denomination of Melo-dramas; still less the
deplorable remnants from the old and established warehouses of
Rowe and Congreve, which have aspired to the more dignified
appellation of Tragedies. The former have had at least the merit
of affording show and spectacle, and might have been tolerably
entertaining to the deaf and dumb students of Mr. Braidwood's
Academy;[13] while the professed tragedies are destitute of every
thing excepting blood and blank verse. In this exalted region of
poetry, therefore, JOANNA BAILLIE stands not merely foremost, but altogether unrivalled, not only most distinguished,
but alone. How or where the spirit of tragedy has slumbered
since the days of Shakespeare and Massinger, of Otway and
Southern,—by what chance their successors have waxed dull of
heart and feeble of fancy, and unfit to receive the influence
which they invoked;—by what strangest of strange dispensations
this rich vein of poetry, strong conception of character, and
vigorous glow of imagination, have become the portion of a
retired, amiable, and unassuming female, is only known to him
who inspired the Jaels, the Deborahs, and the Judiths of Scripture. Of the remarkable persons we have named, and of those
whose names we are yet to review, we consider Miss Baillie as by
far the most wonderful literary phenomenon. In her detail of
the more violent passions, there glows through every scene that
knowledge of the human heart which is derived from intuitive
genius alone, since it could neither be supplied by experience
nor by observation. But poetic inspiration, like the wind of
heaven, bloweth where it listeth; and the same dispensation
which places the heart of a soldier under the rochet of a bishop,
and the narrow soul of a fanatic monk in the bosom of a statesman, has invested a sequestered and gentle-tempered woman

---

13. Thomas Braidwood (1715–1806) moved his school for teaching the deaf and
dumb from Edinburgh to Hackney in 1783.

with a power of analyzing the countless counterpoises and
springs of the human passions, denied to sages, who have spent
lives in metaphysical study, and to the more practical philosophers, who, mixing with the world, have, "with all appliances
and means to boot,"[14] observed in courts and camps the secret
movements by which distinguished characters and great events
are matured, influenced, or achieved. Yet we are obliged to
remark, that even the force of Miss Baillie's genius might, in the
inferior departments of her art, have reaped advantage from a
more extended acquaintance with its rules. Fielding has somewhere said of his hero, Tom Jones, that he had natural but not
artificial good breeding, and was therefore apt to sin against
those arbitrary and conventional regulations of elegant society,
which the *beau monde* establishes from time to time, as the bye-
laws of its own corporation. In like manner, Miss Baillie's execution sometimes falls short of her aim, either by her not knowing, or not attending to attributes, which have, by universal
consent, whether properly or not, been accounted indispensable
to the Drama. She has not hesitated in Rayner to introduce a
drunken negro, and to make the catastrophe of the whole turn
upon a piece of legerdemain, executed by that respectable
character,—highly improbable in itself, and, in point of effect,
unworthy of a pantomime, or even of a melo-drama. Her scenes,
too, are frequently strangely crowded upon each other, with
little attention to the unities of time, place, or action; imperfections which will be found of serious consequence, should a
reviving taste for dramatic poetry ever demand the performance
of the Plays upon the Passions. To these deficiencies in the technical knowledge of her art, we are compelled to add faults which
apparently arise from the want of a correct and well-regulated
taste. The vehemence of her language often outsteps what the
rules of the stage prescribe, and the characters are made to use
expressions more violent and forcible, than either elegant or
dignified. The lower characters sometimes digress into coarse
and clownish dialogue, and those parts of the drama which ought
to be awfully sublime, are occasionally overdriven into the
precincts of the horrible. In this catalogue of the imperfections
of genius, we should disappoint the mean malignant stare of Miss
Baillie's emulous contemporaries, (rivals she has none) did we

14. *Henry IV* Part II, III, i, 29.

not mention her comedies,—the common resort of critical
malevolence, when the force of truth has wrung forth a tardy and
reluctant assent to her tragic supereminence:—What say you to
her comedies? Such is the triumphant question to which we beg
leave coolly and briefly to reply—that we think they are not
comedies at all; but that if the sapient interrogators had read
them with another name prefixed, they would, like us, have
esteemed them good dramatic dialogues, containing some very
pathetic passages, and striking delineations of character, though
devoid of the stage effect, of the humour, of the comic language,
and of the combination of incident, indispensable to performances intended for the stage. Having thus sacrificed to that
weakness of human nature which cannot endure the unqualified
praise of a contemporary, we cannot join in the other popular
objections founded upon Miss Baillie's plan of illustrating a
single passion in the course of each drama. It is no doubt attended with its own peculiar difficulties, especially when the
passion described is of slow growth, and such as only gradually
usurps its predominance over the mind. In this case, the author
is reduced to a dilemma, because if she presents at once in full
tide the passion of which she has not time to trace the fountain,
its violence is likely, as in the plot of De Montfort, to stagger
the faith of those who are either unable or unwilling to comprehend what is not explained to them in particular detail: Or if,
as in Ethwald, the progress of the passion is dramatically traced
from its first breaking forth, to its acquiring universal empire
over the character, it is impossible to avoid gross trespasses upon
the unities of time and place, and the work must necessarily
become rather a dramatic chronicle than a tragedy. But these
difficulties are counterbalanced by this great and important advantage, that the mind of the author, of the reader, and of the
spectator, is arrested during the whole course of the piece by
one strong and overmastering interest, and that not arising from
an artfully conducted chain of incident, but drawn from a display of the deepest recesses of the human heart. The interest
thus imparted, is of a kind far more vivid at the time, and more
important on reflection, than that which depends upon the trick
of the scene, or the artful opposition of characters in contrast
to each other, or even than that excited by striking situation.
Why is it that at a leisure moment we find a volume of Shakespeare more frequently in our hands than any other book, unless

because he considered every part of the drama as subordinate to
the display of passion and of character? It is to such a display,
that the plan so daringly adopted by Miss Baillie, necessarily
pledges her to the reader, and though we may rejoice were its
execution capable of being united with every other requisite to
a perfect drama, we cannot wish it should be sacrificed to the
attainment of any or of all of them.

Miss Baillie's language is well calculated to support the strength
and grandeur of her sentiments. It is formed upon the model of
the old dramatic blank verse, with somewhat too strong an affectation of the antique. It is sometimes, as in the opening scene
of Ethwald, beautifully poetical; but these ornaments are never
misplaced, when the feeling demands bold and energetic expression of passion. We might speak of the art with which Miss Baillie
varies her subordinate personages, giving even to the less important such a peculiarity of language and of sentiment, as marks
individuality of character. It is this art which renders the scene
a mirror to nature; whose character, in manners and mind, as in
the exterior points of countenance and figure, is discriminated
by their endless variety. Many of those touches, though thrown
in slightly, serve, like figures in the distance, to heighten the
interest, and add to the reality of the whole action. The brutal
Woggarwolf, in the tragedy of Ethwald, is an admirable example
of this nice conduct. He is presented to us as a relentless and
merciless marauder, yet with a touch of nature worthy of Shakespeare, his first exclamation, when he hears of his castle being
taken, expresses apprehension for the safety of a favourite page.
The gifted author well knew that the wildest characters retain,
for some fondled object, a hidden reserve of blind and animal
affection. In like manner, the operation of superstition upon
the mind of this bandit when wounded, and the last glimpse
which we are afforded of him heading a monastic procession, as

> Sainted Woggarwolf once a fierce chief,
> But now a cowled priest of marvellous
> grace:

give a variety, and, at the same time, an effect and keeping to
the picture which we can always trace in even the slightest of
Miss Baillie's sketches. We could with pleasure pursue this theme
much further, but our task presses, and we take a reluctant leave
of this interesting subject.

In comedy, the present time has nothing to boast; and in satire very nearly as little. Some miserable attempts have been made by nameless authors, in volumes equally nameless, to distinguish themselves by sounding the rusty trump of personal scandal; but we have seen nothing which merits the generous though severe title of satire. Huddesford, who possessed some humour and power of verse, has not fulfilled the promise of his earlier poems. Gifford, to whose talents we might look for wielding the moral scourge with power and discrimination, has long slumbered over his harp; nor is there a name in Britain which we can couple with his in the department of satirical poetry.

The works of CRABBE, are, however, in some measure allied to satire though not falling strictly under that name. This distinguished and powerful writer has traced for himself a path, which is, to the best of our knowledge, new in poetry. He has assumed for his subject, the middling and lower ranks of life; their ordinary pursuits, pleasures, cares, vices and sorrows. These he has depicted alternately with deep pathos, strong humour, and masculine morality. He has laid aside the Mincian and Arcadian reed, and, assuming for his guide Truth, not merely unadorned, but under her harshest aspect, he has even avoided drawing such pleasing pictures of low life, as he might easily have found originals for without violation of nature. Perhaps we judge incorrectly of the peasantry of England, from those with whose state and manners we have an opportunity to be intimately acquainted. But whatever vice and misery may be found in large manufacturing towns, or in smuggling villages, where the habitual and professional breach of one class of laws brings all others into contempt, and where the very staple of their traffic is the source of idleness, poverty, and vice, we are confident that Mr. Crabbe has used too dark colouring, if his poem is to be considered as a general portrait of the people of Britain. It forms, at least, a very singular contrast to the amiable, simple, and interesting scenes of lower life, which have been presented to us by the regretted Burns. But although strongly opposite in stile, manner, and subject, as the groupes of Gainsborough to those of Hogarth, we acknowledge in each the masterly hand which designs from nature. Indeed the resemblance between Hogarth and Crabbe has very often appeared to us extremely striking. Both have laid their scenes in the regions of low and vulgar life; both have presented their subjects with the squalid and disgusting accompaniments which too often attend them in sad reality. But the want of taste which does not withdraw from our view even the most unpleasing of these circumstances, is amply compensated both in the poet and painter, by the reality given to the picture; by the fund of humour employed in bringing out the comic scenes; by the power and vigour which are displayed in its more serious parts; above all, by the pleasing display of genius armed in behalf of virtue and of moral feeling. Even the defects of the painter and the poet resemble each other: There is in both a want of grace, though no deficiency in pathetic effect; and the serious and ludicrous are sometimes so closely united, as to mar the effect of each. But Hogarth was deficient in sublimity as well as in beauty, and so is not the poet to whom we have compared him. On the contrary, the dark and sublime conceptions of the visions of "Sir Eustace Grey," and the incidents in the tale entitled "The Hall of Justice," trench upon the horrible; and, far from falling short in effect, are almost too powerful for perusal. The same sombre pencil which deepens the gloom and misery attached to poverty and ignorance, has, in these tales, worked upon subjects of more exalted passion, and we behold its productions with interest of that deep and painful kind arising from the narration of a crime of enormous degree, or the sight of the execution of an atrocious criminal, when grief and pity struggle with the feelings of horror and disgust. The former feelings are excited by the tragic power of the poet, the latter by the readiness with which he exhibits in the lowest deep a lower still, by the addition of the horror of incestuous passion, or some similar aggravating enormity, to the vices and misfortunes which his verse details.

In his style, Crabbe somewhat resembles Cowper; his versification being careless and harsh, and his language marked by a quaint and antithetical turn of expression, sometimes humorous, and sometimes substituted in the room of humour. Both poets were perhaps indebted to Oldham's satires for these peculiarities, at least, as Dryden said of him, they want

——the numbers of their native tongue:
But satire needs not these, and wit can
    shine
Through the harsh cadence of a rugged
    line;

A noble error, and but seldom made,
When poets are by too much force betray'd.[15]

It may be farther observed, that the labour which Mr. Crabbe has bestowed upon his characters, and the laudable pains which he takes to invest them with all their peculiar attributes, is in some few instances heavy and tedious, where the subject either excites little interest, or an interest which is not likely to be generally felt. Such heaviness attaches especially to those passages which refer to the clerical profession, and circumstances connected with its exercise. On these Mr. Crabbe is very naturally more minute and particular than can be interesting to the great mass of his readers. But his roughness of style, and occasional prolixity, even his coarseness and want of taste, are trifles in the balance compared to his merits. Mr. Crabbe is an *original* poet, he is *sui generis,*—and in these few words we comprehend a greater praise than can be conferred upon almost any of his contemporaries.

We should now mention the translator of Anacreon, but we are rather willing to withhold the tribute which we should have offered to his genius, than to present it accompanied with our severest censure of the manner in which it has been too frequently employed. We have heard, and we believe, that Mr. MOORE is determined to adopt a different line of composition; his taste and talents are indisputable; may he soon

——Bear no token of the sabler streams,
And mount far off among the swans of
Thames.[16]

Lord STRANGFORD[17] has followed Mr. Moore in his beauties and in his errors. His versions from Camoens are a remarkable instance of the art with which, retaining the sense of an original,

15. Dryden, "To the Memory of Mr Oldham."
16. "He bears no token of the sabler streams,
   And mounts far off among the Swans of Thames."
        —Pope, *Dunciad* II, 297–98.
17. Most of the poets mentioned in this essay are still well known, but a few seem to demand brief identification. Lord Strangford was Percy Clinton Sydney Smythe (1780–1855) and the sixth viscount. He was the secretary of the legation at Lisbon and published his translation of Camoens in 1803.

the colour of the translator's own mind may be flung over it. A voluptuous, effeminate, and sensual style of poetry, may be considered as one of the worst symptoms of a degenerate age. The Sybarites, when they saw their destruction inevitable, are said (if we recollect rightly) to have torn to pieces those poets whose lyres had soothed them in their selfish epicurism, and alienated their minds from virtuous exertion. We would willingly inflict the same punishment, not on the persons, but on the works of those of whom we have last spoken. Let the authors survive for repentance and atonement; if they have virtue for the first, they have talents for that which ought to be its first as its most valuable fruits.

The public have not been lately edified by any precepts in verse; or, to speak in the usual phrase, by any didactic poetry. To these poems we have never been much attached, since it appears that practical knowledge can be ill taught by the metaphorical and periphrastic language of poetry; and that all which is attained by the author is the display of his own capacity for putting that into verse which would be much more intelligible in prose. Accordingly, since the days of the "Fleece" and the "Sugar Cane," didactic poems have been little attended to. Mr. SHEE's[18] Rhymes on Art seem to form a respectable exception; and no doubt the art of painting is so nearly connected with that of poetry that the maxims necessary to understand the former may, better than in any similar case, be conveyed through the medium of the sister art. Mr. Shee has the merit of being familiar, clear, and instructive, and his rules are, we believe, generally considered as well calculated to explain his art. As a poet we do not think him entitled to stand in a high rank, nor are we inclined to deny him what is generally termed a respectable one. The mention of this gentleman naturally reminds us of the heavy loss which both painting and poetry have sustained in the death of Hoppner;[19]—a man whose original and expanded genius cultivated both arts with success. The small collection of tales which he gave to the public in 1806, as he modestly expressed it, "rather to show his love than his skill," possess a humorous gravity and whimsical felicity of expression, superior to any

18. Sir Martin Arthur Shee (1769–1850), later president of the Royal Academy, published his *Elements of Art: a Poem* in 1809.

19. John Hoppner (1769–1810), best known as a portrait painter, published in 1805 *Oriental Tales, Translated into English Verse*.

thing of the kind which has since appeared. They are admirable, in particular, when contrasted with the hard and laborious parturition which Mr. COLEMAN[20] has produced, the string of puns which he wishes to be considered as comic stories. The extreme toil which it costs that poor gentleman to be facetious, damps our disposition to be amused by his wit, as completely as it would spoil our enjoyment of a gala dinner to be conscious that we were eating up the whole year's revenue of our hospitable landlord.

Another painter, WESTALL,[21] a man of feeling and imagination, has published a poetical miscellany, the merit of which seems to illustrate our general proposition, that the alliance between poetry and painting is more than fanciful. His genius is not, however, of the highest order, and his verses are too like those of Warton and Dyer to claim the praise of originality.

There is a capacity for poetry that hovers between taste and genius, and which, in a polished age, dictates more verses than a higher degree of talent. These, of course, have different degrees of merit, as they are the offspring of the heart or of the head, of feeling or of fancy, of real power of poetical expression, or of the mere desire to imitate what we admire, by the assistance of a memory stored with common places from other poets. As we rise in the scale, we find many whom only the pressure of business, or the pursuit of pleasure, or perhaps literary indolence, more powerful than either, has prevented from aspiring to more distinguished honours. Here we may notice the Hon. WILLIAM SPENCER,[22] whose beautiful *vers de société* give us an high idea of his talents, mingled with regret that the avocations of a fashionable life should have occupied hours in which these talents might have been employed to his immortal fame. He has contented himself, however, with the unambitious pretensions of a sonetteer [*sic*] and writer of occasional verses. These little manuscripts which flit around the higher circles of the *gens comme il faut,* which are transcribed by fair hands into red morocco souvenirs, and secured with silver bolts, like the bower

20. George Colman the Younger (1762–1836), the dramatist, also published numerous poems: *Broad Grins Comprising with additional tales those published under the title of My Night-Gown and Slippers* (1802).

21. Richard Westall (1765–1836), another painter, published *A Day in Spring and Other Poems* in 1808.

22. William Robert Spencer (1769–1834), whose *The Year of Sorrow* was published in 1804, had several poems in the *Register*.

of Fairley fair in the old ballad,[23] may perhaps plead privilege
against critical execution. We shall, therefore, content ourselves
with saying, that Spencer has, in many instances, succeeded in
imitating that light, gay, and felicitous expression of occasional
poetry in which the French have hitherto been considered as
unrivalled. The verses in the English Minstrelsy, beginning, "Too
late I staid," are a happy instance of the delicacy of point and
tournure which the Parisian *bel esprit* placed his highest ambition in attaining. Mr. Spencer has also taken the legendary harp
with success, and sung us the ballad of Beth-Gelert. We pray
devoutly that *dejeunés* in the afternoon, and *petit soupers* in
the morning, and all the *et ceteras* of idle occupation which fill
up the hours between them, may leave this gentleman more at
liberty in future to exert his talents and learning in pursuits
more worthy of him.

Astrand by the side of Spencer, on the island of Alcina,[24] but
higher on the shore, and with less chance of floating, we view
with concern the wreck of M. G. LEWIS. Upon this author the
cup of pleasure and fashion has produced a more baneful effect
than upon the former. Spencer is only lulled by the draught into voluptuous indolence, but Lewis has been stimulated to ill-
judged and capricious exertions totally unworthy of his natural
genius. His first work, though he was indebted to the German
for the most striking incident,* and though it was liable to yet
stronger objections upon the score of morality, was indisputably
the work of a man of talent. What he borrowed he made his own,
not by altering and disfiguring, but by improving and beautify-
ing it; and we were willing to hope that the warmth of his descriptions were owing to the want of judgment of a very young
man. In this hope, let us do Mr. Lewis the justice to say, we
have not been disappointed,—he has done all in his power to
obliterate the memory of this original error; but he has not put
off the boy in other respects, He continues to overwhelm us
with puerilities, ghost-ballads, ghost-romances, and diablerie.
We do not unite with the common cry, in denouncing all use of
this supernatural machinery in poetry. There is a feeling im-

---

* [Notes indicated by an asterisk are Scott's.] The story of the Bleeding Nun occurs
with very little variation, in the popular tales of Musæus, under the title of *Die Ent-
führung,* i.e. The Elopement.

23. The old ballad of Hardyknute.

24. Alcina was a witch in Ariosto's *Orlando Furioso,* who turned lovers into beasts,
stones, and trees.

planted in our nature responsive to it, and which therefore may be legitimately appealed to. But it is a spring which soon loses its force if injudiciously pressed upon, and Mr. Lewis has used it unsparingly. He is not sufficiently attentive, besides, to investing his tales of wonder with circumstances of probability. The poet who employs in his art the generally received superstitions of any country, has a right to demand our attention, because, though these were false in themselves, they were, nevertheless, believed to be true. But Mr. Lewis has dragged together hobgoblins from every coast and climate, as if there had been a general gaol-delivery at Pandemonium, or as the whole demons banished of yore to the Red Sea had at once returned from transportation. The same puerility of taste has infected Mr. Lewis's writings in other respects. He accumulates images of horror till they excite disgust, and expects to impress us with terror by details of the shambles or charnel-house. In another situation, a course of salutary criticism might have gradually amended Mr. Lewis's taste, and weaned him from his German lust after marvellous narrative, hyperbolical language, overstrained passion, and distorted imagery. But, moving in a circle where his talents naturally attract the admiration which would be generally bestowed upon them were they exerted with more prudence, we have little hope that our animadversions will be of any use to him.

Mr. REGINALD HEBER may, we fear, be considered as one whom a too easy situation in life is likely to seduce from the service of the Muses, his proper and natural mistresses.—The answer of the wealthy veteran, *Ibit qui perdidit zonam,*[25] has a force in poetry as well as in military enterprise. He who hopes to acquire, by his talents, that distinction which is the road to fortune, is compelled to place himself frequently before the public. But the man of affluence naturally shrinks from the trouble necessary to assert his literary rank, and from exposing himself to virulent criticism and unceasing cabal. He feels that whatever the vulgar suppose, the real pleasure of the poetic talent consists in the power of calling up and arraying imaginary groupes; and that the toil of arresting the glittering visions, of embodying them in verse, and clothing them with suitable language, is usually unsatisfactory labour. But the author of "Palestine" and of "Europe" ought not to think so. The former, a juvenile work, had the faults natural to early compositions.

25. "Ibit eo quo vis qui zonam perdidit." Horace, *Epistles* II, 2:40.

There was a profusion of epithet, an affectation of balanced and sounding versification, and a pomp of eloquence which sometimes exceeded the classical standard. In "Europe," Mr. Heber's latest composition, the unfortunate turn of events, which has baffled the prophecy of the poet, and the sagacity of the statesman, casts an unpleasing gloom over the subject. We do not like to look back upon disappointed hopes and successless efforts, when we remember the glow of expectation which originally preceded our disappointment. Under these disadvantages, however, Mr. Heber's essays place him in a fair rank for poetical fame; for he has a richness of language, command of versification, and strength of ideas, that may lead him to high and distinguished eminence. We sincerely hope that neither the duties of his profession, nor the opiate of ease and affluence, will prevent his again claiming the public notice, or occasion his sinking into the genteel and occasional versifier.

There are other *dilletanti* authors, earls, and knights, whom we might be expected to notice, especially as they have taken the field in form as dramatic poets, and epic poets, and Esopian fabulists. But it would be unfair to review what we have found ourselves unable to read; and we can only pledge ourselves, that when these eminent personages shall produce a play or a poem, or even a single apologue, which has been actually perused by any one above being bribed by a dinner, or the hopes of a seat in the chariot, we shall do our best to imitate an instance of such laudable perseverance.

The very *antipodes* of this class are the poets who daily spring up among the lees of the people, and find admirers to patronize them because they write "wonderfully well *considering.*" This is, abstractedly, one of the most absurd claims to distinction possible. We do not suppose any living poet, Southey for instance, or Campbell, would gain much credit for making a pair of shoes, although they might be very well made *considering.* We hardly think the Agricultural Society, even if Lord Sommerville were preses, would bestow upon Walter Scott a prize for weaving the best piece of cloth, although the "warp and woof" might be very wonderful *considering:* Yet let a weaver, a shoemaker, or a tailor, produce a copy of verses, and he shall find those to extol him above the best poets of the time, and to silence all objection and criticism, by referring, as an apology, to that which should have withheld him from the attempt,—his ignorance and his

want of education. It will hardly be supposed, that, with the
recollection of Burns fresh in our minds—*Vi[r]gilium vidimus*[26]
—we should doubt that, from the lower ranks of society may
arise a poet in the noblest sense of the word, gifted with perception, with energy, with expression, and with sentiment. But
when this divine influence is either withheld, or sparingly bestowed; where the individual, with every advantage of instruction and cultivation, could not have risen above elegant mediocrity; and far more when he could never have hoped to attain
even that humble pitch,—we cannot allow that the literary public can be benefited by his poetical attempts, in a degree sufficient
to compensate the loss which society sustains by turning the
brain of an useful peasant or artizan. It is, indeed, a peculiarity
of the present time, that there are a class of subaltern literati who
act as crimps for the muses, seducing honest ploughmen from
their teams, mechanics from their shopboards, and mild maids
from their pails, to enlist them in the precarious service of Apollo.
We wish we could consider this folly as disinterested in proportion to its absurdity; but such patrons make a stalkinghorse of
the *protegé,* tagging the poetry of the *paysan parvenu* with their
own more worthless *dicta* and commentaries, assuming the airs
of a Mæcenas at a cheap rate, and, under pretence of doing justice
to obscure merit, intruding upon the public their own contemptible personages in the character of its master of ceremonies.
It was thus that Mr. Capel Lofft[27] contrived to ride forward into
public notice on the shoulders of poor BLOOMFIELD,[28] who
was able, partly by real and partly by adventitious circumstances,
to bring his load farther than any one durst have predicated. We
do not mean too curiously to scrutinize the justice of the popularity which this worthy and ingenious man acquired by his first
poem. It was written on a pleasing subject; and with just and
simple description, contained some poetry, though not of the
first order. Our neighbours of England gave it not the less liberal
encouragement, that they might boast an heaven-born genius of

26. Scott remembered this phrase when in 1827 he gave Lockhart his reminiscences
of his meeting with Burns in 1787 at the home of Professor Adam Ferguson. "As for
Burns, I may truly say, *Virgilium vidi tantum*" he told Lockhart, who used the phrase
in his *Life of Burns* and later in his life of Scott. The text in the *Register* lacks the
letter "r."
27. Capell Lofft, the elder (1751–1824), author and barrister.
28. Robert Bloomfield (1766–1823), the shoemaker poet, published his *Farmer's
Boy* in 1800 and his *Banks of the Wye* in 1811.

their own. But there is a meagreness and poverty in Mr. Bloomfield's poetry which place him at a distance incalculably beneath the Ayrshire ploughman, tho' superior unquestionably to almost all the other self-taught bards of the day. His latter verses, addressed to his Mother's Spindle, intimate more power and pathos than any thing we have yet seen of his composition.

The success of Burns had the effect of exciting general emulation among all of his class in Scotland who were able to tag a rhyme. The quantity of Scottish verses with which we were inundated was absolutely overwhelming. Poets began to chirp in every corner like grasshoppers in a sunshine day. The steep rocks poured down poetical goatherds, and the bowels of the earth vomited forth rhyming colliers; but of all the herd we can only distinguish James Hogg, the Selkirkshire shepherd, as having at all merited the public attention; and there cleaves to his poetry a vulgarity of conception and expression which we greatly question his ever being able to overcome. In other respects his talents, though less noticed, are at least equal to those of Mr. Bloomfield. Bloomfield's success has had nearly the same effect in England which the celebrity of Burns produced among the Caledonians; and various self-educated geniuses have sprung forward in the race, most of them, as in the case of Bloomfield and Capel Lofft, with *riders on,* as the jockies phrase it. Even Pratt,[29] dry-foundered himself, has, like the old lame Houynhynm of Gulliver, placed himself in a vehicle drawn by a certain Joseph Blackett,[30] in order to be dragged into celebrity by the exertions of this oppressed animal. But the surprise, groundless as we think it, excited by the first instance of the kind, is at an end, when the world sees that it only requires encouragement to convert some hundred score of tolerable tailors, shoemakers, and lamplighters into very indifferent rhymers;—the wonder is at an end, and with the wonder ends the applause and the profit.

The van and rear of the class of occasional poets being thus reviewed, we turn our attention to the main body. In this vast host we discover those whom reasons and feelings, as various as their talents, have thrown into the same studies. In the poems

---

29. Samuel Jackson Pratt (1749–1814), a voluminous author, also wrote under the pseudonym of Courtney Melmoth.
30. Joseph Blacket (1786–1810), another shoemaker turned poet, published a volume of poems in 1809.

of Mrs. Opie[31] and Mrs. Hunter,[32] and especially in those of the former, we have much of the elegance, simplicity, and tenderness, which ought to mark sentimental poetry. We do not, in this excursion of the feeling or of the fancy, expect grandeur of sentiment, or the ardent vigour of poetical language. It is enough that there be novelty, or at least beauty, in the sentiments, and simple elegance in the mode of expression. Yet excellence in this is as difficult to attain as the successful execution of a bolder plan. The graces of Metastasio, and the charms of the pathetic sonnets of Petrarch, are not more easily caught than the wild and fantastic beauties of Ariosto, nor even than the bold tone of the epic muse. But, though perfection in either kind of composition may be equally difficult of attainment, the sentimental poet has, nevertheless, an advantage over his rivals. To perform exquisitely upon the flute, or upon the violin, is, perhaps, equally difficult; but tolerable execution upon the first is more pleasing, because the notes are sweeter in themselves: Thus the poetry which awakens a natural and amiable train of feeling, which reminds us of the romantic sentiments of youth, and speaks to us again of a fairy-land which we had lost for years, finds in every bosom a judge inclined to receive it with favour proportioned to the modesty of its pretensions. This is more particularly the case, when we can discover that the heart of the poet beats in unison with his lyre. Some of Mr. LISLE BOWLES's[33] sonnets, connected with the remarkable and melancholy circumstances from which they had their origin, are of this affecting and interesting kind. This amiable and elegant writer greatly mistook his own genius, when he departed from a style of composition in which he had acquired well-earned laurels, to write his poem upon the "Spirit of Discovery," which is, to say the best, a very heavy production.

Among the poems which have not received their due share of public attention, we are disposed to reckon Mr. POLWHELE's[34]

31. Mrs. Amelia Opie (1769–1853), wife of the portrait painter, wrote many poems and stories.

32. Mrs. Anne Hunter (1742–1821), author of several volumes of poetry and a contributor to the *Register,* was the aunt of Joanna Baillie.

33. Usually known by his full name of William Lisle Bowles (1762–1850).

34. Richard Polwhele (1760–1838), poet and miscellaneous writer, was one of Scott's correspondents, who sought Scott's aid in having his works reviewed. His letter to Scott of Oct. 24, 1811, saying "You promised to insert some observations on

"Influence of Local Attachment," which contains some passages of great beauty: But its desultory plan has, probably, been unfavourable to its popularity.

We might add to this list the name of Professor SMYTHE[35] of Cambridge, whose beautiful "Invocation to the Southern Breeze" is fresh in the memory of all readers of poetry; of Mr. MONTGOMERY,[36] in whose productions there is often a solemn and tender pathos, peculiarly his own; and we might enumerate many other respectable names; but our plan is limited, and the lyrical bards of England are numerous as the leaves in Vallambrosa.

Some commemoration might be due to those, who, having been former favourites of the public, have decently retired from the stage, warned by increasing age, or the change of taste in their contemporaries: But to address a poet on his past fame, is like calling to the remembrance of an antiquated beauty her former conquests, and conveys rather insult than compliment. Neither are we entitled to mention those persons of poetical talent who have been content with the applause of a small circle, although this class includes the names of MUNDY,[37] one of our best descriptive poets; and of Mrs. TIGHE,[38] whose lamented death we have so recently to deplore.

We therefore close these notices, made in the spirit of kindness towards the authors mentioned, and of forbearance towards those omitted. That the list is perfect we do not pretend; yet it contains as much worth, and as much talent united, as has adorned Britain, at least since the reign of Queen Anne. Nor is it our smallest boast, that the muses have been, of late, generally engaged in the cause of virtue and morality, and that the character of the libertine and spendthrift are no longer the frequent accompaniments of the sacred name of Poet.

my Poems in the Scotch *Register*" must refer to this passage. W. Partington, *Sir Walter's Post-Bag* (London, 1932), p. 73.

35. William Smyth (1765–1849), the historian, had published his *English Lyrics* in 1797.

36. James Montgomery (1771–1854), known today for his hymns, published several long poems which were widely noticed in the reviews.

37. Francis Noel Clarke Mundy, unnoticed by the *Dictionary of National Biography*, published his *Poems* (1768), his *Needwood Forest* (1776), and his *The Fall of Needwood* (1808).

38. Mrs. Mary Tighe (1772–1810) published her *Psyche* in 1805, a work of some influence in Keats's development.

This department of the Register will, in the next volume, be occupied by an Account of the State of Criticism in Great Britain.

⁓ Cursory Remarks upon the French Order of Battle, Particularly in the Campaigns of Buonaparte

Scott's "Cursory Remarks" (*Register*, II, 526–41) fits neatly into the avowed intention of the *Register* to support the country's struggle against the French and to counter the sense of futility expressed by the *Edinburgh Review* in continuing to fight a military genius by showing in a straightforward, rational manner that Napoleon's tactics are quite understandable—and quite vulnerable. Scott's own interest and enthusiasm—later shown in the Waverley novels—for all things military, weapons and their history, as well as tactics and strategy, are revealed in this essay. Faith in British strength with disparagement of French volatility appealed to the basic prejudices of the loyal British reader. The praise of Wellington and trust in his ability parallel the similar faith in the great general which all the ministers showed in backing him to the extent that their resources permitted. The essay also sought to demonstrate both the unreasonableness and ignorance of military matters shown by the Whig anti-ministerialist opposition.

Scott admitted his authorship of this essay: "I have been writing a sketch of Bonaparte's tactics for the Edinr. Register and some other trumpery of the same kind." *Letters of Scott*, II, 482. The essay is listed as Scott's in the *New Cambridge Bibliography of English Literature*.

> But see the haughty household troops advance!
> The dread of Europe, and the pride of France.
> The war's whole art each private soldier knows,
> And with a general's love of conquest glows;
> Proudly he marches on, and, void of fear,
> Laughs at the shaking of the British spear;
> Vain insolence! with native freedom brave,
> The meanest Briton scorns the highest slave.
> ADDISON'S CAMPAIGN[39]

The unparalleled success of the French arms under their present military ruler, has thrown a glare over the causes in which it

39. Joseph Addison, *The Campaign*, 293–300.

originated, peculiarly unfavourable to cool investigation. To account for the overthrow of ancient states, for the annihilation,
not only of whole armies, but of the entire military power of
kingdoms in a single engagement, imagination demands causes
adequate in importance and in splendour to these dazzling consequences, and naturally figures forth a demi-god at the head of an
army of invincible heroes. Were these victories, and the melancholy events which have followed them, matter of remote history, this romantic delusion would be of as little consequence as
if its luminous yet delusive halo invested the brows of Cæsar or
of Alexander; but our safety as a nation is unfortunately deeply
implicated in the judgement which we may form of the French
armies, the genius of their leader, and the causes of their success. One part of the spell flung around them has been fortunately dissipated by repeated practical experiment. No one for a
moment is now tempted to doubt, that, man to man, and regiment to regiment, the French soldiers are, both in a moral and
physical point of view, so decidedly inferior to the British, that
the ancient romantic proportion of two to one has in some
instances scarcely put them upon an equality. Still, however, another part of the charm hovers around us. The general is invested
with a double portion of that merit which he formerly divided
with his armies, and we now hear of nothing but the commanding genius of Buonaparte, which, supplying all deficiencies,
making up for all disasters, conquering all obstacles, gathers
victorious laurels on the very fields from which every other
general, ancient or modern, must have retired with defeat and
dishonour. With this is combined a fearful and inaccurate apprehension, or rather a superstitious terror, of some new-
discovered and irresistible system of tactics, devised and acted
upon by this irresistible leader. Such opinions, were they generally entertained, would form a bad omen for a nation forced
into collision, for all that they hold dear, with the very person
of whose irresistible skill in arms such an ineffable idea is held
forth. We are not however very apprehensive of this dispiriting
creed becoming general among those whose opinion in such subjects is of most consequence,—among the victors of Alexandria,
Maida, Vimiera, Talavera, Busaco and Barrosa. The doctrine of
French invincibility requires no confutation among those who
retreated with Moore, or are now advancing with Wellington;
nor is it to them that, like the ancient pedant in presence of

Alexander, we presume to read our lecture on the art of war.
But we humbly dedicate our few and desultory observations on
the French tactics in the field of battle, to every desponding
statesman out of place, who seeks the character of wisdom by
the presaging notes of a screech-owl, and to all those worthy
common-council men and burgesses, throughout the united
kingdoms, whose digestion is impaired by reflecting upon the
military skill of Buonaparte. When we shall have stripped that
skill of all exaggeration, enough will remain for reasonable apprehension, enough to recommend caution, and to discourage
presumption on the part of his opponents; but, if our researches
have been correct, his system will be found a simple one, neither
implying any transcendant genius in the discoverer, nor necessarily conferring upon the general employing it, that decided
superiority which has been falsely apprehended.

It is scarcely necessary to say, that our observations only
respect the French principle of distributing their forces upon
the day of battle. Other advantages, of a great and important
nature, arise from the combination of the various corps of their
invading armies, maintaining their *liaison*, or correspondence,
by means of the *etats-majors*, or staff-establishments attached
to every division, whose communication with each other, and
with the head-quarters of the emperor, is preserved at all risks,
and with a consummate degree of accuracy and address. Thus
orders are circulated, and combined movements achieved in
consequence of these orders, with the same ease and facility
through various *corps-d'-armée*, occupying positions or moving
upon lines of march an hundred leagues asunder, as in other
services through a single brigade. It is unnecessary to notice the
unity, firmness, and consistency which this regularity and facility of intelligence communicates to the whole plan of invasion.
Another cause of success, which may be shortly noticed, is their
attention to the commissariat and its dependencies. Every
French general is qualified to provide for the subsistence of his
army; every French soldier is accustomed to lighten the general's labour, by looking out for himself and his messmates; and
it must be owned, that if the united efforts of the general and
soldier prove unsuccessful, the latter can sustain hunger and
privation with great patience and firmness. None of these considerations are embraced in our present inquiry; neither do we
mean to investigate the still more powerful causes of success,

which the French well name *les grands moyens,* which embrace *espionage,* bribery, political intrigue, and so forth. Our present subject is limited to the consideration of Buonaparte and his troops arrived on the field of battle, and preparing for conflict. To estimate the extent of his genius, it is necessary to see what discoveries he has made in his profession, what improvements upon those of his predecessors. This requires a momentary glance at the history of the art of war.

In ancient times, when missile weapons were neither frequent nor formidable, the natural arrangement of armies was into masses, which might best support the shock of closing with pikes or swords. Such was the Macedonian phalanx; and such, though more pliant and extended, and capable of subdivision, was the close array of the legions. Against those nations among whom archery was cultivated to a degree which enabled them to maintain a distant but constant and effectual discharge of arrows upon these solid bodies, this was the worst order of battle that could be imagined. Hence the success of the Parthians against the Romans. In the feudal armies, the archery of England maintained the same superiority over the solid array of the French and Scottish, which presented a fair and slow-moving mark to their arrows, and which its own weight prevented from avenging the injuries it sustained. The general introduction of fire-arms (a still more unerring and destructive species of missile) necessarily changed the order of battle from depth to extension, or from the mass to the line. See No. 1. of the annexed diagram.

It was obvious, that, without some improvement upon the art, the long-extended line could not be easily moved without confusion; and before such improvement was discovered, armies acting on the defensive usually took up some position, which they neither did nor could attempt to alter, during a general engagement, without hazard of utter ruin. This ancient order may therefore be represented by a line without intervals, as that in No. 1.; not that there were not actually intervals in the ancient order, but because it was not subdivided for the purpose of facilitating motion. In like manner, we must be understood as speaking abstractedly and generally when we talk of the line being stationary. The wings and centre were moved in retreat or advance according to the vicissitudes of battle; but it was without principle or combination, which are necessarily implied in a

modern military movement. They advanced, if victorious, or
retired, if discomfited; but they did not attempt such manœuvres
for the purpose of achieving conquest or avoiding defeat.

The genius of Frederick of Prussia brought into practical use
an improvement upon this order of battle, the effect of which,
whether applied to attack or defence, was to give the general the
power of changing his array, and executing such movements,
even during the heat of action, as must be decisive of the event,
unless the same activity, pliability of disposition, and military
talent, were displayed to counteract his purpose, as he brought
to its execution. This grand step in the art military consisted in
subdividing the long line (No. 1.) into a number of brigades,
(No. 2.) each of which could be easily moved and manœuvred
without the risk of confusion or interference. By this simple
principle of subdivision, to which his troops and his officers
were heedfully and regularly trained, the King of Prussia, instead of making his dispositions before the action, and then trusting the event to fortune and the valour of his troops, was enabled totally to change his arrangement in the very moment of
advance, nay, even in the battle itself, and to gain such positions
as must ensure the defeat of the enemy, who found themselves
pressed probably on the very point, which, at the commencement of the action, was least menaced, and which was proportionally ill provided for defence. This is the guiding principle of
the Prussian tactics, to facilitate which all their discipline tended,
and which repeatedly gave Frederick conquest when employed
against the most formidable armies; which, however brave,
numerous, and skilful, did not possess the principle of activity
thus maintained by the Prussians. In a word, the method of subdividing extensive lines with a view to facilitate their movements,
the principles and machinery by which these subdivisions, and
consequently the whole order of battle, can be accurately moved
and reunited upon new ground, either in the former, or in any
new relation, were brought to perfection, if not in a great measure invented, by Frederick the Second.

The Prussian tactics were transferred to France by the writings
of Guibert;[40] and although modified, as we shall presently see,
to the circumstances of their own armies, do at present form the

40. J. A. H. Guibert, Comte de (1743–90), whose celebrated work, *Essai general de
tactique,* was published in London in 1770.

leading principle of all their movements. So little do those know
of the modern art of war, who are daily exclaiming against the
sluggish and heavy tactics of Frederick, as incompatible with,
and supplanted by, the vivacious movements and new discoveries
of the modern French school of war. The Austrians also adopted
the new principle of movement; but unfortunately they had not
genius enough to discover, that, like a mechanical power, it was
capable of being applied in an endless variety of modes. They
seem to have considered it as only applicable to the ancient
order of an extended line, (as in No. 2.,) and to have overlooked
the obvious consideration, that, having once divided the line of
battle into moveable brigades, it became as easy to reduce it into
a column of those brigades, as it is to form a regiment into a
column of companies or half companies. About the year 1793,
the Austrians might have been able to engage Frederick upon
somewhat resembling his usual application of the principle which
he had invented; but they were unfortunately unprepared for
the tactics of a new enemy, who applied the same principle in a
manner suited to the nature and resources of their own armies.

The King of Prussia, whose troops were excellently disciplined,
and whose numerical force was usually much inferior to that of
his antagonist, applied his principle of manœuvre in the oblique
order, inclining his line so as to turn his antagonist's flank. Thus
his order, though moving obliquely, retained the ancient principle
of extension, and continued to be a line, though not drawn parallel to that of his enemy. It suited his purpose well, but it did not
apply equally to that of the armies of France. These wanted (at
least at the commencement of the revolutionary war,) the skill
and discipline which the Prussian regiments possessed, and they
had the numerical superiority which the Prussian monarch
wanted. It was, therefore, their object so to employ their armies,
that they might derive the utmost advantage from that superiority, and encounter the least possible risque from their deficiency
in practice and discipline. It was plain that the subdivisions of
Frederick might not only be arranged in line, but that they
might be placed behind each other in *reserve;* by which we do
not mean the usual reserve used in all disciplined armies, which
supports the troops in action, and is in fact very nearly engaged
as soon as they,—but a substitution and succession of several
strong divisions, or corps d'armée, placed at a considerable
distance in the rear of each other, and none of which is brought

into action until that in front of it has for a time sustained the heat of the contest, and, by doing so, exhausted the strength of the enemy. An army so placed may be termed an open column of divisions, each of which in turn either makes or sustains attack. (No. 3.) In either case, their advantage over the extended order, so pertinaciously adhered to by the Austrian tacticians, is demonstrable.

In the case of attack, the numerical superiority and preponderating weight of a column impelled against an extended line, must undoubtedly break it. Now, an order of battle, consisting of a number of lines short in extension in proportion to the depth with which they are formed behind each other, is, upon the general and abstract view, an open column, moving on the principle, and possessing all the advantage and disadvantage, of that order. The leading division, supported as it is by those behind it, and acting *de fort en foible,* probably breaks the extended line of the enemy. It is true, that the manœuvre is a hazardous one, for the division which so penetrates an enemy's line is immediately exposed to a murderous cross-fire from the divided portions betwixt which it has passed, and whom the slightest alteration or inclination will place on both its flanks; and such a body, if unsupported, is almost certainly destroyed.*

It is here that their system of *reserve* enables the French to avail themselves of the numerical superiority of their whole army. If that first division is defeated, those who escape throw themselves into the rear of the reserve, for facilitating which the French regiments are often exercised in the manœuvre of rallying upon a new position after total dispersion; the second reserve advances to support or to revenge it, and advances perhaps at the moment when the enemy, having made a flank movement upon the first line, are themselves exposed to be flanked by the second. If the enemy, by reinforcements or obstinate valour,

---

*The French are also partial to the attack by brigades in column, which have, on their scale of action, the same effect, and are liable to the same disadvantages, as the formation of their general order of battle. Thus, at the battle of Vimiera, General Loison's brigade of 2,500 men were thrown into confusion, and driven back with great slaughter, when their column was flanked by three or four hundred of the 50th regiment under Colonel Walker. Thus, also, the charging columns at Busaco suffered the most dreadful carnage. And this mode of resisting the French attack in column is said to have been particularly recommended by the late General Moore. The French, however, usually possess such superiority of numbers as renders them prodigal of the lives of their soldiers, for the certainty, or even the chance, of carrying an important point.

defeats the second reserve, a third advances to the charge, with all the advantage of fresh and unbroken strength, against a foe who has already undergone the loss, fatigue, and confusion of having sustained two desperate attacks. If the attack of the third reserve also is sustained, that of the fourth becomes irresistible, unless the system which exposes an extended line to the attacks of a concentrated succession of attacks, is in the mean time abandoned, and a similar concentration of force affords relief to the party attacked, and counteracts the movements of the French. But if, on the other hand, the centre of the army thus attacked be at length broken, while its wings, either by distance or by being themselves occupied, are prevented from closing to its relief, total defeat may be considered as unavoidable. Its ranks are broken, its flanks exposed, and flight alone can save any part of it. It is for this advantage that the French are willing to make any sacrifice of lives; for they well know that, if it be once attained, valour and discipline are alike unavailing, and the best troops are exposed to be destroyed by those of a very inferior description, if the officers of the latter know but how to avail themselves of the position they have gained.

Hitherto we have supposed the simple case of the French divisions attacking in succession a stationary line; but the advantage of their disposition is the same, if the enemy has either originally begun the attack or has become the assailant, and advanced in pursuit after sustaining and repelling the first charge of the French. In either case the attacking enemy has the disadvantage of encountering a succession of detached corps d'armée, each of which he finds drawn up in its own position, prepared with every advantage of freshness and good order to renew a combat, which his troops have sustained for the whole day. That we may not be accused of vague and theoretical reasoning, we will detail the incidents of the battle of Marengo, in which the Austrians were assailants, and where the French sustained the attack upon the principle, and solely by means of their numerous and powerful reserves.

Upon the 13th June, 1800, the Austrian General, Melas, having united his forces with those of General Otto, then in retreat before Buonaparte, judged himself able to commence offensive operations. He crossed the Bormida at day-break to attack the French army under Buonaparte, which, as the following detail

shews, was disposed in different divisions in the rear of each
other, yet each sufficient for a certain time to sustain the attack,
and waste the forces of the assailants. Generals Gardanne and
Victor, with two divisions of the vanguard, defended the village
of Marengo from seven in the morning till about nine. Perceiv-
ing that the place must be carried by the Austrians, who advanced in columns, Gardanne defiled the greater part of his
troops by an oblique movement, so as to flank them on their
advance; but this manœuvre, as well as a charge of French cavalry on the advancing column, was in vain, and the position was
stormed by the Austrians. A reserve under the command of
Buonaparte now succoured the defeated vanguard; and this
second division of the French army, united with the remains of
the divisions of Gardanne and Victor, again awaited the attack
of the victorious Austrians. The light troops of the Premier
Consul were driven in upon his line; his line was charged by the
Austrian cavalry; and the stand made by Lasnes, whose division
supported that charge, was rendered ineffectual by the disorder
of the centre, which gave way, and exposed Lasnes's flank. The
French line then yielded ground in every direction. Buonaparte,
not yet an emperor, endeavoured to execute some movements
to flank the advancing Austrians, and offered to head the 72d
brigade, which he ordered to the service; but his officers remon-
strated on the exposure *tam chari capitis*,[41] and it would seem
the troops were unable or unwilling to execute so desperate a
manœuvre under any meaner authority. The Consul then
ordered a retreat by intervals upon the troops of a third reserve,
that of General Monnier, whose division arrived to sustain his
right wing. But although the French right wing by this timely
aid not only sustained the attack of the enemy, but even recovered some of the ground they had lost in the morning, they
found themselves obliged to abandon this advantage, in order
that they might cover, and in their turn be protected by, the
centre and left wing, which continued a retreat that gradually
assumed the appearance of a route. The whole French line, including all the divisions which had been successively engaged,
were now driven before the Austrians in the greatest disorder as
far as San Juliano, a village considerably in the rear of that of
Marengo, where the conflict had commenced. Thus far, there-

41. "Quis desiderio sit pudor aut modus / Tam cari capitis?" Horace, *Odes* I, 24.

fore, the Austrians, after a heavy loss and a toilsome struggle, had been victorious over every division opposed to them, however supported or reinforced. But here the secret of Buonaparte's tactics may be remarked. In the front of San Juliano lay a fresh and untouched French army. It was their last reserve, under Dessaix, and was formed in two lines, their flanks sustained by battalions *en potence,* and by close columns of infantry, by a train of flying artillery on the right, and on the left by the French cavalry under Kellerman, which, repulsed in the beginning of the action, had been rallied on this point to renew the conflict. The position which they occupied was a species of defile, closed on one flank by a wood, on the other by a very extensive and thick plantation of vines. The retiring army of Buonaparte threw themselves, rather in flight than retreat, behind this new and formidable protection. Had they not known that such was in their rear, it may be well doubted whether they would not have been utterly broken and almost disbanded before they reached it. It was four [in the] afternoon when the Austrians, who had been engaged in combat from seven in the morning, came in front of this new and untouched division of the French army. They were instantly charged by Dessaix at the head of the ninth light brigade, while in that confusion which success, as well as defeat, always must occasion. Their progress was checked; and though Dessaix was slain and his followers repulsed, yet Buonaparte had obtained time to bring his battalions into order, and, uniting them with the reserve, he advanced as to a new battle. Even this charge of a new and fresh division the Austrians for a time sustained; but the confusion it occasioned among their fatigued and disordered ranks, gave an opportunity to Kellerman, who with his whole cavalry attacked their flank, and forced six battalions, whom the rapidity and fury of his movement had separated from the rest, to throw down their arms. The tide of the battle was then completely turned. The Austrians, hitherto successful in every point, but now totally unsupported, were routed and chaced beyond the Bormida with immense loss; while the French, who the whole day had been beaten from position to position, being sustained by repeated reserves, were at last enabled to wrest victory out of the hands of an enemy too fatigued to hold it.*

*See "Recueil de Plans de Battailes, &c., gagnés par Bonaparte, en Italie et en Egypte, et par deux Officiers de son Etat Major. A Paris et Leipsic." The following

In all the grand general actions of Buonaparte, the same principle can be discovered, namely, that of combining a prompt and vigorous mode of action with a concentrated order of battle, which it has been generally his good fortune to oppose to indecision, want of energy, and a prejudice in favour of an extended line. Where circumstances, as in the battle of Wagram, have, as it were, compelled his enemies to present a more collected front than usual, he has employed a still greater degree of concentration on his part, so as to ensure his having the last reserve which can be brought up. In short, he does not gain the battle by the perseverance of the soldiers engaged in it, but by renewing it by means of numerous reliefs. The perseverance is in the general and his plan of tactics, not in the troops; and the principle consists not in requiring it from the latter, but in making up for their want of it. And it is a most admirable plan for a general, circumstanced like Buonaparte, whom extended means of every kind, as well as the great unity and promptitude of combining different marching columns upon a given position, enable always to appear in the field with a numerical superiority. The old mode, by which a general used to avail himself of the advantage of numbers, was by extending his wings, so that their extremities might outflank and surround his enemy, as in the battle of Rosbach. But by this extension the line is exposed to be attacked by the concentrated force of the enemy in any given point, as really happened at that battle. (No. 4.) The system of Buonaparte is the very reverse of this, and consists, as we have seen, in condensing his line, leaving it in length barely equal at most to the enemy's front, and often much less extended, but strengthening it in depth, by placing one division in

---

observations on the same engagement, by an author calling himself a Russian Staff Officer, but whose style and information argue him to be a Frenchman, may be received as corroborating those in the text:—"*La journée de Marengo, où le Grand Consul parut, et fut en effet si fort an-dessous de sa reputation, prouve qu'à cette époque il n'avait dans l'art des battailes aucune supériorité sur ses rivaux; mais elle lui apprit a connaître une importante vérité; savoir, qui'l n'est presque jamais un premier mouvement qui décide la victoire, que au contraire elle reste définitivement au général qui, après quelques heures d'un engagement opiniâtre, tient à sa disposition un corps respectable de troupes fraîches. Le succès d'une réserve est dans ce cas rarement douteux, et il devient infailliblement la cause d'un succès décisif, si elle profite pour faire une attaque impétueuse des derangemens, des fluctuations inévitables dans la ligne ennemie, pendant le cours d'une action générale, et que son mouvement victorieux ait été incessamment soutenu par un changement analogue dans les mouvemens du corps de battaile.*"—Essai sur le Systeme Militaire de Bonaparte, &c. p. C.H.S. Officier D'Etat-Major Moscovite. London, 1811. Dulau et Cop. et Pannier.

rear of another. It is this system of repeated reserves which enables him to avail himself of the superiority of numbers to its fullest extent, and to compel the enemy to put forth their whole strength in struggling with a force equal to their own, while he can bring up, at the chosen moment, reinforcements sufficient to throw the odds against them. That moment he waits for with the utmost coolness and patience, and even partial success does not induce him to anticipate its arrival by a premature motion in advance.

The post of the emperor, or *quartier-general,* is at the head of the strong and numerous reserve which supports the centre. From that point all orders are issued, and to that point, with inexpressible celerity, all communications are made. In general, the French permit the enemy to commence the attack, and content themselves with maintaining a severe fire of musquetry and artillery. No regiment of infantry or cavalry is permitted to advance beyond the line of battle in order to charge; for in French tactics they adhere strictly to the military rule, that the particular movement of each battalion must always bear reference to the general movements of the whole body,—a rule which is of course most easily attended to in a condensed and concentrated array, through which orders can be transmitted with accuracy and promptitude. On the other hand, they are prompt to avail themselves of the partial and unsustained advance of any part of the opposing force. Thus at Austerlitz the imperial horse guards of Alexander precipitated themselves on the French line, and broke through it. But it was an unsupported movement of indignant impatience; and no sooner were they in the rear of the line which they had broken, than they were themselves flanked and routed, or cut to pieces by the cavalry of Buonaparte's reserves. At Talavera, too, the gallant impetuosity of the guards endangered, by a rash advance, the victory of the day. But they were supported and covered by directions of a general, whose eye nothing escapes. The French then do not hazard these partial and dangerous movements, especially in the commencement of an action, considering it, and justly, as of more importance to preserve the unity of their order, than to grasp hastily at any subaltern advantage. They are aware that when the day is far advanced, the victory must remain with that party who can last bring into the field a strong force of fresh troops. It is often in the very moment that the enemy suppose themselves victors that this unexpected apparition turns the scale of battle. Their advantages cannot have been acquired without loss, tumult, and disorder, and it is while they are in that state that they are suddenly pressed by fresh troops, who in this moment are permitted to indulge all their national vivacity of courage and enterprize. Thus in one of Buonaparte's bulletins concerning the battle of Friedland, it is stated, that after the conflict had continued a great part of the day, the emperor resolved to put an end to it, (here is a proof he was rather apprehensive of the result,) and came up with a strong reserve. We must leave it to those who wish to prosecute the study, to trace this principle of movement (it is a general one, and subject to various modifications) through the great general actions fought by Buonaparte,* cautioning him at the same time, that he is not to expect to discover it in the encounter of small armies, where all the ground is under the eye of both generals, and where neither could make a strong detachment in reserve without the other being aware of its existence, and making a similar reserve on his side to encounter it. He must also observe, that in some of Buonaparte's grand engagements, although the principle of the formation be the same, yet its operation is not so simple or so obvious at first sight as in the battle of Marengo. In some of these, as at Wagram and Jena, the same concentration, arising from a more than usual number of reserves, enabled the French general to render his own line impenetrable, whilst he turned his enemy's flank, or availed himself of any opening in their line to pierce it. But these latter uses to which reserves may be applied, are only resorted to by Buonaparte when the conduct of the opposing general is more than usually incautious.

It remains to shew in what manner the French masque their formation, and occupy the attention of the enemy along the

---

*We again fortify an opinion formed long before the printing of this work, by the evidence of the Russian Staff-Officer, (if such he be) whose essay we have already quoted: —"*Les victoires d'Jéna, de Ratisbonne, de Wagram, furent dues au même principe, à le même manœuver. Ainsi que je l'ai avancé, les Français laissent ordinairement commencer a leurs ennemis les premiers mouvemens. Or, ces premiers mouvemens n'étant jamais qu'une attaque isolée au lieu d'être dirigés comme devant être le commencement d'un mouvement général, quelque desordre qu'ils puissent causer dans la ligne des Français, ces derniers ont dans l'emploi immédiat de leur réserve les moyens non-seulement de réparer leur defection; ils rendront funeste a leurs ennemis, le mouvement victorieux mais inconsidéré, d'une troupe qu'on ne soutient pas.*"

full extent of their long order of battle, while in fact they only oppose a short and condensed front to the centre of their line. This is accomplished by means of their numerous light troops, which were at first formed after the example of the irregular sharpshooters of America, as the readiest mode of training their conscripts. But the genius of the French soldier seems particularly adapted to this light and skirmishing species of warfare. The loose order, or rather the dispersion of these tirailleurs, enables a number comparatively small to occupy the attention and harass the movements of the enemy's extended front, if unprovided with similar forces. Thus these numerous irregulars act as a screen to their own lines, while it is impossible for those who are assailed by them to discern whether they are supported by battalions, or in what order the French general is arraying his forces in the rear of this swarm of hornets. Thus they remain in complete ignorance of the French disposition, and dare not of course attempt to change their own; and while the wings waste their force, nay sometimes sustain heavy loss in encountering this harassing, and, as it were, unsubstantial enemy, their centre has to sustain the full weight of the French line, concentrated as we have described it. This mode of warfare was peculiarly severe on the Austrians; for it happened, by some unfortunate fatality, that in her passion for the Prussian discipline, that power judged it fit to convert the greater part of her Croats, the finest light troops in the world, into heavy battalions, and thus diminished their strength of this particular description of force at the moment when the fate of battle was about to depend upon it. The excellence of those light corps which Austria retained could not supply their great inferiority of numbers; and thus in that sort of minor battle of advanced guards, which is maintained by the light troops, and of which it is usually the object not to beat back the enemy, but to distract his attention, and, by engaging him in a confused struggle with a foe not the less formidable because yielding and almost invisible, to bring him up to their own line crippled and disheartened, the French acquired a superiority, which enabled them, without the least risque of being outflanked, to contract their own line within the extent necessary for employing the so-often-mentioned principle of reserves.

But it may be asked, to what tends this exposition? The French have been almost uniformly victorious, and how avails it to what their victories can be ascribed? Our answer is twofold. Such an

investigation as we have attempted leads us to due appreciation
of the talents of Buonaparte, instead of blind terror or blinder
admiration. We have no wish to insinuate a disrespect for his
talents, having (as they unfortunately possess) the disposal of
such extraordinary force at their command; in the words of a
warrior speaking of his enemy, we grant him

> ——Strong, and skilful to his strength,
> Fierce to his skill, and to his fierceness
> valiant.[42]

But it will remain to be inquired whether his genius is of such a
transcendant and overpowering nature as a distant contemplation of his exploits might induce us to believe. His plan, of which
we have endeavoured to develope the principle, is indeed well
fitted to ensure the most numerous of two encountering armies
the full superiority of its numbers; but there is no brilliant genius
requisite to the formation. It is not an invention like Frederick's
discovery of a new principle of moving an extended line. The
latter is like the discovery of a mechanical power, and must in
one shape or other be useful while armies are opposed to each
other. The system of Buonaparte is only a peculiar mode of
employing the same power previously discovered, which may be
destroyed by any counteracting system, or superseded by any
improvement on the application of the principle upon which it
turns. In all his great engagements, (that of Austerlitz perhaps
excepted,) Buonaparte seems never even to have attempted
manœuvering, that is, he never attempted to gain for his army
a position which must give it an immediate and decided advantage over the enemy. Now this art we take to be the consummation of military ability, as being that by which military skill
supplies the lack both of strength and of numbers. In the battles of the King of Prussia and other distinguished generals, we
are led to augur the fortune of the day from the dispositions
their ability enabled them to make relative to their enemy; and
in the progress of the action we gradually observe our expectations realized. But Buonaparte's dispositions never authorize
any conclusion as to his final success; and the imperfection of
his positions, as well as the inferiority of his troops, is frequently

42. *Troilus and Cressida*, I, i, 7–8.

conspicuous by the defeat of his army during the greater part of
the day, until at length the fortune is turned by that in which
his secret seems to consist, the appearance, namely, of a numerous reserve, fresh and in order. But it may be asked, is that not
ability which secures to itself the effect of bringing up the last
reserve? Undoubtedly it is, but of a subordinate and somewhat
vulgar nature. It is the game of a chess player, who, conscious of
superiority by a single piece, goes on exchanging man for man,
because he knows that the lower he can reduce both parties, the
more his numerical superiority will be likely to gain the ascendant.
Independent, therefore, of the waste of human blood, which conquerors seldom attend to, Buonaparte's road to victory seems
greatly to depend upon his bringing a predominating force into
the field, and upon his enemy's pertinacious adherence to the
infatuated system of exposing an extended line to the action of
a deep and reinforced column.

But the second object of our remarks is yet more important.
Not only do we think the system of Buonaparte too obvious
and too coarse to claim the praise of very high genius for the
general who has trusted so constantly to it, but we conceive that
it also admits of being easily counteracted.* Supposing that an
enemy not inferior, at least not very much inferior in numbers,
encountered Buonaparte with a line condensed like his own,
covered in front by sharp-shooters, supported by numerous and
powerful reserves, and capable, from its concentration, of suddenly executing general and combined movements, his ordinary
scheme is entirely disconcerted, and the two armies meet upon
equal terms. Now where this is the case, uniform experience
shews, 1st, That the bravery of the French, however ardent, is
rather of a volatile and spirited nature, than what we term steadi-

---

*The Russian Staff-officer gives the grand secret in a few words:—"*J'ai dit que la
bataille d'Austerlitz avoit été pour Bonaparte le présage de ses victoires futures, qu'il
était le maître DU GRAND SECRET. D'après ce que je viens de dire, et on ne peut
contester que mes assertions ne reposent sur des faits nombreux, ce Grand Secret n'a
pu en être un que pour les généraux sans intelligence que les souverains du continent,
ont constamment opposés a l'usurpateur. Qu'y a-t-il en effet de plus connu que
l'emploi d'un corps de réserve, et de plus simple que l'usage qu'en font les Français?
Ils l'emportent par leur mobilité, l'ensemble dans les mouvemens. . . . Généraux!
qui cherchent en vain la cause d'un tel avantage, ou feignez de ne pas l'apercevoir,
supprimez vos bagages, ordonnez a vos généraux subalternes d'étudier leurs manœuvres,
de combattre a la tête de leurs divisions: aux capitaines de l'infanterie d'être a pied à
la tête de leurs compagnies: changez l'organisation et la composition de vos états-
majors, et vous serez aussi les maîtres du Grand Secret.*"

ness and intrepidity; and, 2dly, that where sufficient skill is united to the latter qualities, they, like what is called *bottom* by the prize-fighters, secure superiority in a long action. 3dly, The French general must be necessarily embarrassed and disconcerted by the neutralization of the very plan on which he had rested for conquest. For these combined reasons, we conceive, that if deprived of the benefit of this favourite manœuvre, the balance would probably incline against the French: Nay, we are able to shew an example in modern war, where Buonaparte's own system was successfully employed against himself by the Russian General Benningsen, at the battles of Pultusk and Eylau. In sustaining the French attack at Pultusk, the Cossacks and other light troops of the Russians formed as it were an outwork, or advanced battle, to their mainline, and not only completely overpowered the *eclaireurs* and *tirailleurs,* who were thrown forward, as usual, to protect and mask the advance of the French columns, but greatly embarrassed, interrupted, and crippled the columns themselves before they could reach the Russian position, properly so called. At Eylau, the counterpart of the French system was equally successfully provided against and counteracted by the Russians. Reserve after reserve was brought up by the French, but at the close of a long and desperate battle, the last reserve brought into action was that of the Russians. In both these battles, the Russians had decidedly the advantage,—a fact which might have remained concealed from Europe, but for the clear, distinct, and able statement of Sir Robert Wilson[43] in his late publication, which he himself invites the reader to contrast with the partial and studiously confused bulletins of Buonaparte, which form part of his appendix. It may be supposed strange, that the generals of a much more uncultivated people should be able to imitate, and by imitating to foil, a system of tactics, before which the generals of Austria and Prussia had given way. But it should be remembered, that the Russians had conducted wars upon a very broad scale, and though their operations were against barbarians, they were, perhaps for that very reason, more certainly brought back to general principles, and freed from the prejudice of military men, who, having only studied in one school, expected their antagonist strictly to conform to their own game and their own rules for playing it.

43. Sir Robert T. Wilson's *Brief Remarks . . . Campaigns in Poland* was reviewed in the *Quarterly* for Feb., 1811.

Let it be remembered, that it was a Russian Emperor, who, by simply covering his line-of-battle by a chain of closed redoubts, instead of the combined fortified lines then in use, broke, at Pultowa, those Swedish infantry, whom every general in Europe, nay, Marlborough himself, regarded with respect and apprehension. The French themselves were comparatively undisciplined when they devised this very system of reserves, as affording them the means of availing themselves of their numbers against the superior skill of their adversaries. We cannot forget the reproaches cast upon Lord Wellington as a *Seapoy General.* Had he not learned his art upon a broad and extended plan, such as India alone has yet afforded to a British general, where else could he have acquired the art of providing for the necessities of a large army, the principles of combination necessary for conducting its extended movements, in short, the complicated branches of military skill by which he is now driving before him those hordes, whose greatest disgrace it is, that they cannot shelter their abominable rapine and atrocity under the barbarous ignorance of Seiks or Mahrattas.

It may indeed be pleaded too justly, that the acknowledged imperfections in the Russian commissariat, the deficiencies of their staff, and, above all, the deplorable neglect of their government to supply and reinforce their armies, deprived them of the fruits of victory; while the active energy of Buonaparte drained his whole acquisitions of every soldier, or man who could be made such, to resume the field with a force superior to that which had foiled and defeated him. These considerations, however, do not respect our present subject, which refers merely to the field of battle, on which, we repeat, the Russians have neutralized Buonaparte's favourite manœuvre. It may be briefly noticed, that the inhabitants of the peninsula, less fortunate in facing him in the field, and who at Tudela experienced discomfiture from the effects of that system which we have detailed, have yet shewn, that when a general battle is lost, the advantages of the victory may be in a great degree intercepted. The inveterate and desperate hostility of the Spaniards and Portuguese, so widely diffused through the peasantry of the country, has utterly destroyed the boasted system of intercourse and communication, by which the march of one French column was made to correspond with that of all who were acting in the same kingdom. Near as the events and positions were, it is almost impossible that Massena could have known the fall of Badajos when he broke up from Santarem, or that Soult anticipated the retreat of Massena when he himself fell back into Spain, instead of advancing into Alemtejo, to make a diversion, and afford support to the *enfant gaté* whom Fortune was dropping out of her arms. But the general and inveterate enmity of the peasantry entirely annihilated all the fair system of unity and constant correspondence, which in Germany the French armies maintained at any given distance. Couriers, aids-de-camp, orderly men, and disguised spies, were alike the objects of suspicion to the Ordenanza, who, rather than miss securing their letters, would steadily rip up their bowels,—a sad interruption to a regular and friendly correspondence. And thus these two great generals seem to have known little more of each other's motions, than if they had been next door neighbours in London. The self-devoted patriotism, with which the Portuguese destroyed every part of their own property, which could afford supply or assistance to the invading army, rendered the genius of the French for the commissariat department equally unavailing. Nay, even *les grands moyens* themselves have proved fruitless in a country, where Lord Wellington has declared, that none, even of the lowest description, forgot, through any compelled intercourse with the French, the duty which they owed to their country. We glance at these subjects, though distinct from that which we proposed to enlarge upon, merely to shew, that as the French system of tactics in the field of battle is far from infallible, so neither are the other means which they employ in facilitating the operations of the campaign less liable to derangement, where the population of an invaded country is confident in their own leaders, and true to their own cause.

We now close these desultory observations, by stating, in justification of the tone of decision which we have presumed to adopt, that the theory they contain was deduced from an attentive perusal of the plans of Buonaparte's battles published at Paris. Yet we should have hesitated to offer them to the public on our slender authority, had we not found our opinion confirmed three years after we had embodied it in writing, by the excellent work of Sir Robert Wilson, and by a very striking treatise, entitled "Essai sur le Systeme Militaire de Bonaparte, par C.H.S. Major d'Etat Muscovite," which we have liberally quoted in our notes. These authorities coinciding with our own opinion so much beyond our expectation, led us to give our sketch to the public, in hopes that, thus supported, it may operate as a sedative in tranquillizing the mind of those who do not know more of the practice of war than we do ourselves; and we shall not quarrel with the true-blue Englishman who may think with Corporal Trim, that one home-thrust of the bayonet is worth it all.

DIAGRAM,

Referred to in the preceding Article.

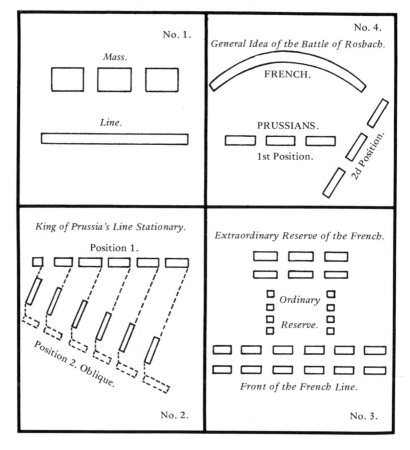

ༀ The Inferno of Altisidora

Scott made no secret of his authorship of "The Inferno of Altisidora," which he wrote as a preface to his poems: "The Poacher," an imitation of Crabbe; "Oh say not, my love," an imitation of Moore; and a fragment of his own *Bridal of Triermain*. Scott called his essay in a letter to James Ballantyne "a wild sort of an introduction" to the imitations and asked for Ballantyne's assistance in finding the appropriate quotation from *Don Quixote*. See *Letters of Scott*, I, 412; II, 525–26 and note. The essay is listed in the *New Cambridge Bibliography of English Literature*.

"The Inferno of Altisidora" (*Register*, II, 582–99), owes something to Swift's *Battle of the Books* but rather more to the essays by Henry Mackenzie in the *Mirror* and the *Lounger*. The narrator of "The Inferno" is similar to the old bachelor of Mackenzie's essay (38) in the *Lounger* (Oct. 22, 1785) who has a dream of various married couples who ask for a dissolution of their marriage. "Lady Rumpus" is a character mentioned in the *Lounger* essays. The *Mirror* is also mentioned in "The Inferno," and the setting in Edinburgh makes the connection with Mackenzie even stronger. The subject matter of the essay—the various reviewers of the day—connects it with Scott's essay "On the Present State of Periodical Criticism" and often parallels the statements in that essay. The reference to *Don Quixote* in the essay is a further reminder of Scott's admiration and love for Cervantes.

> "*A uno dellos nuero, flamante y bien enguardernado le diéron un papirotazo, que le sacaron las tripas, y le esparcieron los hojas.*"
> —Cervantes, *Don Quixote*, Part II., lib. viii, cap. 70.

> "They tossed up a new book fairly bound, and gave it such a smart stroke, that the very guts flew out of it, and all the leaves were scattered about."
> —Motteux, *Translation*

TO THE PUBLISHER
OF THE EDINBURGH ANNUAL REGISTER

Sir,—The character of your present correspondent is perhaps very little to the purpose of his communication; but who can resist the temptation of a favourable opportunity for speaking of himself and his own affairs? I am, then, a bachelor of fifty, or, by'r lady,[44] some fifty-five years standing, and I can no longer disguise from myself, that the scenes, in which I formerly played a part of some gratifying degree of consequence, are either much

---

44. An allusion to Falstaff: "his age some fifty, or by'r Lady, inclining to three-score." *Henry IV*, Part I, II, iv. 467.

altered, or I am become somehow less fitted for my character.
Twenty years ago I was a beau garçon of some renown, escorted
Lady Rumpus and Miss Tibby Dasher to oyster parties, danced
with the lovely Lucy J——, and enjoyed the envied distinction
of handing into St. Cecilia's Hall the beautiful and too-early-lost
Mis B——t. But, as the learned Partridge[45] pathetically observes,
non sum qualis eram; and now, far from being permitted to
escort the young and the gay through that intricate labyrinth,
entitled the Entrance to the New Theatre Royal, I observe it is
not without obvious reluctance that I am selected as a proper
beau to the General Assembly. Nor indeed can I disguise to myself, that I owe even this humble distinction to the gravity of
my physiognomy and habit, which the discerning fair consider
as peculiarly calculated to overawe the beadles, by conveying
the impression of a Ruling Elder. My apartments in Argyle's
square, those very lodgings where my *petits soupers* were accounted such desirable parties, have now acquired a certain
shabbiness of aspect, and seem to me contracted in their very
dimensions. Nay, what is worse than all this, my annual income,
though nominally the same, does not produce above half the
comforts it used to compass. Amid these disconcerting circumstances, one would have thought that I might still have derived
some benefit from a smattering of literature, which, having
decorated my conversation in my better days, might be supposed still in some measure to recommend me to society. But I
know not how it happens, that even in this respect matters
seem strangely altered to my disadvantage. The time has been,
when I could thrust my head over the threshold of Mr. Creech's
shop,[46] and mingle in the first literary society which Scotland
then afforded, and which (no disparagement to the present men
of letters) has hardly been equalled since. I was personally
known to Adam Smith, to Ferguson, to Robertson, to both the
Humes, and to the lively Lord Kaimes. At a later period, my
company was endured by the Man of Feeling, and other distinguished members of the Mirror Club. I have talked on prints and
pictures with Johnie M'——n, have shaken my sides with the
facetious Captain Grose over a bottle of old port, and one evening had the superlative distinction of hearing the tremendous Dr.

---

45. Henry Fielding, *Tom Jones*, Book 18, chapter 5. Partridge so remarks to Allworthy.
46. William Creech's bookshop was a favorite meeting place for literary men.

Johnson grumble forth wit and wisdom over a shrinking band of
North British literati; so that I may say, with the magnanimous
Slender, "I have seen Sackerson loose, and taken him by the
chain."[47] These, sir, are pretensions to a respectable place in
literary society, and might entitle me to some deference from
my juniors, who only know most of these great men in their
writings or by tradition. Yet now I find my opinions in taste
and criticism are almost as much out of fashion as my toupee
and my small silverbuckles. Every stripling, whom I remember
an urchin at the High School, seems to have shot up into an author or reviewer, for the purpose of confuting my sentiments
by dogmatical assertion, or overwhelming my arguments by professional declamation. This is so melancholy a truth, that I have
learned to rank myself in conversation according to the rule of
precedence settled at processions; and never attempt to declare
my own opinion till I am sure all the younger members of the
company have given their sentiments. But, notwithstanding
every compromise which I have endeavoured to make with the
spirit of the time, I feel myself daily becoming more and more a
solitary and isolated being; and while I cook my little fire and
husband my pint of port, I cannot but be sensible that these are
the most important occupations of my waking day.

I was thus whiling away my evening, with a volume of Don
Quixote open before me, when my attention was caught by the
account which Altisidora gives of the amusement of the devils
in the infernal regions. "I got to the gates of hell," says she,
"where I found a round dozen of devils in their breeches and
waistcoats, playing at tennis with flaming rackets; they wore
flat bands, with scolloped Flanders lace, and ruffles of the same;
four inches of their wrist bare to make their hands look the
longer, in which they held rackets of fire. But what surprised
me most was, that, instead of tennis-balls, they made use of
books, that were every whit as light, and stuffed with wind and
flocks, and such kind of trumpery. This was indeed most strange
and wonderful; but what amazed me still more, I found that,
contrary to the custom of gamesters, among whom the winning
party is at least in good humour, and the losers only angry, these
hellish tossers of books of both sides did nothing but fret, fume,
stamp, curse, and swear most horribly, as if they had been all

47. *Merry Wives of Windsor*, I, i, 268.

losers. "That's no wonder at all," quoth Sancho, "for your devils, whether they play or no, win or lose, they can never be contented." When I had proceeded thus far in my author, the light began to fail me. I finished my last glass of wine, and threw myself back in my easy chair to digest what I had read. The ludicrous description of Cervantes became insensibly jumbled with my own reveries on the critical taste and literary talents of my contemporaries, until I sunk into a slumber. The consequence was a dream, which I am tempted to send you as an introduction to some scraps of poetry, that, without it, would be hardly intel-ligible.

Methought, sir, I was (like many of my acquaintance) on the high-way to the place of perdition. The road, however, seemed neither broad, nor flowery, nor easy. In steepness, indeed, and in mephitic fragrance, the place of my peregrination was no bad emblem of the descent of Avernus; but, both in these and in other respects, it chiefly resembled a deserted *close* in the more ancient part of our good city. Having been accustomed to the difficulties of such footing in my younger days, I picked my way, under low-browed arches, down broken steps, and through miscellaneous filth, with a dexterity which no iron-heeled beau of the present day could have emulated. At length I came in sight of a very large building, with a court-yard in front, which I conceived to be the Tartarus towards which I had been descend-ing; I saw, however, neither Minos nor Æacus, neither Belial nor Beelzebub; and, to speak plainly, sir, the building itself seemed rather to resemble your own Pandemonium, than either that of Milton, the Erebus of Virgil, or the dread abode of Hela. Cerberus was chained near the door; but, as he had got rid of two of his heads, and concentrated their ferocity in that which he retained, he did not greatly differ in appearance from an English bulldog. Had it not been for certain whips, scourges, gorgon-faces, and other fearful decorations of infernal archi-tecture, which were disposed on its front by way of architrave, like the fetters and chains in front of Newgate,—had it not been, I say, for these and similar emblems of disappointment, con-tempt, and mortification, and for a reasonable quantity of fly-ing dragons and hissing serpents that occasionally flew in or out of the garret windows, I should rather have taken the place for an immense printing-house than for the infernal regions. But what attracted my attention chiefly, was the apparition of a body of fiends, of different stature, size, and ages, who were playing at racket with new books, exactly in the manner described by Cervantes in the passage I have quoted, and whose game was carried on and contested with most astonishing perseverance in the court-yard I have mentioned. The devils, being, I presume, of real British extraction, were not clad in the Spanish costume of laced bands and scolloped sleeves, and they seemed to have transferred the pride which Altisidora's fiends took in the length of their wrists, as mine more demoniacally piqued themselves on the longitude and sharpness of their claws. Neither was the party equipped in the same livery, but exhibited all sorts of dresses, from the priest's to the soldier's, and from that of a modern fine gentleman to the rags of a *polisson,* whose cloven hoofs peeped through his second-hand boots. They all wore vizards, however, which, although not complete disguises, (for the by-standers pretended to distinguish them by their mode of playing, and I heard them whisper, "That's Astaroth," "that's Belphegor," and so forth,) yet served, like the wire masque of a fencer, to save their faces from the awkward accidents incident to so violent a sport. I did, indeed, remark one old gentleman,[48] and, 'twas said, he had been a notable man in his day, who made a match to be played bare-faced; but whether, like Entellus of old, he had become stiff and unwieldy, or whether he was ill-seconded by his few and awkward partners, so it was, that he was soon obliged to give up the game, which the rest continued to prosecute with the utmost vigour.

As few of the volumes, which it was their amusement to buffet, stood many bangs with the racket, the whole ground was whitened with their fragments; and it would have grieved your very heart, sir, to see the waste of good paper and pica. The incessant demand of the players for new materials was as constantly supplied by a set of little ragged urchins, nowise differing from printers' devils, except that each had at his back a small pair of bat's wings, which, I suppose, were only for shew, as I did not observe the imps make any use of them. The books, which they brought in quantities from the interior of the building, they tossed one by one into the air, and it seemed their object (but which they rarely attained,) to throw them out of

---

48. Richard Cumberland (1732–1811), conductor of the short-lived *London Review* (1809), introduced the novelty of signed reviews.

the reach of the gamesters' rackets, and, if possible, over the
low boundaries of the court-yard. On the other side of these
limits waited an immense and miscellaneous concourse of spectators, whose interest seemed to be excited by the fate of each
volume. The general appearance of the game resembled tennis,
or rather battledore and shuttle-cock; but I was unable to trace
the various and apparently complicated principles acted upon
by those engaged in it. This I observed in general, that when, by
its natural lightness and elasticity, or by the dexterity of the
diablotins by whom it was committed to the air, or by the
stroke of some friendly racket, or, in fine, by a combination of
these causes, a volume was so fortunate as to clear the barrier, it
was caught up like a relique by the spectators on the outside.
You have seen, sir, boys at a review chace each other for the
fragments of smoking cartridges, which may give you some
idea of the enthusiastic regard with which these fortunate books
were received by this admiring multitude. On the contrary,
when any one was struck to the ground, or shattered to pieces
within the inclosure, its fall was solemnized by whooping and
hisses and groans from the good company. So far I could understand the game well enough, and could easily comprehend
further, that the imps by whom each book was thrown into the
air, had deep bets in dependence upon its being struck across
the line. But it was not so easy to comprehend the motives of
the different players. Sometimes you beheld them anxious to
strike a volume among the spectators, sometimes equally indus-
trious to intercept its flight, and dash it to the ground. Often
you saw them divide into different parties, the one attempting
to keep up a favourite book, the other to bring it down. These
partialities occasionally gave rise to very diverting bye-games. I
sometimes saw a lubbard fiend, in attempting to give an impulse
to a ponderous volume, strike it right up into the air, when, to
the infinite delight and laughter of the beholders, it descended
with added momentum upon his own noddle, and put him out
of combat for some time. I also observed the little bat-winged
gentry occasionally mix among the racqueteers, and endeavour
to bias their game by bribing them to play booty. Their offers
were sometimes accepted with silent shame, sometimes rejected
with open contempt; but I observed in general, that those whom
these bustling but subordinate imps were able to influence, were
the worst players, and most frequently exposed to the ridiculous

accidents which excited the contempt of the spectators. Indeed, the gamesters were incalculably different in strength, activity, and dexterity; and one of superior address was very often able, by a well-timed back-stroke of his racket, to send in, or to bring down, a book, which all his comrades had combined to destroy or to save. Such a game, it may be easily believed, was not played by such a description of beings without infinite noise, clamour, and quarrel. Sometimes a book would be bandied between two of them without any further regard for the volume than as they could strike it against each other's face, and very often one party seemed determined to buffet a work to shivers, merely because another set had endeavoured to further it on its journey over the lists. After all, a great deal seemed to depend on the degree of *phlogiston* which each manufacturer endeavoured to throw into his volume, and which, if successfully infused, afforded an elasticity capable of resisting the downward impulse of the most unfavourable racket. In some few cases, the mob without made a scramble for a favourite, broke in, deranged the play, overset the racqueteers, and carried off in triumph, works which apparently would never have reached them according to the usual practice of the game. These cases, however, were uncommon; and when, through a violent and unfair blow, some tome, which had been waited for with anxiety without the barrier, was beat down and trampled on by the players, its fall only occasioned slight murmurs among the respectable part of the expectants, without any desperate attempt to rescue it. A single friend or two sometimes essayed to collect the fragments of a volume, and to raise an outcry against the usage which it had sustained; but, unless supported by the general voice of the exterior mass, they were usually jostled down by the players, or silenced by a smart knock with a racket. The fate of a volume, also, *cœteris paribus,* depended in some degree on its size. Your light *twelve-mo,* sir, (to use your own barbarous dialect) flew further with a favourable impulse, and afforded a less mark to the assailant, than the larger and more ponderous quarto. But neither was this rule without exception. Some large volumes spread their wings like wild swans, and went off triumphant, notwithstanding all the buffets of opposition; and, on the other hand, you might see a whole covey of crown octavos, and duodecimos, and such small deer, drop as fast as a flight of plovers who have received a shower of hail-shot while upon the wheel.

In short, the game depended on an endless complication of circumstances and principles; and although I could easily detect many of them when operating singly, they were yet so liable to be balanced and counterbalanced, that I would sooner have betted on throwing doublets thrice running at backgammon than upon the successful escape of any single volume from the rackets, and its favourable transmission to the other side of the court-yard. But, after I had long watched this extraordinary scene, I at length detected a circumstance which altogether confounded the few calculations which its uncertainty had previously permitted me to form.

I observed that there mingled among those engaged in the game, as well as among the gazing crowd, a man in the extremity of old age. His motions were as slow as the hour-hand of a watch, yet he seemed to be omnipresent; for wherever I went, I saw him or the traces of his footsteps. Wherever I turned my eyes, whether upon the players, or upon the populace who watched their motions, I beheld him; and though I could with infinite difficulty find out his occupation while gazing upon him, yet, by watching him from time to time, I discovered that his influence was as powerful as its operations were slow and invisible. To this personage, whom I heard them call *Tempus,* various appeals were made on all hands. The patrons of the wrecked volumes claimed his protection almost unanimously; the defeated players themselves, though more coldly, desired him to do justice between them and their more successful opponents, or to make register of the undue violence by which spectators in some cases rescued their lawful prey. The old gentleman, to do him right, was as impartial as the justices of peace in a small debt court, when none has a tenant at the bar, and as inexorable as the same bench when dinnertime draws near. He continued his tardy but incessant manœuvres, now crawling among the feet of the gamesters to collect and piece together some of those volumes which had suffered the extremity of their fury, and now gliding unseen and unnoticed among the spectators, to wile out of their hands certain works which they had received with the loudest jubilee; and he succeeded in both cases, as nurses do in securing the play-things of children, which they have either broken in a pet, or admired to satiety. The use which he made of his power and his perseverance, was very different in these different cases. When he had slyly possessed

himself of some of these works which had been most highly applauded, I detected him stealing towards a neighbouring ditch
(the Lethe of the region) into which he discharged his burthen,
without the least regret on the part of those from whom he had
abstracted it. On the other hand, in his slow and imperceptible
manner, he would every now and then unfold to some of the
more grave and respectable among the by-standers, fragments
and favourite passages out of books he had rescued from among
the feet of the racket-players, and, by the impression these
made, he gradually paved the way for a general and brilliant
reception of an entire volume. And I must observe of the books
thus brought into notice, that they were said to be rarely liable
to a second declension in public favour, but, with a few worthies,
who, like them, had stood the test of *Time,* were, I was informed,
deposited in an honourable and distinguished place in his library,
for the admiration and instruction of future ages.

The general feeling of surprise and consternation, with which I
hitherto regarded this extraordinary scene, began soon to give
way to curiosity and to the desire of making more minute observations. I ventured to draw as near as I durst to the old father
I have described, who was then employed in collecting and piec-
ing a huge quarto, which had received an uncommonly severe
buffet from a racket, and on the front of which I could spell the
word MADOC.[49] "Good father," said I, as respectfully as I could,
"do you account that volume a great treasure?" "Since I saved,"
answered he, "a poem in the same measure, the work of an old
blind man, out of the hands of some gay courtiers, I have hardly
made a more valuable acquisition." "And what then do you
purpose to do with it?" pursued I, emboldened by his affabili-
ty."—"Reserve it under my mantle, as I did the former, for an
age worthy of it"—"Good Tempus," resumed I, "if I do not entirely mistake your person, I have some reason to complain of
hard measure from you. Is it not you that have thinned my hair,
wrinkled my forehead, diminished my apartments, lessened my
income, rendered my opinions antiquated, and my company un-
desirable; yet all this will I forgive you on one slight condition.
You cannot have forgot a small miscellany, published about
twenty years ago, which contained some copies of verses sub-
scribed Amyntor?"—The old personage protested his total want

---

49. Jeffrey had harshly reviewed Southey's *Madoc* in the *Edinburgh Review.*

of recollection.—"You will soon remember them," rejoined I:
"suffer me but to repeat the verses to Lydia, when a fly settled
on the tip of her ear."—"I have not time," answered the
obdurate old brute, although he was Time itself—"Yet promise
me," cried I, endeavouring to detain him, "that you will look
back among your stores for this little volume, and give it that
interest in the eyes of posterity, which was refused to it by
contemporary stupidity and malevolence." "My son," replied
he, gliding from my grasp as he spoke, "you ask of me impos-
sibilities. Yon ditch, to which is consigned all the refuse of this
Pandemonium, has most assuredly received the volume in which
you are so much interested. Yet do not be altogether disconcerted. A set of honest painstaking persons have erected gratings
upon the common-sewer of oblivion, from one interval to another, for the precise purpose of gathering the scraps of printed
paper thrown into it, without being deterred by the mean and
nameless purposes which they have served. No lame beggar rakes
the kennel for stub-nails with half the assiduity that these gentlemen fish among all sorts of trash for the names and offal of forgotten rhymers; for Love esteems no office mean, or, as the
same old friend has it,

> Entire affection scorneth nicer hands.[50]

If thou hast any luck," continued he, looking at me with infinite
contempt, "thy fragments may be there fished up by some future
antiquary, and thy name rendered as famous as the respectable
sounds of Herricke or Derricke, or others that are only now
remembered because till now they have been most deservedly
forgot." With that, his usual constant though imperceptible motion conveyed him out of my hold and out of my sight.

I endeavoured to divert the mortification which this colloquy
had excited, by turning my attention once more to the game of
racket, which was continued with more fury than ever. These
hellish tossers of books, as Cervantes calls them, curst, swore,
threatened, roared, and foamed, as if the universe depended on
the issue of their gambols. Verse and prose, sermons and stage-
plays, politics and novels, flew to pieces without distinction;
nor (what you, sir, would probably have felt afflicting) was

50. *The Faerie Queene*, I, viii, 40:3.

more respect paid to the types of Bensley or Bulmer, or to your own, than to those employed on half-penny ballads and dying speeches.

In observing the manner and address of the different players, my attention was at length powerfully fixed by the dexterity of one individual dæmon. He was, in stature and complexion, the identical "wee reekit devil"[51] of my poor friend Robert Burns; but, being ambidexter, and possessed of uncommon activity and accuracy of aim, he far surpassed all his competitors.[52] He often shewed his dexterity by striking the same volume alternately in different directions, leaving the gaping crowd totally at a loss whether it was his intention to strike it over the lists, or to shiver it to atoms; and he had an unlucky back-handed blow by which he could sometimes intercept it, while all hands were in the air to receive it with acclamation. Sometimes he seemed to repent him of his severity, and, in one or two instances, endeavoured to give a new impulse to works which had suffered by it. But this seemed to defy even his address; and indeed I observed of the players, that they were not only, as might be expected from the philosophic observations of Sancho upon their diabolical nature, much more prone to assault a book than to favour it; but even when they made the latter attempt, they went about it awkwardly, and were very rarely successful. But, in shattering calf-skin and letter-press, the dexterity of this champion was unequalled, which produced him much ill-will from his less successful brethren; till at length, like Ismael, his hand was against every one, and every one's against him. A dæmon, in particular, who had exchanged a jockey whip for the racket, seemed to bear him particular spleen, and I generally observed them and their followers attempt to strike the books at each other's noses. The latter gamester, although he played some capital strokes, and was indisputably the second-best[53] in the field, could not at first be termed equal to the other in agility, although, as he grew warmer, he evidently improved in his game, and began to divide the opinion of the spectators, chiefly aided by some unknown individuals closely masked, but who, like the disguised heroes of

51. The phrase from Burns is "A reekit wee devil looks over the wa'." The poem is "Kellyburnbraes."
52. Jeffrey was only about five feet tall. "It were impossible to be angry with anything so diminutive," Southey wrote William Taylor. Memoir . . . Taylor, II, 102.
53. William Gifford, editor of the Quarterly Review.

romance, were easily distinguished from the vulgar. I observed that the rivalry between these two leaders was attended with some acts of violence, especially after either of them had taken a cordial out of a small dram-bottle, to which they occasionally applied. These flasks, I was informed by a by-stander, contained an alcohol called *Spirit of Party;* infamous, like all ardent spirits, for weakening the judgement, dazzling the eyes, and inflaming the imagination, but rectified in a different manner according to the taste of those who used it. "It is a pity that they are so much addicted to the use of it," added he; "but, were you to ask them its nature, the one would pretend that his was pure *Pit-water,* and the other protest that he himself only used a little genuine and salubrious *Hollands;* although his enemies pretend that he, or at least that some of his followers, preferred a French liqueur double distilled, *a la Burdett.*"[54]

My curiosity now became ungovernable; and, as the lively genius aforesaid was standing near the court-yard wall leaning on his racket, after having played, as we used to say at the High-school, a very hard *end,* I could not help addressing him for some explanation. "I see, sir," said I very respectfully, "upon some of these loose leaves with which your dexterity and that of your companions has been sheeting this area, certain works to which our upper world is no stranger. But, what greatly surprises me is, to behold fragments of some books bearing the names of well-known authors, who, I am pretty confident, have not yet given such productions to the public." "My friend," replied he, in a very peculiar tone of voice, which I have certainly heard somewhere about Edinburgh, "you must know that what you now behold is an emblematical representation as well of what is to happen, as of what has befallen in the earthly walks of literature and criticism. You remember, I doubt not, the occupation of Anchises in the shades?" "I rather think I do not," replied I. The goblin proceeded:

> "Inclusas animas superumque ad lumen
>   ituras
> Lustrabat——[55]

---

54. Pit-water: the Pittites or supporters of the government; the Hollands were a powerful group of Whigs led by Lord Holland and with whom Sydney Smith was on friendly terms. Burdett is Sir Francis Burdett, most radical of all members of Parliament.
55. *Aeneid,* VI, 679–80.

"In something the same manner our sport announces the reception of the future labours of the press, the fates and fortunes which books yet unborn are to experience both from the critics and from the world in general. In short, as critics play the devil upon earth, so we devils play the critics in hell. I myself am the image, or emblem, or *Eidolon,* of a celebrated"——Here his discourse was interrupted by a quarrel among the gamesters. A racqueteer, whom I had observed playing my obliging informer's back-game, and who, though in a parson's band[56] and gown, had distinguished himself by uncommon frisks and gambols, was complaining loudly that one opponent had given him a black eye with his racket, and that another, in the trencher-cap of an Oxford student, had torn and dirtied his band. My friend went with all speed to his assistance, leaving me to regret the interruption of his communications. Indeed the urbanity of this goblin seemed so great a contrast to his diabolical character, and to the inveteracy with which he pursued the game, that I could not help concluding in his favour, like the liberal-minded Sancho Panza on a similar occasion, that there may be some good sort of people even in hell itself.

I became aware, from his kind explanation, of the opportunity afforded me of collecting some literary intelligence from so authentic a source. I hastened to gather some of the scattered leaves which bore the mark or signature of celebrated living names; and while I glanced them over, I exulted in the superiority which my collection would afford me in the conversaziones of the upper world. In the midst of this task my ears were assailed with a discordant sound, which imagination, with its usual readiness to adapt external impressions on the senses to the subject of a dream, represented as proceeding from a battle royal of the fiends. But, as the din predominated over my slumber, I plainly distinguished the voice of my beldame landlady screaming to her noisy brats in the tone of a wild-cat to its litter, that their caterwauling would disturb the "old gentleman's afternoon nap."

I was no sooner thoroughly awakened by her ill-judged precautions in favour of my repose, than I took pen and ink, and endeavoured to secure the contents of the fragments which yet

---

56. Sydney Smith's attack upon Oxford education in the *Edinburgh Review* for October, 1809, brought a reply from Edward Copleston and began a lengthy controversy.

floated in my imagination. I am sensible I have succeeded but indifferently; nor can I pretend to have made by any means an exact transcript of what the visionary fragments presented. In this respect I am in exactly the same predicament with the great Corelli, who, you know, always insisted that his celebrated piece of music, called from the circumstances, the Devil's Concerto, was very inferior to that which his satanic majesty had deigned in a vision to perform upon his violin. As, therefore, I am conscious that I have done great injustice to the verses from the imperfections of my memory, and as I have, after all, only the devil's authority for their authenticity had I recollected them more accurately, I will not do any respectable author the discredit to prefix his name to them, trusting that, if my vision really issued from the Gate of Horn, these fragments will retain traces of resemblance sufficient to authorize their being appropriated to their respective authors. I retain some others in my budget, which it is not impossible I may offer to you next year.

Meanwhile, I am, sir, (for any nonsensical name will suit as well as my own) your humble servant,

CALEB QUOTEM*[57]

On the Present State of Periodical Criticism

This essay (*Register*, II, 546–81) is certainly by Scott, even though he never declared it to be his own. At the end of his essay, "On the Living Poets of Great Britain," in the first volume of the *Register* he concluded: "This department of the Register will, in the next volume, be occupied by an Account of the State of Criticism in Great Britain." The opening sentence of the essay refers to this promise.

The best proof of Scott's authorship of the essay is in a letter of Scott to William Gifford of October 25, 1808, in which Scott advises Gifford about procedures for the new *Quarterly Review*. He attributes the great success of the *Edinburgh Review* to its independence from booksellers

---

*The Editor, in the plenitude of his conviction that honest *Caleb* is entitled to all the honours of the Gate of Horn, doth fervently entreat the continuance of his visionary lucubrations.

57. Caleb Quotem is the general factotum in George Colman the Younger's *The Review; or the Wags of Windsor*, a popular farce for many years.

"who have contrived to make most of the other reviews mere vehicles for advertising & puffing off their own publications or running down those of their rivals" (*Letters of Scott,* II, 102). Its second source of strength has been its policy of paying all its contributors very generously. The fourth paragraph of the present essay begins with a survey of periodical publications, and in the sixth paragraph their imperfections are attributed to the cause that the reviews "had gradually fallen under the dominion of the publishing bookseller." The second point—that of generous payment—is elaborated upon at length emphasizing that it is a means of gaining the services of able young men. As Scott phrased it: "There are many young men of talent & enterprize who are extremely glad of a handsome apology to work for fifteen or twenty guineas" (*Letters of Scott,* II, 103). In the essay the idea was worded: "Young men just entering upon life, especially if they belong to Scotland, are seldom in a situation to afford their time gratis." The example of Czar Peter working in the trenches but receiving the pay of a common soldier is cited in both letter and essay.

These two points which occupy a prominent part of the first third of the letter are supported by other points of similarity in Scott's letters. In his letter of November 18, 1808, to George Ellis, Scott stated: "The common Reviews, before the appearance of the Edinburgh, had become extremely mawkish; and, unless when prompted by the malice of the bookseller or reviewer, gave a dawdling, maudlin sort of applause to everything that reached even mediocrity" (*Letters of Scott,* II, 128). Almost two paragraphs of the article develop this point: "a dull and stupifying mediocrity began to be the most distinguishing feature of the English reviews. . . . there was a visible tameness and disposition to lethargy in the English reviews at the close of the 18th century."

The paragraph toward the end of the article, which remarks that the rivals find it easier to imitate the caustic tone rather than the ability of its articles, is also made by Scott in his letter to George Ellis in phrases that anticipate the article: "The Edinburgh folks squeezed into their sauce plenty of acid, and were popular from novelty as well as from merit. The minor Reviews . . . have given us all abuse, and no talent." (*Letters of Scott,* II, 128) The discussion of Richard Cumberland's *London Review,* a short-lived experiment of having all reviews signed, parallels his letter to Charles Kirkpatrick Sharpe of December 30, 1808, where Scott defends the custom of the unsigned review and elaborates upon the prediction that to propose "that each contributor shall place his name before his article . . . must prove fatal to the undertaking." Scott concluded the letter describing the contributors to the new *Quarterly* with the same quotation from *Henry IV* that he used in describing the qualifications of the contributors to the newly founded *Edinburgh Review:* "no foot land-rakers, no long-staff sixpenny strikers, but with nobility and tranquillity, burgomasters, and great oneyers." (*Letters of Scott,* II, 143)

Although Scott neither republished nor claimed this essay, its quality can scarcely be the reason for this neglect. It is an excellent survey of the periodical as it had been conducted in the latter part of the eighteenth century and at the time of the composition of the essay. The author is knowledgeable and has an intimate, first-hand acquaintance with the literary and publishing world. The essay provides an over-all view of periodicals and periodical literature and criticism in 1812, when the general-literary-critical review and magazine as it was to fashion itself in the nineteenth and twentieth centuries was being established. Scott was acute enough to recognize that the trend inaugurated by the *Edinburgh* and the *Quarterly* could not be reversed.

Southey recognized Scott's hand in the essay and wrote him on September 8, 1811: "I saw the last volume . . . and there I could trace your hand in a powerful but too lenient essay, upon Jeffrey's journal." (Southey, *Life and Correspondence,* III, 316). W. J. Couper also assumed that this essay was by Scott. (*The Edinburgh Periodical Press* [Stirling, 1908] II, 78n.) Margaret Ball in *Sir Walter Scott as a Critic of Literature* (New York, 1907) also attributes the essay to Scott.

It is not without some apprehensions that, in prosecution of the plan laid down in our first volume, we approach the province of Periodical Criticism, impeded as our road must be with jungles, thorns, and thickets, and rendered dismal by the gibbetted reliques of unfortunate authors. The dark and mysterious forest of Massilia, in whose gloomy recesses human sacrifices were offered to invisible and malignant dæmons, impressed hardly more horror upon the veterans of Cæsar:

> ————barbara ritu
> Sacra deum, structæ diris altaribus aræ:
> Omnis et humanis lustrata cruoribus arbor.[58]

Our field of research, like the sacred grove of Lucan, is also subject to its fated periodical revolutions, its monthly or quarterly almutens, when the master of the sign, as astrologers said of old, sits in full power upon the cusp or entrance of the planetary house, as Lord of the Ascendant, and the bookseller, the printer, nay, the very devil himself, can hardly brook his presence:

> ————Medio cum Phæbus in arce est,
> Aut Cœlum nox atra tenet, pavet ipse Sa-
> cerdos

58. Lucan, *Pharsalia,* III, 403–405.

Accessus, dominumque timet deprendere
luci.[59]

Yet have we not entered rashly or unadvisedly upon our dread
adventure, but have availed ourselves, like the knight errants of
old, of such arms as might best secure us in an encounter with
the magicians of the maze of Criticism, and in some respects
bring the contest nearer to equality. Are these wizzards [sic]
periodical in their exertions? We are annual.—Are they numerous
and confederated? We also are plural.—Can they shroud themselves in obscurity by virtue of the helmet of the sable Orcus?
We have the invisible cap of Jack the Giant-killer. Nor shall we
lack the prayers of the oppressed to forward our chivalrous
undertaking. Wherever, through the wide realms of literature,
there is one who has writhed under the scourge of this invisible
tribunal; wherever there is a gentle minstrel who bewails his
broken harp, a fair maiden who weeps over her mangled novel,
a politic knight who bemoans his travestied lucubrations, or a
weary pilgrim who mourns his anathematized travels, we find a
friend and a beadsman in the sufferer. Then with good courage,
and St George to speed, we boldly press forward upon our pur-
posed achievement.

The early state of periodical criticism is of little consequence
to our present purpose. At first the art pretended to afford
little more than a list of the works of the learned in the order of
publication, with some brief and dry account of the contents of
each, a sort of *catalogue raisonée* in short, where the books published within a certain period, were arranged according to order,
with such a view of each as might inform the book-buyer whether
it fell within the line of his reading or collecting. These earlier
journalists contented themselves with intimating what the work
under consideration actually contained, without pretending to
point out its errors, far less to supply its omissions by their own
disquisitions. As for satire and raillery, the laborious compilers
of these dry catalogues, many of whom actually expired under
the task they had undertaken, had neither leisure nor spirits for
such flights of imagination. These were abandoned to the editors of newspapers and journals, whence flying shafts of satirical
criticism were often discharged amid the thunder of political

59. Ibid., III, 423–25.

artillery. It was not from reviews, but from Mist's Journal, the Daily Journal, the Gazetteers, &c., that those vollies of abuse against Pope were hurled forth, which, contemptible as they now appear, had but too much effect upon the poet's irritability. It is hard to guess what would have been the feelings of the Wasp of Twickenham, had he lived in the present day, when ten or twelve periodical works, devoted to criticism alone, claim as their proper subject, or rather their natural prey, every new publication which issues from the press. But the grave authors of the "Works of the Learned," and other early publications approaching to the nature of reviews, could not long preserve the neutrality to which at first they confined themselves. It was scarcely to be expected, that a critic of competent judgement should, in giving an account of a new work, resist the temptation to express the information or pleasure he had received from particular passages, still less that he could refrain from manifesting his own superiority, by pointing out occasional omissions or errors of his author. And thus reviews gradually acquired the form and character which they now exhibit, and which is too well known to require definition. But within the last ten years, a very important change has taken place in the mode of conducting them, a change which, as it has inexpressibly increased their importance and influence upon literature, claims for its causes a candid and critical attention.

The discerning reader will easily perceive that we allude to the establishment of the Edinburgh Review; a journal which in its nature materially differs from its predecessors, and has given in many respects an entirely new turn to public taste and to critical discussion. It becomes our duty to state in what particulars the ancient system was innovated upon, and where the charm lies which has enabled a journal of such recent establishment, not only to take the lead, and give the tone to most of its predecessors, but in a variety of instances utterly to supersede their authority, and reduce whole cartloads of criticism to a melancholy inactivity in the publisher's warehouse. For this purpose, it is necessary to take a view of the state of the popular reviews previous to 1802.

The imperfections of these journals may be traced to one great cause. Each of the leading English reviews, though originally established by men of letters, had gradually fallen under the dominion of the publishing bookseller. We have no wish to join

in the common cry against this class of tradesmen, which is
chiefly swelled by the deep-mouthed discontents of neglected
authors. On the contrary, we feel great sympathy for their situation, and are humbly of opinion, that not only the authors, but
even the age, are very ready to transfer the depression of neglected genius, and other consequences of their own egotism or
stupidity, to the broad shoulders of the gentlemen in the Row.
A bookseller, to live by his trade, must buy so as to sell with
profit. If the demand for any work, be it ever so ingenious, is
insufficient to pay for print and paper, is it reasonable to expect that the tradesman can pay for the copy-right? The shame-
ful fact, that the Paradise Lost was bought for ten pounds,
throws infamy indeed upon the taste of the age, but not on the
conduct of the purchaser, who did not sell an edition in eight
years, and was probably a loser by the bargain. In short, a
bookseller, even supposing him a judge of literature, has it not
in his power with common prudence to make the author of a
new work an offer which may be fully adequate even to his own
ideas of its value; for the risk arising from the caprice of the
public must be covered by such an insurance as makes no small
deduction from the price of an author's labour. But this deduction becomes much greater, and almost intolerable, if, which is
far more commonly the case, the bookseller is obliged to provide some guarantee against the consequence, not only of the
public fickleness, but of his own ignorance. Few of these
gentlemen are, and, fortunately for the state of their warehouses, few even affect to be, judges of literary merit. They buy
copy-rights as a blind man might purchase a lot of horses, at
such an average price, that the success of one book may compensate the loss upon twenty. In this point of view, the accompts between the worshipful Company of Stationers, and the
no less worshipful Society of Authors, come, upon a general
balance of the ledger, nearly to an equality, although, no doubt,
the personal accompts with some individuals may stand greatly
in favour of the bibliopolists. We are, therefore, fully sensible
how much this trade is a lottery, and it is without the least wish
of censuring those engaged in it, that we point out the divers inconveniences attending those reviews which are under mercantile
management.

   A periodical publication has been often said to resemble a
mail-coach. It must set out at a particular day and hour, it must

travel the road whether full or empty, and whether it conveys
bullion to the bank of England, or a sample of cheese to a grocer
in Thames street. In such a case, the prudent owner of the
vehicle purveys such horses as are fittest for this regular, fatigu-
ing, and, in some points of view, derogating duty. He buys no
"fine framped steeds," that are fitted for a chariot or curricle,
nor yet brutes that, by their clumsy make and bulk of bone, are
qualified only to tug in a drayman's cart; but he labours to
secure, of

> "Spare-fed prancers many a raw-boned
> pair;"[60]

such as have, perhaps, seen their best days, and acquired discretion to submit to their necessary task, while they retain vigour
and animation sufficient to tug through it speedily and hardily.
The bare-worn common of literature has always afforded but
too numerous a supply of authors who hold a similar description;
and who, by misfortune or improvidence, or merely from having
been unable to force themselves forward to public notice, are
compelled to subject talents worthy of better employment, to
whatever task a bookseller shall be pleased to dictate. In London
particularly, where the pursuit of letters is a distinct profession,
whose students cannot easily provide for themselves in the more
ordinary walks of life, there are, and must be, many men of learning, of mental vigour, even of genius, whose circumstances do not
entitle them to despise the regular and fixed emolument which
may be procured by stated employment in an established review.
Amongst these, then, the bookseller might easily select such as
could at once labour at the most reasonable rate, and to the best
effect; while he may be supposed also to have possessed the authority necessary to direct their industry into those channels
which had obliquely the effect of advancing his own trade. It
was, accordingly, a thing so well known, as to be observed even
by the dullest, that from the publisher's name in the imprint of
a new book, readers were enabled to calculate, with absolute
certainty, the nature of the treatment it would receive in the
corresponding reviews. From this it naturally followed, that the

60. "And high-fed prancers, many a raw-boned pair." Crabbe, *The Borough,* Letter
XI (Inns), 40.

more heavy, or, to speak technically, the more dull of sale a
work happened to be, the more this tender assistance was necessary on the part of the reviewers, and the more eagerly it was
called for by the proprietors of both works. A man of genius,
and many have been engaged in such labour, might sometimes
wince a little under the burden which was thus imposed upon
him, since to produce a panegyric without merit is as difficult
as to make bricks without straw. But the strongest minds are
bent to circumstances,—even Johnson submitted to Cave the
bookseller, a sheaf of his powerful and varied effusions, with
the humiliating acknowledgement, *emptoris sit eligere;* and it
may be readily supposed, that few, who have resembled him in
poverty and in talents, have been more nice and fastidious than
Johnson. It thus happened in the general case, that the reviewer,
like a fee'd barrister, sacrificed his own feelings and judgement
to the interest of the bookseller his employer; and it followed,
almost of course, that, without bending the whole force of his
mind to so ungracious and unsatisfactory labour, he was satisfied if he discharged it in a workman-like manner, and, without
aiming at excellence, was contented if he could not be justly
charged with ignorance of his subject, or negligence in the mode
of treating it. In this manner, a dull and stupifying mediocrity
began to be the most distinguishing feature of the English reviews, even of such as were written by men of acknowledged
learning and admitted talents. Articles doubtless occasionally
appeared of a very different description, where the reviewer,
pleased with a theme which corresponded with his own taste
and pursuits, threw off the labourer, assumed the author, and
analysed with a kindred spirit the productions of genius or the
researches of philosophy. In other cases, the gentleman of the
trade, whose book was to be reviewed, sought out among his
own customers, or the literary friends of the author, some person whom he supposed qualified to treat the subject well, and
disposed to use the work favourably. Such a voluntary assistant,
though he might not possess more ability than the person on
whom in stated routine the task would have devolved, took it
up nevertheless with the eagerness of novelty; and if, at the same
time, he was paying a tax to friendship, or endeavouring to
throw a double lustre upon opinions which he himself professed,
his article was likely to possess a spirit and energy which might
raise it above the cold uniformity of those with which it was

mingled. But exceptions, arising from either of these causes, were comparatively of rare occurrence, and, upon the whole, there was a visible tameness and disposition to lethargy in the English reviews at the close of the 18th century.

A spirit of indolence is usually accompanied with a disposition to mercy, or rather those whom it has thoroughly possessed cannot give themselves the trouble of rousing to deeds of severity. Accordingly the calm, even, and indifferent style of criticism, which we have endeavoured to describe, was distinguished by a lenient aspect towards its objects. The reviewer, in the habit of treating with complacency those works which belonged to his own publisher, was apt to use the same general style of civility towards others, although they had not the same powerful title to protection. A certain deference was visibly paid to an author of celebrity, whether founded upon his literary qualities or on the adventitious distinctions of rank and title, and generally there was a marked and guarded *retenue* both in the strictures hazarded and in the mode of expressing them. If raillery was ever attempted, there was no horse-play in it, and the only fault which could be objected by the reader was, that the critic was

Content to dwell in decencies for ever.[61]

This rule was not, indeed, without exceptions; the mind of a liberal and public-spirited critic sometimes reversed the sentence of his employer, and, unlike the prophet of Midian, anathematized the works on which he was summoned to bestow benedictions.[62] Neither was it meet that the critical rod should be hung up in mere shew, lest in time, as it is learnedly argued by the Duke of Vienna, it should become "more mocked than feared."[63] The terrors of the office were, therefore, in some measure maintained by the severity exercised upon the trumpery novels and still-born poetry which filled the monthly catalogue, whose unknown, and perhaps starving authors, fared like the parish-boys at a charity school, who are flogged not only for their own errors, but to vindicate the authority of the master, who cares not to use the same freedom with the children of the squire. Sometimes

61. Pope, *Moral Essays,* Epistle II, 164.
62. Balaam defied Balak by blessing and not cursing the Israelites. Numbers, chapters 22–23. Scott makes this same allusion in *The Lord of the Isles,* III, st. 31.
63. *Measure for Measure,* I, iii, 27.

also "fate demanded a nobler head."[64] The work of a rival bookseller was to be crushed even in birth; a powerful literary patron,
or perhaps the reviewer himself, had some private pique to indulge, and added a handful of slugs to the powder and paper
which formed the usual contents of his blunderbuss. Sometimes
political discussions were introduced, before which deference
and moderation are uniformly found to disappear. Or, in fine,
the sage bibliopolist himself occasionally opined that a little
severity (so it came not the way of his own publications) might
forward the sale of his review, and was therefore pleased to cry
havoc, and let slip the dogs of war.[65] But the operation of each
and all of these causes was insufficient to counteract the tendency of this species of criticism to stagnate in a course of dull
and flat and luke-warm courtesy. Something of the habitual
civility and professional deference of the tradesman seemed to
qualify the labours of those who wrote under his direction; and
the critics themselves, accessible (not, we believe, in almost any
case, to pecuniary interposition,) but to applications for favour
in divers modes, which they found it difficult to resist, and mixing, too, in the intercourse of private life with many of those
who afforded the subjects of their criticism, were seldom disposed to exercise their office in its full, or even in its necessary
rigour. These were days of halcyon quietness for authors, especially for that numerous class, who, contented to venture their
whole literary credit on one dull work written upon as dull a
subject, look forward less to rapid sale and popular applause
than to a favourable criticism from the reviewers, and a word or
two of snug, quiet, honied assent from a few private friends. The
public indeed began to murmur that

> Lost was the critic's sense, nor could be
> found
> While one dull formal unison went round.[66]

But the venerable and well-wigged authors of sermons and essays, and mawkish poems and stupid parish histories, bore each

64. Gray, *The Fatal Sisters*, 43.
65. *Julius Caesar*, III, i, 270.
66. "Lost was the Nation's Sense, nor could be found,
   While the long solemn Unison went round."
                              Pope, *Dunciad*, IV, 611–12.

triumphantly his ponderous load into the mart of literature, expanded it upon the stall of his bookseller, sate brooding over it
till evening closed, and then retired with the consolation, that,
if his wares had not met a purchaser, they had at least been
declared saleable, and received the stamp of currency from the
official inspectors of literary merchandize. From these soothing
dreams, authors, booksellers, and critics were soon to be roused
by a rattling peal of thunder; and it now becomes our task to
shew how a conspiracy of beardless boys innovated the venerable
laws of this lenient republic of literature, scourged the booksellers out of her senate-house, overset the tottering thrones of
the idols whom they had set up, awakened the hundred-necked
snake of criticism, and curdled the whole ocean of milk and
water, in which, like the serpentine supporter of Vistnou, he had
wreathed and wallowed in unwieldy sloth for a quarter of a century. Then, too, amid this dire combustion, like true revolu-
tionists, they erected themselves into a committee of public
safety, whose decrees were written in blood, and executed without mercy.

As in many other great revolutions, the causes which gave rise
to this change of system were slight and fortuitous. A few young
men, who had just concluded their studies at the University of
Edinburgh, and were united together by a similarity of talents
and pursuits, conceived a project (designed, we believe, to be
temporary,) to rescue this province of literature from the state
of degradation into which it had gradually sunk, and to give to
the world what for many years it had not seen—a fair, but, at the
same time, a bold and impartial review of such works as appeared
to merit public attention. The scheme of publication, although
deeply laid, contained some staggering preliminaries. The associated critics, while they asserted the most uncontrouled freedom from the influence of their publisher, stipulated, it is well
known, a subsidy at more than treble the rate allowed to the
best as well as supplest mercenaries which London could afford.
The mention of this circumstance, though it may seem to savour
of minute inquiry, is in truth neither trivial nor petulant. Young
men just entering upon life, especially if they belong to Scotland, are seldom in a situation to afford their time gratis, or, if
in such a situation, are still more seldom disposed to bestow
their leisure hours in labour of any kind. Besides, every one
knows the inadequate recompence usually made to a Scottish

barrister during the early years of his practice, and it was probably not injudiciously conceived, that a more ample guerdon
might seduce some of that well-educated and peculiarly acute
class of young men to lend their aid to the new undertaking,
which was carefully cleared of every thing resembling mercenary
drudgery, while the *honorarium* it held forth made the ordinary
professional emoluments kick the beam. In one respect that
mercantile part of the matter was managed with equal delicacy
and prudence. No distinction was permitted between the Dilletanti writer, and one whose circumstances might render copy-
money necessary or acceptable. If Czar Peter laboured in the
trenches, he drew his pay as a common soldier;[67] and thus the
degrading distinction was excluded between those whose fortune or generosity inclined them to labour for nought, and the
less fortunate scholar, to whom reward was in some degree an
object; the pride of the latter remained unwounded, and,
mingled as he was among many critics of wealth and rank, it
remained a secret known to none but himself, whether he was
actuated by any additional motives besides the desire of literary
distinction. The report, too, of this uncommon premium gave a
sort of eclat to the undertaking, and shewed that the associated
critics claimed a merit and consequence beyond the ordinary
class of reviewers; that their band, like the confederates of Gads-
hill, were "no foot-land-rakers, no long-staff sixpenny strikers,
but nobility and tranquillity, burgomasters and great oneyers."[68]
In short, this subordinate circumstance (for it must be supposed
that we hold it highly subordinate to the principal causes of
success) gave the undertaking at its outset an appearance of
seriousness; for which, considering the youth of those upon
whom the execution was to rest, they might otherwise hardly
have gained the necessary credit.

   In another circumstance, the Edinburgh Reviewers judiciously
took a difference from their brethren of England. Their criticism
was professedly limited to works which, in one shape or other,
deserved the public attention; and, that ample time might be allowed for selecting such subjects, their term of publication was
made quarterly instead of monthly. At the same time, and as a

67. Scott in a letter to William Gifford of October 25, 1808 had made this same
comparison between the policy of the *Edinburgh Review* and Czar Peter. *Letters of
Scott,* II, 103.
68. *Henry IV,* Part I, II, i, 84.

part of the same arrangement, it was announced to the public,
that it was the object of this new publication to be distinguished
rather by the selection than for the number of its articles; that
the editors did not assume any merit for conveying priority of
literary intelligence, and therefore left such a space of time
betwixt their periods of publication as might avail for mature
consideration of the works fit to be reviewed, as well as of the
judgement to be passed upon them. It cannot be doubted that
this deliberate mode of proceeding at once added to the real
merit of the review, and greatly raised its character with the
public. The reviews had been hitherto published monthly, and
it was a necessary consequence, that those numbers which appeared in what is called the publishing season, which lasts from
the end of November till after the King's birth-day, were overwhelmed with important discussions which the critics had
neither time maturely to consider, nor room to treat at length.
Hence we have frequently seen the reviewer under the inconvenient but unavoidable necessity of continuing a single article
of importance from one number of his review to another, by
which division his argument sustained deep and material injustice. It was a yet more serious inconvenience to the editor,
that he was obliged to bolster out his summer numbers with an
extra proportion of those insignificant and still-born productions which never for an instant either did attract, or ought to
have attracted, the attention of the public. But at all times their
plan admitted too much of this trumpery. The monthly catalogue, where, as in the cauldron of Acheron, all mingles that
mingle may, while it occupied a degree of room widely dispro-
portional to its no importance, had, in a secondary point of
view, an effect disadvantageous to the character of the reviews,
and those by whom they were written. We have already stated
our belief that the booksellers principally interested in the success of these works took care for their own sakes to procure
respectable assistance for what are called the leading articles.
But what man of talent would be bribed to the analyzing and
reporting this dunghill of shreds and patches, this "mass of all
things base,"[69] or write these paltry and brief notices, which
were strung together, and appended to the more dignified articles, like the shreds of paper which form the tail of a boy's kite?

69. "A ridge of all things base." Crabbe, *The Borough*, I, 43.

Or, if such a critic were willing to stoop to the task of a scavenger, and was condescending enough to sift this heap of cinders, could a bookseller be expected, upon mercantile principles, to compensate his labours according to the writer's merit and not to their worth? It is probable, therefore, that these departments in many cases slipped into the hands of a low description of hackney scribblers, whose very names tended to throw disrespect upon the employment of reviewers, and who may be supposed little scrupulous as to the indirect modes by which they mended the pittance allotted them. As, therefore, in this subordinate department, the partiality of private friendship, and the rancour of personal malignity, could be summoned into activity, unsuspected and undetected, it seems farther probable, that, if there were any real grounds for actual corruption and bribery, to which we believe the superior class of reviewers were strangers, they might perhaps occur in this ill-scoured sink, this lowest dungeon of critical publication. In disclaiming, therefore, any intention of reviewing what was naturally destined to obscurity, the Edinburgh critics at once cleared their hands of a huge, ill-arranged, and most uninteresting class of subjects, and relieved themselves from the necessity of associating in their labours those discreditable compeers, upon whom the task of considering it must necessarily have devolved. They did more— by this arrangement, they pledged themselves to the reader, that they would exercise no absolute and peremptory *fiat* of acquittal or condemnation without treating the subject at some length, and giving the grounds of their sentence, so that, if just, they might be assented to, if ill-founded, they might be opposed and confuted. Thus every thing in their plan bespoke the purpose of men capable and confident in their powers, bending themselves gravely to a purpose from which they had studiously excluded all that was trifling, vulgar, or insignificant.

The associated critics having thus provided for the expences of their campaign, calculated the duration of their marches, and estimated the importance of their proposed achievements, the Edinburgh Review appeared in October, 1802. A circumstance is said to have occurred in the very outset, unimportant in itself, but tending strongly to shew the necessity that some review should exist altogether free from bookselling influence, as well as to evince the strong opinion of the right of management which the trade retained as to all such works. A very respectable book-

seller, selected as the London publisher, took upon him to decline
or delay publishing the first number of the Review, alleging (it is
said) very frankly, the detriment it was likely to occasion to the
sale of a certain expensive work in which he was concerned, and
which the Northern Aristarchs had treated with slender cere-
mony. The future services of this gentleman were of course
declined, and it was made sufficiently manifest that the publishers were to derive no other advantage from this work than the
direct emoluments which the sale might produce to them.

The first numbers of the Edinburgh Review asserted the character which it has in most respects maintained to this day. The
style was bold, caustic, decided, and intolerant. To mark as far
as possible the new principles of their criticism, the adventurers
hung out the bloody flag in their title-page, and by the appropri-
riate motto (*Judex damnatur si nocens absolvitur*) intimated
their intention to discard the courteous rules and indulgent
civility, under the restraint of which their contemporaries had
been hitherto content to wage their drowsy warfare. It was a
sort of imprecation on themselves and their infant publication,
if they withheld their arm from battle for pity, need, or respect
of persons.

> "Such and such evil God on Guyon reare,
> And worse and worse, young orphan, be
>   thy paine,
> If I or thou due vengeance do forbeare."—[70]

Most readers must remember the hubbub occasioned by the
first issuing forth of this unruly northern whirlwind. The confusion is before our eyes and in our ears, as if it had happened
but yesterday. A hailstorm, or rather the alarm of a mad-dog in
Kensington Gardens, about four o'clock on a fine Sunday, is the
best emblem we can propose to those who did not witness the
universal consternation of the book-writing and book-selling
world. The Edinburgh critics meanwhile, like their countryman
Lismahago in a similar situation, beheld, with a Sardonic grin,
the confusion they had occasioned, and proceeded to fire their
second barrel among the astonished multitude, regardless alike
of the piteous state of those who fell into the ditch in attempt-

70. *The Faerie Queene*, II, i, 61:5-7.

ing to scramble out of gunshot, or supplicated mercy on their
knees, and of the threats of the hardier few who gathered stones
and mud, or waved canes and umbrellas, to repel their assaults.
"Remarks," "Observations," "Defences," "Vindications," came
forth without end; nor were there wanting those who endeavoured to retort the injuries they or their friends had received in
the scuffle, by circulating pieces of personal abuse and scurrility
against the supposed authors of the fray. But the public, after
viewing so new a scene for some time with amazement, began to
learn that an insulted author is an animal not better furnished for
defence than the poor sloth, which can only annoy its hunter by
its plaintive and discordant screams. A writer who complains of
the severity or even the rudeness of criticism, is like one who
should tell of the inhumanity with which his adversary kicked
or cudgelled him; for the disgraceful nature of the injury attracts
more scorn than his sufferings can inspire pity.

We do not, however, know whether the *pococurante* disposition of the master critic, although a quality as remarkable as any
by which he is distinguished, could have actually borne him
through in his undeviating course of severity in despite of fear
and favour, had he not resided at a distance from the capital in
which his review had excited this ferment. Lampoons, libels, and
all that pop-gun train of scandal's artillery, may annoy the most
stoical and indifferent philosopher, if he be placed within the
actual range of their explosion, and view them primed and levelled
against him from every bookseller's window; but these paper
pellets, which may have some little teazing effect when discharged
across a street in town, lose their force entirely in the space between London and Edinburgh. A single copy or two may reach
our northern metropolis, perhaps by the medium of some
"damn'd good-natured friend;" but, as they never get into general circulation, or become subjects of discussion in society, a
man must be very irritable indeed who can disturb himself at the
mere knowledge of their existence. Had Pope lived two hundred
miles from London, he would probably never have heard of the
puny attacks which called down vengeance in the Dunciad; and
we cannot help taking notice, that the only personal assault
which the editor of the Edinburgh Review ever gave himself the
trouble to answer, was written and published in Edinburgh.

The same accidental distance from London probably fortified
the Edinburgh critics in adherence to their general plan of an

impartiality bordering on rigour. They were separated from the great body of English authors, and a gulf, as it were, placed between them, so that, while their works were under consideration, no personal image of the writer could excite either favour or commiseration in the mind of the critic. They escaped also the manifold ties that warp almost insensibly round one who is fond of literary society, and which wind him into partiality which it is difficult to discard, and expose him to solicitations which it is impossible to parry. Edinburgh, indeed, it may be said, has a literary society of its own, the members of which frequently subject themselves by publication to the censure of periodical criticism. But, in the first place, the literati of Edinburgh are generally engaged in other pursuits in life, and are not, we have observed, apt to feel sore under the lash of criticism, as probably more indifferent to literary fame than their brethren of the south, who frequently make that, and the emoluments which accompany it, the prime object of life. The critic may therefore exercise his faculty even on those with whom he lives and converses, we do not say with security, but at least with little fear of converting a friend into an enemy. But, secondly, if the ties of private friendship sometimes occasion a tendency to partiality, of which we cannot deny there may be found traces even in the Edinburgh Review, the narrowness of the sphere in which such temptations occur necessarily renders their influence rare and occasional. Lastly, we must observe, to the honour of the literary society of Edinburgh, that if there exist any causes why a critic who is their fellow-citizen and daily companion should delight to honour them more than perhaps they merit, there is little room for that darker motive of partiality, which arises from the feuds, factions, and heart-burnings in which he might be elsewhere involved. There is, indeed, a difference between two classes of our philosophers, which we (to use Sosia's[71] expression) shall leave to the "other we," our physical associates, to make plain, and which, if we (meaning we ourselves) rightly comprehend the matter, resolves into a dispute whether the world at the creation was roasted or boiled into its present form. But we do not find our Neptunists and Vulcanists[72] inclined to draw daggers on this

71. See Dryden's *Amphytrion; or, The Two Sosias.*
72. Scott refers twice to this geological dispute between the Wernerians and the Huttonians or the Neptunists and the Vulcanists in letters of February 29 and April 4, 1812. *Letters of Scott,* II, 84, 101.

question; (at which we are rather surprised, considering that it seems incapable of proof, and is of very small consequence,) on the contrary, they discuss their roast and boiled together in a very sociable manner. As for our literary class, it is well known that our Celt sits down with our Goth, our war poet with our peace poet, our Marian with our Elizabethan, and all with our critic; so, until the lion lie down with the kid, and the child play upon the hole of the asp, we can hardly expect a more edifying accordance of opposite natures. Perhaps this may be owing to the narrow circle in which these gentlemen move; perhaps to the predominance of barristers among their number,—a class of prudent persons, who account all angry debate too valuable to be thrown away in gratuitous controversy, and keep it carefully corked up in guinea and two guinea bottles, for the use of those who may chance to need it at the bar. But whether the ludicrous cause we have assigned, or one more honourable to those who are by profession in the daily habit of maintaining controversy with temper, and enduring contradiction without animosity, gives stability to the amicable and pacific state of our little literary republic, the fact is certain, that the critics who are members of it can draw from thence no food to stimulate malevolence, though it is possible they may find some motives for indulgence or partial preference. And these secondary causes had doubtless their effect in establishing the character of the Edinburgh Review, since candour, like other virtues, is most easily adhered to where there are the fewest temptations to dis-obey its dictates.

All these, however, were but accidental advantages, which could only further this undertaking in proportion to the internal vigour and stamina with which it was supported. The aim was judiciously taken, but it remained to prove the elasticity of the bow and the nerves of the archer. And, after laying due weight upon the particulars we have enumerated, as contributing to the success of the Edinburgh Review, it must be allowed that the talents of the editor and his associates would have been of them-selves sufficient to force the work into public notice under the most disadvantageous circumstances. The tone of the editor's mind necessarily pervaded and regulated the principal articles. It was bold, uncompromising, and intolerant, fraught deeply with various science, yet still more remarkable for prompt arrange-ment of the knowledge he possessed; distinguished for the clear, summary, and perspicuous statement of argument or theory, but unequalled for the ready and acute felicity of brilliant illustration. With these high gifts was combined a fluent eloquence upon almost any given topic, the coruscations of a lively wit, and the power of pungent sarcasm and unmerciful irony. The possessor of such talents could hardly be ignorant of the superiority which they afforded him over all whom he met in the ordinary walks of life, and over most of those whom he conversed with through the medium of their literary essays. And perhaps this sense of his own uncommon powers has given rise to the most striking feature in the Edinburgh Review, an indifference, namely, to the work treated of, and a tone of superiority, both over the book and the writer, often just, but sometimes offensive to the reader, and always irritating to the author. It is scarce necessary to observe, that the despotic exercise of authority, though it may subdue, seldom can reform; and, considering the cause of literature as alone in question, a tone of haughty and uniform superiority on the part of the critic is sure to harden the author in the offences charged against him. The latter is of a class not famous in any case for pliability or meekness; he is probably conscious that, whatever his general inferiority may be, he must have bestowed more thought and research upon the immediate subject of his work than the reviewer by whom his labours are vilipended, and his wounded pride finds a reasonable pretext for resisting counsels, which, however just and useful, have been conveyed with supercilious contempt or acrimonious censure. By adopting this tone of general severity, therefore, the real advantage which literature might have derived from the Review was greatly diminished. There is prudence in the maxim which recommends us to glean knowledge even from an enemy; but few are able to practise so humiliating a lesson, or to derive the same profit from contumely and reproach, which they might have been disposed to deduce from friendly advice and gentle reproof. It will be readily admitted, that we only object to the indiscriminating use of severity. We have already stated our sense of the degraded state of lethargy into which the critical art had fallen for want of a little animated and independent satire, and we can have no wish that those days of gentle dulness should return, when all the disquisitions of criticism, like the messes of the Romans, were sweetened with honey and oil. In the name of public justice, let conceit be flogged and pickled, immorality

ducked and pilloried, and folly brayed in a mortar. It is when
works conveying, perhaps useful, nay important information,
are ridiculed for the want of graces which were not necessary to
their matter—it is where writers of talent may have erred in the
application of their powers—it is where early genius, in a premature attempt at distinction, may have fallen short of the mark
at which it aimed, that we would recommend to a critic who
shares that information, talent, and genius, to suspend the lash
of ridicule, and to essay the effects of a friendly and warning
voice. It would have the appearance of cant, were we to expatiate
on the pain which a contrary tone inflicts upon the sufferer; nor
can we expect that such an argument should influence a professional critic, to whose occupation such infliction is indispensable.
But in the Memoirs of the late amiable and ingenious Kirke
White, we find a scene of which no good man would willingly
hazard a repetition, whether for the sake of exhibiting his wit,
or of extending his reputation. To crush the spirit and annihilate
the hopes (as far as the reviewer was able) of such a young man,
was not merely harsh and unjust cruelty to the individual, it was
defrauding the public of all they had to expect from awakening
talent, and smothering the fire of genius ere it had struggled
through the damps of timidity and modesty.[73] There is at least
the same cause for forbearance and moderation, where information really useful in itself is communicated by a person perhaps
not well fitted by taste or education to come before the public
as an author. In such a case, a critic is bound by his duty to the
public, rather to consider the merit and value of the work, than
the talents or manner of the author. The latter is often peculiarly
obnoxious to ridicule; for the creeping style of the laborious
antiquary, the egotistical verbiage of the traveller, the stately and
self-important dogmatism of the experimental philosopher, may
be easily rendered ridiculous, while the value of their discoveries
remains unimpeached. But the boy in the apologue could not
have justified his imprudence in cutting off the supply of the
golden eggs by pleading that it was a goose which produced them:
and, as every one who reads must be conscious that our most
valuable information has not always been obtained by men the
best fitted to put it into an elegant shape, a discerning critic

73. Southey in his biography of Henry Kirke White prefixed to the *Remains of
Henry Kirke White* (1807) had stressed the unfortunate effects on the young poet of
the severe review of his *Clifton Grove* (1803) in the *Critical Review*.

ought rather in such cases to consider the intention and effect of
the information conveyed, than amuse himself and his readers by
bantering the shape and fashion of the vehicle which brings it before his tribunal.

It remains we should notice the effect of this tone of dogmatical superiority in the reviewer, when it is assumed towards
authors of some name and an ascertained rank in the literary
world; and, to say the truth, it is in such a case that we consider
the critic as most justified in assuming an independent at least,
if not a lofty tone of censure. Too much deference to merit generally admitted, too much delicacy in pointing out the errors of
an author of acknowledged rank, would in fact be a cowardly
dereliction of his own critical authority, and an admission that
he had cited to his bar one who should have sate upon his bench.
It is, therefore, in such instances that a moderate and manly,
nay somewhat a peremptory assertion of the dignity of his craft
becomes a reviewer well, if it be supported with the skill and
knowledge necessary to render it more than an empty assertion.
And we are reconciled to a certain severity of criticism in such a
case for two reasons; both because it is ten to one that such an
author will peruse the article respecting him either with good-
humoured conviction, or with contemptuous indifference; and,
secondly, because there is ground for a fair and manly contest
between the assailant and the party assailed, and not unattended
with risk to the reviewer himself, since he cannot fall into the
error of over-loading his critical artillery without somewhat en-
dangering his reputation by the recoil. Yet even in this struggle,
"where Greek meets Greek,"[74] the Edinburgh reviewers are apt
to forget, that fair and generous opposition of sentiment ought
to be like open war between civilized powers, undebased by the
use of undue advantages and poisoned weapons. Above all, the
critic should remember, that the form of the fight gives him the
right of attack,—an advantage to be used with courtesy, not with
atrocity. The author, by the very act of publication, gives, as it
were, his cheek to the smiter; he must, like the Duke of Austria
in the old romance, who undertook to receive a buffet from
Richard Cœur de Lion, "stand forth, and hold his head fair as a
true man." We think this advantage ought not to be abused on

---

74. "When Greeks joined Greeks, then was the tug of war." Nathaniel Lee,
Alexander the Great, IV, scene 2.

the reviewer's part; that the combat ought to be maintained according to the laws of courteous chivalry; and our literature, if possible, preserved from disgraceful wrangling between the professors and the judges of literature, and from the revival of such controversies as disgraced learning in the days of Scioppius and Scaliger.

Another leading innovation, introduced by the example of the Edinburgh Review into the art of periodical criticism, is perhaps strictly connected with, and derived from, the tone of superiority assumed by these critics over the subjects of their lucubrations. It is the right which they assume of at any time deserting the work which gives the title to their article, and, without further reference to it than a few lines of general vituperation, proceeding to canvass the subject matter according to their own views. Former reviewers accounted it their principal and indispensable duty to give an account of the work upon their table, and conveyed all their own remarks in such a form as might bear upon and be applicable to their immediate text-book. But the Edinburgh reviewers have often flung it aside, as an extemporaneous preacher shuts the Bible after he has read his text, and it is well if, on such occasions, they have again adverted to it during the whole of the article. It cannot be denied that this mode of considering a subject, in a general point of view, gives scope to the genius of the critic, and an ample opportunity for the display of his own knowledge; nor are we inclined to join the cry of the neglected and discontented authors, who complain that the edifice of the critic is often run up with bricks surreptitiously abstracted from their own contemned Babel. On the contrary, the Edinburgh Miscellany must be admitted to contain many original and luminous essays upon subjects the most generally interesting, written in a style alternately powerful and lively, and forming a species of composition which, if it cannot be properly termed a review of any work, is often much better worth reading than if it were. It is no doubt true, that the example of this leading publication has induced those of minor fame to neglect the natural and usual discharge of their functions, in order to wander into disquisitions quite beyond their own depth and talent. But we cannot so far adopt the severity of the northern critics, as to make them responsible not only for their own mode of writing, but for the errors and absurdities of all who, emulous of their fame, may attempt to imitate them in it.

We shall therefore content ourselves with observing, that this novel practice is peculiarly convenient for the numerous class of grown gentlemen who are desirous to have a superficial knowledge of the topics of the day, without being peculiarly anxious about its accuracy, or disposed to encounter much toil in the acquirement. To this body of readers, reviews, magazines, pamphlets, and all the light-armed forces of the press, have been always a principal resource; and, as it is quite the same to them whether the scantling of information which they require comes from the reviewer's mother-wit, or is only an abstract or report from the author before him, it is probable that the variety, liveliness, and perspicuity of the lucubrations on general subjects in the Edinburgh Review have tended not a little to extend its popularity, although they may not be strictly consistent with its title and professed purpose.

Hitherto we have spoken only of certain peculiarities in the conduct of this celebrated and popular journal, of its general and uncompromising tone of severity, and of the unceremonious neglect of the various works which it professes to review, but which have often as little connection with the article to which they give the title as the sign of the inn with what passes in the tap-room. Something remains to be said of the nature and taste of criticism which it exhibits; and it is with some regret that we must necessarily consider it separately, as exercised upon topics of general literature, and as connected with party politics.

Upon the first of these points we confess our inability to deduce any precise canons of criticism from the sixteen volumes which are now before us. Nor do we consider this as matter either of surprise or censure. A series of unconnected decisions, each resting upon its own specialities, pronounced perhaps by different judges of the same court, can scarcely afford coherent materials for compiling a code of laws. But perhaps the articles of a review still more resemble the pleadings of an ingenious barrister upon various points of law, or the theses of a learned sophist on different points of controversy, in which the sole object, besides that of displaying the versatile genius of the advocate, is the maintaining some isolated and unconnected proposition by arguments which, upon another occasion, may be changed or exploded, without incurring the charge of inconsistency. Thus the same premises may be used on various occasions, as authorizing the most opposite conclusions. For example, the decided and extended popularity of one author may be represented as arising from his dealing more in the common-places of poetry than his contemporaries, and another may be consoled by the assurance, that if his work be caviare to the multitude, it is the more valuable to the few who can estimate the just representation of the most ordinary feelings of our nature, which are precisely those upon which the common-places of poetry are founded: nay, if it be necessary, both these propositions may be abandoned, to charge a third poet with want of popularity, as a conclusive sentence against him, pronounced by the silent practical judgement of the public. Now, although each of these dogmata may be supported by very plausible and ingenious reasoning, it must certainly puzzle any author, disposed to act under such high authority, to discover whether, by using the most hackneyed language and subjects of his art, he is most likely to secure the applause of the multitude, or that only of the select few; and if he should determine on pursuing the road to popularity, recommended in the reviewer's latest opinion, he would be still uncertain whether, when attained, it is to be considered as a mark of merit or reprobation. In the same manner, if an author be dubious what degree of labour or distinct description he ought to bestow on the detail of those minute particulars which form the accompaniments of his picture, he may find difficulty in reconciling two articles[75] in the Review for April, 1808, in one of which the author of a tale of chivalry is *censured* for the pedantic specification of donjons, keeps, tabards, scutcheons, tressures, caps of maintenance, portcullises, and wimples, while, in another, the poet of the village is distinctly *applauded* for the minute and Chinese accuracy of detail which inventories the whole household goods of a thievish smuggler, including ill-sorted packs of cards, unpaired pistols, frocks, wigs, hats, and bludgeons. To us it appears, that both poets, in completing their pictures, were obliged to fill up the back-ground with the objects best suited to the nature of the scene and character of the actors, and that whatever advantage might be on either side in

---

75. This was the number of the *Edinburgh Review* which so disturbed Scott. The reviews are those of his own *Marmion,* which is censured for the very things the reviewer praises in his review of Crabbe's *Poems.* Scott is quoting here almost word for word. "Fine ladies and gentlemen now talk, indeed, of donjons, keeps, tabards, scutcheons, treasures, caps of maintenance, portcullises, wimples." *Edinburgh Review,* XII, 32.

the mode of execution, the minute specification in question was
to both a rule of art which they could not easily elude or disobey,
any more than Teniers could have finished his Flemish carousals
without introducing tubs, barrels, pots, ladles, and other vulgar
utensils, or than Spagnolette could have brought out his group
of banditti without the necessary accompaniments of chains,
axes, torturing engines, and bloody armour.

It would be easy to point out similar instances of critical inconsistence in the reviews which refer to different works of the
same author, and to shew that the unfortunate wight has been
sometimes censured for taking, in his second work, the tone
which the critic had approved and recommended in the first.
But we are satisfied to have adduced proofs of our proposition
from leading articles upon popular works, composed, it is understood, by the same ingenious critic; and where therefore the conclusion which we have drawn is not liable to be evaded by ascrib-
ing the apparent inconsistence which they display to their being
written by different hands. So that, if the author be disposed to
pardon what Dryden calls the horse-play of the reviewer's raillery,
he may be confounded by the capricious distribution of favour
or censure, which seems to have been adopted from the involun-
tary exercise to which a cat subjects an unfortunate captive. This
tone of uncertainty, and variation of opinion, or rather of humour,
seems necessarily to arise from the leading principle of the Review,
which renders each article an independent essay. It is impossible
for the critic, while considering every new work as an isolated
subject for the display of his own genius, to maintain perfect
consistence with what he may have formerly advanced upon
similar occasions; nor would his doing so amuse or interest the
generality of the readers, who are accustomed to consider each
Review as an ephemeral publication, the contents of which are
banished from their recollection before the next number makes
its appearance. These will, of course, expect a new disquisition,
as lively and brilliant as the preceding, upon every fresh work
which an author may send forth, and will care very little whether
such disquisition be founded on the same, or upon new and inconsistent critical doctrine. We have, therefore, been often
tempted to compare these distinguished articles in the Edinburgh
Review to the prefaces and critical essays of Dryden, abounding
in striking passages, animated language, and acute reasoning, but
written to serve some instant or pressing purpose; and so far from

having any regard to an uniform or general system, that they are
often in direct opposition to each other. They are, in short, like
a series of decisions of certain courts of law, in which each question is studiously separated from all others by a detail of circumstances, and decided as upon grounds proper to itself, until the
lawyer, instead of being able to extract general principles of law
from the train of practice, is utterly perplexed by the maze of
contradictory judgements, and only consoled by the reflection,
that in the hour of need he can never fail to discover a precedent
in favour of his own cause, whatever sort of precedent that cause
may chance to stand in need of. That the law would grievously
suffer in the parallel case supposed cannot be doubted for a
moment; and if literature does not sustain the same disadvantage
in that before us, it is because the decisions in the court of
criticism are not necessarily binding upon the parties over whom
they are pronounced. But it is evident that, in this desultory mode
of delivering his opinion, the critic abandons the chance of rendering real service to letters, by establishing, or at least acting
upon, something like permanent rules of taste; and that, however amusing the revolutions of his doctrine may be to the
public, they can only serve to confound the unfortunate author,
for whose benefit, one would suppose, admonition and reproof
were principally intended. In short, we conceive this determination to be equally brilliant, and striking, and witty, and new,
upon every article of importance which comes before them, is,
in the critical court, a sacrifice of the high duties of the judge's
office to the love of amusing and of dazzling an extensive circle
of readers. Were we to attempt to make any general deduction
from a style of criticism so shadowy and variable, we should say,
that subjects of pathos, bearing immediate reference to domestic
feelings and affections, seem to come most home to the critic's
bosom. The wilder flights of fancy find little there which is
responsive; and had our northern Aristarch[76] sat in judgement
at the Grecian recitations, we are certain he would have given
his vote for Euripides, while we shrewdly suspect the flights of
Pindar would scarcely have atoned for their irregularity by their
beauty and sublimity. There is something in this distinction appropriate to the very art of criticism, which, although, in a good

76. Scott referred to Jeffrey as the Aristarch in a letter of February 10, 1810.
"Even the critical Aristarch Jeffrey was melted into tears." *Letters of Scott*, II,
298.

and kind disposition, it cannot be supposed to harden the heart, may have no small effect in blunting the ardour of fancy. Under the analytical process of such an observer, traits of natural feeling are like the perfume of the violet, which is only increased by the dissection of the botanist, while those beauties which address themselves to the imagination are, like the colours of the same flower, defaced under his scalpel. This, however, is descending more minutely in our observations on the character of the journal than is here necessary.

There are general subjects, and we record the fact with pleasure, upon which the Edinburgh critics have exhibited no variation or shadow of turning, but have passed and uniformly adhered to their well-advised and well-merited censure. We allude to that class of poetry which, while it is particularly addressed to the young and gay of both sexes, is calculated to exhibit a sentimental refinement of the strains of Sedley and Rochester of old. We rejoice to say, that the northern blight has so far affected the bays of the modern "men of wit and pleasure about town," that, when they shall sprout again, we may confidently expect a very different foliage. Nor do we notice with less pleasure their sturdy defence of morality in general, and their animated exertions against the negro trade in particular,— a cause which they early adopted, and contributed, we believe, not a little, by well-timed and well-written articles, to conduct to its present fortunate and honourable consummation. This tenacity upon points of morality may be well allowed to counterbalance a thousand variations of the reviewers' opinions upon matters of taste.

Our approbation of the theological articles of the Edinburgh Review cannot be so unqualified. They are deeply tinged with party spirit; but of that we shall speak presently more at length. But they also exhibit an unbecoming mixture of buffoonery and "fool-born jest"[77] with subjects of the deepest political and religious import. The tone with which the methodists in particular are treated, is that of a jealous clergyman who affects in his coterie to ridicule those of his flock whom his pulpit eloquence is unable to withhold from the tabernacle. But the matter is grown too ominously serious for this jocular mode of discussion. If it is intended to convert the methodists from their more

77. *Henry IV*, Part II, v, 5, 54.

enthusiastic tenets, let the effort be made in such a manner as
will neither irritate the feelings which prompt them, like other
men, to repel contumely by contempt, or shock those of reveren-
tial awe, with which they, above all other sects, are trained to
regard every thing connected with religion. There is much good
and much evil in methodism, and it is difficult to conceive how
it should have been made the subject of ludicrous discussion by
those very men who pretend to regard the question of catholic
emancipation as a matter of such serious and vital importance,
unless indeed they allege the novelty of the sect as sufficient excuse for treating its doctrine with familiarity, and think with
Œnobarbus,

> ——'tis better playing with a lion's
> whelp
> Than with an old one dying——[78]

Upon metaphysical subjects, the Edinburgh Review vindicates
the ancient reputation of our metropolitan university, long celebrated for that species of cobweb reasoning, as Paisley is for our
national gauze. The *non est tanti,* always an ungenerous argument, might be more decidedly applied to pure metaphysics than
to any other pursuit, were it not that, like the abstract propositions of algebra, they afford a facility of generalizing or analyzing at pleasure questions of political and moral importance, and,
if they bewilder weaker minds, afford to those of a firmer tex-
ture, an acuteness of perception and argument not to be acquired
by any other study. Upon no subject, indeed, has the manager of
the Edinburgh Review displayed more of his characteristic acuteness, than upon those where metaphysics are treated, either
separately or as applied to practical subjects. There is at once a
force, a dignity, a simplicity, and a precision in his mode of expression peculiarly fitted, not only to impress upon the reader
the importance of the subject, but to enlighten and delight the
attention which he has previously fixed. He never uses words of
a dubious import, or in an imperfect sense; his illustrations, although numerous and splendid, never exhibit that doubtful
analogy which tends to mislead the reader, or bewilder him in
the puzzling consequences of an imperfect and inaccurate

78. *Antony and Cleopatra,* III, xiii, 94.

parallel. The reviewer not only fully comprehends all which he
means to say, (no small virtue in a metaphysician,) but he has
the happy art of expressing himself in language as plain as it is
precise, and of conveying, in the most distinct manner, to every
reader of moderate intelligence, the propositions which his own
mind has conceived with so much accuracy. It is but his just
praise to say, that, as a guide through the misty maze of speculative philosophy, none has trod with a firmer step, or held equally high a torch which has glowed so clearly.

Several disquisitions of great classical value have at different
times appeared in this work; and the scientific department is sustained by masterly talent. On historical and archiological [*sic*]
subjects, the journal does not merit the same commendation.

The fault which we are under the necessity of charging against
this able review with the most unqualified censure, is the spirit
of political party which pervades it in so remarkable a degree.
We are far from saying that reviewers are not entitled, nay
called upon, in the fair discharge of their duty, to express their
own political sentiments whenever the nature of the subject
requires them to do so. Accordingly, though we might feel disposed to combat the opinions delivered by the Edinburgh reviewers in many of their political articles, we do not pretend to
question their right to treat these questions in the way which
appeared to them most fitting. But the evil lies in the strain of
party feeling, which visibly infects those articles of general literature with which politics have least to do, in a sort of narrow
factious spirit of distributing censure or approbation with an eye
to the political predilections of the author, rather than to the
literary merits or demerits of his work. In former reviews, the
effect of the critic's politics was confined to a few articles,
where every reader was prepared to expect that he should give
way to his partialities, and therefore considered his argument
with the necessary allowances; but on the modern system, these
prejudices are like the plague in Leviticus, which not only infected warp and woof, linen and woollen, but left its foul stains
upon the walls, the mortar and the stones, upon subjects whose
natures seemed incapable either of admitting or retaining the
tokens of pestilential infection.[79] It is not enough that the
critics have "relaxed their brows severe," and softened their

79. Leviticus, 13:47-59; 14:33-57.

tone of censure in favour of those authors with whom they may stand connected by party alliance, and by the *sodalitium* of clubs and societies. This partiality, although it falls under the imprecatory censure of their fulminating motto, may be pardoned to the weakness of humanity. There are even other temptations under which the critic who yields to them may claim our commiseration, if not our pardon. A severe attack upon a popular demagogue, or an incendiary scribbler, may draw down his vengeance, not perhaps on the person responsible for the review, (for the manager himself may consider the attempted retribution only as matter of contempt,) but upon friends engaged in political life, and bestirring themselves in that stormy ocean, where a gale from any quarter is hazardous. Here, therefore, the call of friendship is likely to predominate; the provoked Cerberus must be propitiated, and, instead of dragging him to day with the arm of Hercules, the reviewer, in woeful inactivity, sits down, like Theseus beside Pirithous, and sacrifices his own honour and duty to the security of his friend. We are much mistaken if such feelings did not somewhat paralyze the attack upon Cobbett, which, whatever the Edinburgh reviewer may suppose, gained him more credit with the moderate part of the public than ought to have been sacrificed to the fear of exposing any of the critical fraternity to the illiberal virulence of the Political Register. We write these things rather in sorrow than in anger, and own ourselves more disappointed upon recent occasions, that we had formerly seen the lion pawing to deliver himself from the sordid soil with which he was encumbered, and have had more than one glimpse of the service which the acute and generalizing powers of the leading critic, if freed from the adhesive slime of party, might render to a country which at no former time so greatly needed the light of a vigorous and intelligent mind. Amid the sacrifices which have been made to party-spirit, (if indeed we are to regard it as consummated,) a more powerful understanding and more varied talent have never been immolated than by the individual to whom we allude with a mixture of respect and sorrow.

But, omitting and pardoning the departure of the journal from its duty, whether for fear or favour, and cancelling at once its sins of omission, the Edinburgh critics must still be arraigned for the strange and unjustifiable despotism of visiting, upon the literary productions which have no concern with politics, the

supposed political attachments of the authors. It is inconceivable
to what trivial motives may be traced the shade of censure which
pervades a whole article. A dedication to an obnoxious character,
the praise bestowed upon one public man, or the omitting to
praise another, the censure inflicted, or the compliment withheld in a passing paragraph, are quite sufficient to colour the
whole character of a work in the Edinburgh Review. This has
even been carried still farther; for there are instances in which
the author has not left a single opening through which his political opinions could be glanced at; and yet he has been arraigned
upon his general character, and his productions, literary, philosophical, or historical, turned the seamy side without, solely because his party-faith did not square with that of his reviewer. In
such cases the Edinburgh critics seem to adopt the opinion of
Sir Lucius O'Trigger,[80] who held it sound reason to call a man
to account for a sentiment he had never uttered, and was so
subtle a disputant as to differ from one who was not at the moment giving any opinion at all. So sweeping a charge of gross
and glaring partiality, of which the purpose is to write *up* the
characters of men of their own party, and to write *down* that of
all others, it may be said, ought not to be hazarded without some
proof. Now for this our limits are unfortunately too narrow; but
if any reader will have the curiosity to divide the authors reviewed for these last five years into two classes, we pawn our
credit, that out of those whom the Edinburgh critics are visibly
inclined to favour, and those upon whom they exhaust the
rigours of criticism, he will be able to form a black and white
list, in which Pittites and Foxites shall be as regularly arranged
in opposite columns as in a division in the House of Commons.
This partiality does not, it is true, altogether weigh down the
scale of favour, or lighten that of censure, but we distinctly aver,
that it gives a strong cast to the beam. It is the leaden bias, which,
however concealed from sight, and small in proportion to the
circumference of the bowl, however liable to be more or less
counteracted by the manner in which the player delivers it from
his hand, has still a subtle and controuling influence upon the
course which his cast pursues. In a word, as every mess dressed
by a Spanish cook relishes somewhat of garlic, this unfortunate

80. Sir Lucius O'Trigger, a character in Sheridan's *The Rivals,* a favorite play of
Scott's.

spirit of party gives more or less a tone and colour to the most
ingenious criticisms in the Edinburgh Review. In some cases, it
cools the praise which it dares not altogether suppress; in others,
it mitigates and qualifies the censure which it cannot entirely
withhold. The critic keeps one eye upon the author's merits,
and industriously watches with the other his political acts and
opinions; and where an individual is marked as falling under the
ban of the party, a direct attack upon his literary reputation is
perhaps the least he has to dread, since there are, in the course
of such an extensive work, a thousand modes of obliquely assail-
ing him, by illustration, comparison, or allusion. And these
insidious animadversions are the more dangerous, because in
such a passing observation the critic is at liberty to assume the
premises on which they are founded, which, in a direct attack,
he is under the necessity of supporting by proof. Now, considering how widely party differences extend through a free country
like Britain, and how much the good, the learned, the wise, and
the accomplished have differed upon political points, we cannot
but regret that the Shibboleth of party should be fixed upon as
a pass-word to the favour of a court of literature. What we now
think of Winstanly, who declared that Milton's fame had become
"extinguished and stunk, because he reviled our sovereign lord
king Charles," will be the opinion of future times concerning
all critics, whether Whig or Tory, Pittite or Foxite, who shall
make their literary decisions truckle to party politics.

Having said thus much upon the predominance which a party-
spirit has gained in the general conduct of this able journal, it
becomes less necessary to notice those articles in which, by
general admission, as well as by the very charter of their office,
the reviewers are called upon to deliver political opinions. In this
department the Edinburgh Review once asserted an independence
of public men and party leaders, as absolute as their abjuration
of bookselling management. The controversy with a certain
noble peer upon the Sources of National Wealth, the angry retort
of his lordship, and suppressed rejoinder of the critic, are not yet
forgotten, and may be contrasted with the fond indulgence extended to a later and still poorer production of the same noble
lord upon Indian affairs. But the progressive course of human
affairs will not always permit a systematic assertion of the lofty
independence with which the generosity of youth commences
its career. Every step which a political adventurer makes in his

advances into public life, convinces him how little unassisted
and isolated talent is able to raise its possessor to the distinction
of which he is laudably ambitious. At every turn a friend is to
be acquired, or an enemy to be soothed and conciliated; the
jealousy of party favours no man's views who does not place
himself with entire devotion in its phalanx, and the voice of the
boldest and most independent patriot is lost and drowned, unless the crowd upon one side or other of the House shout in
chorus to it. And if it should be observed by a reasoner, attentive to the circumstances of parties, that the situation and habits
of the manager of the Edinburgh Review have removed him from
this gradual entanglement in the toils of a party, it will only remain to inquire, whether this has been the case with his principal
and most powerful assistants; and whether friendship for these
persons, and gratitude for the support they have uniformly afforded him, may not be as potent a bribe to a generous mind as
the direct and sordid temptation of ambition or self-interest. So,
however, it has happened, that the Edinburgh Review has become the distinct and pronounced eulogist and defender of a
party in the House of Commons, whose cause they advocate
with as much keenness and address as eloquence and talent. We
are not entitled to censure them for adopting opinions which
may not coincide with our own; but upon some occasions of
great and predominating interest, we have longed to have seen
them throw off their harness and their trammels, and give, with
the independence that always claims hearing, and the native
talent and acquired information that uniformly command attention when audience is gained, their unbiassed judgement upon
affairs, before the momentous importance of which every thing
like the selfish interest of a party ought to become invisible. But
of late we have been able to trace no symptom of a "self-denying
ordinance," nor do we see any chance of purchasing the countenance or councils of the Edinburgh Review at a cheaper price
than a total change in the ministry of the country. This cold and
pettifogging *esprit de corps* never disgusted us more than when
the Spanish war has been the subject of discussion. We willingly
wave descending to particulars; but it is impossible to read these
articles without suspecting a lurking desire on the part of the
writer to see his original predictions of evil success verified by
the event; nor are we much assured of the contrary by the reviewer's late assurances, that he detests Buonaparte almost as

much as his Majesty's Chancellor of the Exchequer, and the other ministers who have so obstinately withheld from the friends of the journal the seats to which they were so clearly entitled, upon the brocard, *dentur [sic] dignioribus.*

With these reflections we dismiss this celebrated journal, regretting that we should have had occasion to mingle so much censure where there is ample room for praise and admiration. The length at which we have treated the nature and conduct of a work which has so strongly influenced the modern taste in criticism, will enable us to dispatch rapidly what we have to offer upon periodical publications of the same nature.

> But lo! to fierce encounter in mid air
> New wizards rise.———[81]

The determined party-spirit exhibited in the Edinburgh Journal has already excited a formidable antagonist in the Quarterly Review, conducted upon nearly the same plan, and avowedly supporting opposite opinions in politics. The rapid and extensive circulation of this journal, when opposed to a redoubted opponent already in possession of the field, with no less than ten or twelve thousand subscribers, seems to justify the censure we have ventured to attach to the narrow, partial, and exclusive principles upon which the Edinburgh Review has been conducted. For, although the Quarterly Review has exhibited many articles of great beauty and talent, it will hardly be said that it could, in its very nonage, have made a stand against the Edinburgh work, had the latter added to its extensive reputation for eloquence, acuteness, wit, and talent, the yet higher praise of moderation and impartiality. The opening, however, has been afforded, and the enemy has availed himself of it. The general sense and feeling of a great proportion of the country has at once enabled a rival publication, under the numerous disadvantages with which such must always struggle during its infancy, to place itself in opposition to these giants of criticism with a support originally respectable and constantly increasing. As politicians, we see this with pleasure, since, without being sworn to either party, our feelings incline most strongly to the cause espoused by the Quarterly critics, even if we were not seduced

81. Pope, *Dunciad,* III, 265–66.

by the superior eloquence which, upon party subjects, they have almost uniformly displayed. As moderate men, we rejoice in an opportunity of hearing both sides of a political question ably stated and supported, by persons whose powers and opportunities of information are so far beyond those by whom such points are usually disputed in periodical publications. But as friends to the general cause of literature, we cannot but deprecate the tendency on both sides to involve its interest in the tumultuous and partial discussions to which politics uniformly give occasion. It gives us no pleasure to see either party prepare his whitewash to be used whenever the other shall have applied his blacking-ball. These obvious partialities, by which the author's political creed is made the gage of his literary proficiency, we censure alike in both cases; or, if we impute more blame to the Edinburgh Journal, it is because it led the way to the introduction of so unjust and mischievous a criterion of judgement.

As to other particulars, the plan and conduct of the Quarterly Review has been closely formed upon that of the Edinburgh; so that, in taking a view of the principles of modern periodical criticism, what has been said of the one will be found to apply pretty nearly to the other. They are both conducted by persons of high literary distinction, and superior to all bookselling influence; and the very party-spirit, of which we complain so heavily, is undoubtedly the means in both cases of procuring voluntary contributions from persons high in situation as in talent, who, in these bustling times, could scarcely have been enlisted out of mere regard to literature. The Quarterly Review has on some occasions appeared to lose sight of politics while treating of abstract points of literature; but on others it has been as violent and acrimonious as the critics of the North. We will leave them, therefore, to arrange their pretensions to public favour, being pretty certain that it will be finally determined by the shew of hands in favour of their respective politics.

The establishment of these two works, as the Gog and Magog of criticism, had greatly thrown into the shade the ancient and established reviews of Great Britain. Even the Monthly and Critical Journals, long at the head of this class, are considerably shorn of their beams. They partook of the evils which we have already seen attached to the old *regime,* and although different attempts have been made to new-model them upon the fashionable plan of discipline, they have not been as yet able to regain

much weight with the public. The most obvious feature in their
rivals' criticism is its stern, caustic, and uncompromising tone. It
seemed also more easy to imitate the northern Aristarchs in this
point than in the extent of their information, or the lively and
forcible arrangement of their argument. But severity and rudeness have now lost their novelty, and the public, who were at
first disposed to believe that such language could never have
been employed without some cause existing to merit it, now
regard violence of expression as the *vox signata* of criticism,
used in every case as a matter of course, and having no more
actual meaning in her court than the legal fiction in a writ of
latitat. On another principle an attempt was made, and very
creditably supported, to extend the period of the publication
adopted by the Edinburgh reviewers from a quarterly to an
annual period. But the advantages which attended the departure
from the monthly plan were not found equally to accompany a
further prolongation of the term, and, after some time allowed
for the experiment, the Annual Review returned to the old system, and, if we mistake not, is now published monthly. It was a
moderate and sensible work, under the conduct of a most
respectable publisher; but, from the taste which the public had
acquired for what is pungent and picquant in this species of
writing, it fell short of the success which it merited. Various
other attempts to establish new reviews, upon the principles so
successfully adopted in Edinburgh, have also failed. But one of
these was on a plan so new as to demand separate notice.

We allude to the London Review, a work instituted by the
late Richard Cumberland, with the professed purpose that each
piece of criticism should bear in front the name of the party by
whom it was composed. There was something generous and
spirited in the conception of this plan. "The man," said the
venerable author, "who, in this genuine spirit of criticism, im-
partially distributes praise or blame to the works he reviews, has
no more need to hide his name than the tradesman has who
records himself over his shop-door,—for whom has he to fear, or
of what to be ashamed? Learning has no truer friend, genius no
better counsellor, no safer guide. Every one must confess that
there is a dangerous temptation, an unmanly security, an unfair
advantage in concealment. Why then should any man, who seeks
not to injure but to benefit his contemporaries, resort to it?
There can be no reason why he should do that with the best

intentions which evil men are fain to do for the worst of purposes. A piece of crape may be a convenient mask for a highway, but a man that goes upon an honest errand does not want it, and will disdain to wear it." This was the language of a veteran and accomplished author, whom literature has now to regret; and we feel ourselves called upon to pay it some attention, as immediately connected with our present subject. Upon accurate consideration, however, we are of opinion the reasoning of Mr Cumberland will be found rather specious than solid. In the first place, it must be observed that there is no real concealment in the system of reviews now generally adopted. For, although the author of each individual critique may not be known, there is uniformly an editor who is answerable both to the public and to the individual, not perhaps for the soundness of every opinion which may be advanced in his journal, but for its general adherence to the language used among decent persons, and the fairness and candour which become men of literature. The author, therefore, who complains of a deficiency in either point, cannot want a party who must either be responsible for the article, or give up the writer's name, that he may answer for himself. But, besides the security afforded by reference to an avowed and responsible editor, the writers of the leading articles in the reviews of any eminence, are in general pretty well known both to the public and to the individual authors who are the subjects of their criticism. The different manner and style of the principal contributors to the Edinburgh Review, for example, are easily detected, and, like the champions of old, who, though sheathed in armour, were known by their bearings and cognizances, they are distinguished farther in the battle than the groom and yeoman who entered into it barefaced; so that the usual cant of "shots from ambuscade" and "arrows discharged in the dark," however it may be suffered to continue as legitimate permissible syllables of dolor in the mouth of a wounded sufferer, has no foundation in the actual state of things. To what purpose, then, it may be asked, should a mystery be affected which is so easily seen through, or why should not those who are the known authors of critical articles adopt Mr Cumberland's plan, and openly prefix to them their names? Our answer is founded upon the forms of civilized society, which are always calculated to avoid personality where free discussion is required. It would be scarcely possible to secure a free, or at least a

peaceable, debate in the British House of Commons, without
adherence to the style of what is called parliamentary language,
since many things must be distinctly said by one statesman of
his antagonist, which could not with propriety, or even safety,
be hazarded between man and man in the common intercourse
of life. In like manner there is in criticism an impersonal language, which, though every one knows it is used by a particular
individual, has more weight with the public, and gives less just
offence to the author censured, than if the criticism had been
declaredly written in the first person singular. It is in some degree
a deception, but it is one to which we willingly give way, as it
tends to save the decorum of society, and to give the critic an
opportunity of discharging his duty frankly, without any appearance of personality upon his part, and without giving the
party reviewed a strong temptation to push criticism into
controversy. It remains also to be noticed how often the reviewer may gain a hearing from the public by use of the emphatic pronoun *we,* which might have been denied to the criticisms
of an obscure individual upon the work of an established literary
character. The difficulty, finally, of enlisting individuals to fight
with their visors up, may have hastened the conclusion of Mr
Cumberland's unsuccessful attempt to establish a review upon
his new plan. Every one has heard of the celebrated harlequin,
who could not go through his part with spirit unless when he
wore the usual mask, although conscious that his identity was
equally recognized whether he used it or not; and we cannot
help thinking that those critics whose opinions are best worth
hearing will be most ready to deliver them under the modest
disguise of an anonymous publication, although they know that
in many cases it is a secret which all the world knows, and in
others, one which any party interested may discover if he
pleases. For all these reasons we are led to conclude that the
present system, while no real objection lies against it, is best
fitted to preserve harmony in the literary world, and to encourage a free and unrestrained spirit of discussion, without risk
of its degenerating into personal controversy, or being tram-
melled and chilled by over formal and timid civility; one or
other of which extremes might, we think, be the consequence
of the system practised in the London Review.

   With the notice of this anomaly in the reviewing system, we
must conclude our account of the present state of Periodical

Criticism in Britain. We have it not in our power, nor would the labour be repaid by any useful result, to report upon the various works now current in this department, far less to arrange their precedence. What we have chiefly attempted in this sketch is to give some idea of the spirit and principles of that which is decidedly the foremost in the field. Its surprising and unprecedented success has rendered the Edinburgh Review the mirror in which the others dress themselves, and from which they endeavour to select and imitate the qualities which recommend that journal to popular favour. The tone of criticism, therefore, at the commencement of the nineteenth century may be characterized as harsh, severe, and affectedly contemptuous, dwelling rather in general and excursive discussion, than in that which applies itself to the immediate subject; but requiring, from those very circumstances, an elevation of talent and extent of information unknown, or at least unnecessary, to the humble labourer of the preceding period. If the art has been emancipated from the commercial trammels of the bookseller, it has unfortunately become more deeply involved in the toils of the political statesman. This last yoke, however, if equally rigorous, is less sordid than the former, and the professors of the art of criticism have risen in rank and reputation accordingly; nor can it be denied that these periodical publications have at present an interest and importance altogether unknown in any former part of our literary history.

ᐧᐧ View of the Changes Proposed and Adopted in the Administration of Justice in Scotland

This essay (*Register*, I, 342–72) reveals an important, if neglected, side of Scott. His many years in the law courts demanded a large share of his time and energy, and contributed not a little to his insight into a wide cross section of human life, particularly among those citizens who enjoy litigation and the drama of the courtroom. It is a commonplace of Scott criticism to observe how skillfully and how frequently Scott used this experience and knowledge in his portrayal of characters and description of law-court scenes in the Waverley novels. Not so well documented, and patently of less interest to those whose interests are primarily literary, is Scott's knowledge and skill in the law. This essay, admittedly dry and technical to any reader unversed in the subject of Scottish jurisprudence, reveals Scott's mastery of his professional subject. It further reveals his use of the opportunity to write an essay upon the changes he considered desirable in the Scottish judicial system as a result of the knowledge he had gained by serving as secretary to the commission looking into the desirability of changes.

The essay is clearly organized, moving from a description of the various courts in Scotland as then existing, and then to the changes proposed. The essay also has some perceptive insights into the special problems of Scotland and the desirability of recognizing differences between the Scotsman and the Englishman. However technical the essay may be, the passages describing such differences provide a lighter moment, especially when the Scotsmen are compared to Englishmen as "more sagacious, conceited, disputatious, and irritable; much fonder of the exercise of power, and infinitely less disposed to bend to the authority of their superiors." Scott thought that Scottish juries—the bill provided that trial by jury be extended to civil cases formerly decided by a judge or judges—would find it almost impossible to come to unanimous agreement.

In the Historical Department of the present Register, we have endeavoured, as is necessary at the commencement of such an undertaking, to lay before our readers a summary of the most remarkable events which have occurred in the period to which it relates; accompanied with such a sketch of the predisposing causes as might enable them fully to understand the events themselves, and duly to appreciate the political consequences to which they may be expected to lead. In framing this summary, it will not be imagined that the changes proposed, and those actually adopted, in the administration of justice in this our native country, should have escaped our recollection. They were too interesting to us as Scotsmen, and, if we do not egregiously misapprehend its import and bearings, the system, at one time under the contemplation of the legislature, was by far too important to every person who understands the value of the constitution under which he lives, to have justified us in passing over the subject in total silence, or in bestowing on it that subordinate degree of attention which a slight change in one department of the municipal law of this part of the empire ought to attract, in a work professedly national.

From feelings of this kind, it was, at one time, our intention to devote a portion of that division of our work, to which we have given the title of THE HISTORY OF EUROPE, to this important subject; but, on farther consideration, we became satisfied, that, for several reasons, this plan ought not to be

adopted. There was some hazard that a full exposition of the
subject of our enquiry, its origin and consequences, might not
prove very interesting to a large class of readers; while, at the
same time, we could not content ourselves with a slight and
general revision, as if the attention of the legislature had been
directed to some insignificant arrangement in the proceedings
of a petty territorial court, preserving inviolate the great principles and land-marks of the law. We have, therefore, set apart
this section to a "View of the Changes proposed and adopted
in the Administration of Justice in Scotland;" and shall attempt to lay before the public a sketch of the evils most severe-
ly felt in the system of Scottish jurisprudence, and of the
remedies intended to remove those evils, which have, successively, been under the contemplation of the legislature; accompanied
with such remarks as have occurred to us on the probable consequences of what has been *done,* and of what has been *rejected.*

It is not necessary for our present purpose to trace the history
of the Court of Session, our supreme civil court, from its establishment, in 1532, and to explain the nature and extent of its
jurisdiction, or the manner in which that jurisdiction is carried
into effect. At the time when the first of the bills which have
given rise to these observations was introduced into Parliament,
and for nearly a century before it, this Court was composed of
fourteen Ordinary Judges, (as they are termed,) and a Lord
President. In this tribunal the cognizance of all personal and
real rights was vested. The trial of public wrongs, or crimes and
misdemeanours, belongs exclusively to the Court of Justiciary,
and of revenue questions, to the Court of Exchequer; but over
every other dispute which can occur in the multifarious intercourse of human society, whether they regard a man's property,
his *status,* or his character, the Court of Session, either originally, or by appeal, has a supreme and universal jurisdiction. The
system of personal rights, recognized by that law which it ad-
ministers, is founded on the law of Rome; that admirable code
of equity, almost unknown to our neighbours of the sister kingdom, till the time of Lord Mansfield. Its real rights have the
same roots with those of every other feudal nation. And all
these the Court of Session decides without the assistance of a
Jury.

Each of the fourteen Ordinary Judges may be said to form a
separate and independent court; for, with certain minute excep-

tions, foreign to our present purpose, every cause is submitted
to his opinion in the first instance; and his judgment, if not
altered by his brethren sitting in what is termed the *Inner House,*
has the force and effect of a decree of the Court of Session. The
merits of the case are first stated in a writ, called a *summons,*
sued out by the party by whom the action is instituted, and in
defences for his adversary; both vaguely, incorrectly, and inarti-
ficially prepared. The cause is then pleaded, *viva voce,* by the
counsel of the parties. If the issue chances to be precise, the
Lord Ordinary may give his judgment; but it is seldom that the
cause advances so rapidly in its progress. In some cases, the summons is to be altered; in others, writings, material to one of the
parties, are to be recovered. From the necessity of adducing a
proof by witnesses; from difficulties arising in the discussion of
the cause; from the reluctance of hazarding a judgment on an
argument at the bar,—a reluctance laudable in its motive, but
productive of much inconvenience, of various descriptions; and
often from pretexts, impossible to be parried, to which a litigant, anxious to *delay* an event, which, he is conscious, cannot
be *evaded,* has recourse; the Judge orders the case to be stated
in writing. A written argument is prepared, still more loose than
the original summons and defences. In the preparation of this,
a considerable time is almost always employed. Additional information may be thought necessary by the Judge; he has an
unlimited power of reviewing his own judgments; and, when he
has given his final determination, the losing party may remove
his cause to the whole court, where the same sort of pleading
goes on. He may then, if he thinks fit, betake himself to the
House of Lords, which is the last round in the ladder of litigation.

In this rapid and general sketch of the mode of dispensing
justice in our Supreme Civil Court, it must not be forgotten,
that, in those cases which rest exclusively on parole evidence,
the Court has no opportunity of seeing and examining the witnesses, on whose testimony their judgment depends. Commissioners are appointed by the Court, or the Judge who has
directed the proof to be taken. These Commissioners, as is unavoidable, are not all equally qualified for the discharge of the
delicate and important duty assigned to them:—their province
is to state the result of the evidence led in their presence; but
they are not empowered either to bring witnesses before them,

or to commit for prevarication or perjury. We are not disposed
to enumerate all the consequences of this mode of procedure.
To say nothing of the expence to both parties, or of the inconvenience produced by the mistakes, or indecision of the Com-
missioner, every one must be sensible that it is calculated to
create difficulties, almost insurmountable, in the discovery of
truth; and that it deprives the Judge of all access to those
minute and undescribable circumstances by which alone the
credibility of the evidence laid before him can be correctly appreciated. To adopt a maxim, already applied to the subject we
are considering, *Alia est auctoritas præsentium testum, alia
testimoniorum quæ recitari solent.*

The evils produced by these infallible recipes for misdecision
were the subject of various publications, at the time the proposal for improving the administration of justice in Scotland
was first submitted to the wisdom of the legislature; and we are
not inclined, nor do we deem it necessary, to resume them in
detail. It is evident, in the *first* place, that the establishment of
one court, possessed of an exclusive jurisdiction, tended to
repress that emulation to which all eminence in science, as well
as all excellence in the inferior departments of life, may, perhaps, be ultimately referred. It is evident, in the *second* place,
that, if, in the language of the English law, it be true, that
multitudinem decem faciunt, a court of fifteen men, trained to
polemical habits from their youth, is more fitted for the dex-
terities of a popular debate, than for the gravity and decorum
of judicial deliberation. From these radical errors in the constitution of the Court, aided by the defects in the mode of pleading, and of adducing parole evidence, to which we have adverted,
arose, uncertainty in the state of the law; the delay of justice;
and expence, which either deprived the poor of their remedy,
without a struggle, or which compelled them to withdraw from
the field of litigation before the course was finished; and a want
of confidence in the judgment of the Supreme Court, which
sometimes induced parties to prefer a dereliction of their rights
to the calamities of a law-suit, and sometimes to submit their
differences to a tribunal of their own nomination, whose decisions never can be so satisfactory to the parties themselves, or
so beneficial to the public, as the judgments of a well-constituted,
and well-regulated court of justice. These imperfections, as is
manifest from their nature, admitted of being removed without

injuring, or even tampering with, the essence of the law; and that law was well worth the preserving. Our system of real rights has attained a point of perfection unknown to any other country in Europe. If, in the other department of law, the pre-eminence is not so decided, we are entitled, without the imputation of national vanity, to say, that the personal rights of the subject are as well defined, and his character and *status* as securely protected, as they have ever been, under any government with which the history of the world has made us acquainted. While a sense of the imperfections of that law, arising, as they obviously did, from the rudeness of the age when the Court of Session was established, suggested the necessity of a partial change, the considerations to which we have last adverted rendered it peculiarly requisite to preserve the fabric entire, and to make the reparation, as nearly as possible, in the style of the original building.

It does not appear that any serious plan for altering the constitution of the Court of Session was entertained from 1724, when an act* passed, declaring that there should be no future nomination of extraordinary Lords, till the year 1785, in the course of which, a bill was introduced into the House of Commons, by Sir Ilay Campbell,[82] then Lord Advocate, for diminishing the number of Judges to ten, and for increasing their salaries. The measure was obviously salutary in itself, and would probably have led to other improvements; but it was an inadequate remedy, and it soon was abandoned. A few years afterwards, an attempt was made, by the late Lord Swinton,[83] to excite the attention of the public to this interesting and important subject. His proposal was, that the Court should be divided into two Chambers, each consisting of six Judges, the remaining three being allowed to retire; that, in a certain description of causes, the Court, at their discretion, might allow a Trial by Jury, which should proceed before that Chamber, of which the Judges of the Court of Justiciary were to be members; that in all cases regarding a sum below £12 sterling, the decree of a single Judge should

*10 Geo. I. c. 19.

82. Sir Ilay Campbell, Bart. (1734–1823), Scottish judge, lord president of the court of session. In 1809 he published a forty-page pamphlet: *Hints Upon the Question of Jury Trial, as Applicable to the Proceedings in the Court of Session.*

83. John Swinton (d. 1799), a Scottish judge and author of *Considerations Concerning a Proposal for Dividing the Court of Session into Classes or Chambers* (1789: reprinted 1807).

be final; and that it should be competent for the twelve Judges
to reserve questions of difficulty for their own consideration.
This plan, which promised to lessen, if not entirely to remedy,
the defects long felt in the procedure of the Court, without any
abrupt or violent innovation, did not attract any notice at the
time it was announced; and the pamphlet in which it was detailed, with all its bearings, (a work of great learning and uncommon merit,) was, till very lately, entirely neglected and forgotten. Soon after the formation of the last ministry, it came
to be understood, that a reform in the law of Scotland was in
the contemplation of his Majesty's Government; and on the
18th of June, 1806, Lord Grenville, then at the head of the
Treasury, laid before the House of Lords a series of resolutions,
as the basis of a bill, to be introduced in the course of the following Sessions of Parliament.

Of the alterations in the establishment of our courts, proposed
by Lord Grenville, in which the forms and principles of the law
of Scotland were to be adhered to as much as possible, and the
true meaning and spirit of the articles of Union were to be in-
variably maintained, the essential parts were these: That the
Court shall sit in such number of separate Chambers as may be
found most convenient; each of which shall possess the same
functions that formerly belonged to the whole Court: That a
precise statement of facts shall be given by each party; and that
the issue may be tried by a Jury, sometimes before the Court of
Session, and sometimes before the next Circuit: That it shall be
competent to complain against verdicts of Juries, as having been
given contrary to evidence, or by misdirection: That the judgments of inferior courts may be appealed from, without the
circuity previously necessary: That every judgment of the separate Chambers shall be subject to review, in a Chamber of
Review, "to be constituted in such manner as shall hereafter be
appointed by act of Parliament:" That appeals to the House of
Lords shall only be competent against the judgments of the
Chamber of Review: That all questions formerly cognizable by
the Court of Session, acting as the Court of Teinds, in virtue of
a statute passed in 1707, shall, with certain insignificant exceptions, henceforward be tried by the Barons of Exchequer; and
that the unlimited power of increasing the stipends of the
clergy, the exercise of which has of late been deeply felt, and
loudly and justly complained of, as an intolerable grievance,

shall be restrained, in the manner to be afterwards declared.

These resolutions, though allowed to lie on the table till the ensuing Sessions of Parliament, did not excite any general attention to the subject to which they related; and from this apparent apathy very opposite conclusions were drawn by the friends and opponents of the measure originating with Lord Grenville. That measure, it was said by the latter, had not been provoked by any complaint from the inhabitants of Scotland, who knew nothing of the grievances under which they were supposed to labour, till they heard of the *panacæa* by which these grievances were to be removed. Even after the resolutions had been adopted by the committee, announcing the existence of defects, which required the interposition of the legislature, the people of Scotland persevered in the same obstinate silence; no resolutions were passed, and no petition was presented, stating the necessity of any alteration in the establishment of the courts of law, or approving the plan of reform to which the first Lord of the Treasury had given his sanction. Of the same facts, a different explanation was given by those who favoured the project of reform. They remarked, that the resolutions introduced into the House of Lords, at the end of the Session 1806, had been circulated throughout Scotland during the summer, and had produced no objection from any public meeting; and as mankind are generally prejudiced in favour of their ancient usages and institutions, the silence observed on the disclosure of a measure so extensive, and so hostile to some of the most established of those usages, was construed into a direct and distinct approbation of it.

We differ from both these theories, and are decidedly of opinion, that the circumstances on which they are built, when fairly examined, do not warrant any inference whatever, as to the sentiments of the people of Scotland on the expediency of the great legislative measure for altering their system of law; and that they admit of a solution more honourable to our national character than is implied in either of the hypotheses we have just stated. It is not correct to hold, that the whole arrangement of our judicial establishments was felt to be perfect, merely because no complaint was preferred, at a time when a plan for improving them was under the consideration of Parliament; in the face of the notorious fact, that its defects were very generally perceived; of which the two pamphlets we have alluded to, and a proposal for forming two courts, prepared by three of the Judges, found, it is said, in the Secretary of State's office, on the change of ministry in 1806, are, of themselves, satisfactory proofs. But it is preposterous and extravagant to infer an universal approbation of a measure, the merits of which depended on its details, from the single circumstance, that the measure was not resisted before its details were known. The silence of the people of Scotland arose from different causes. Lord Grenville's resolutions were no more than a general sketch and outline, which were to be filled up in a bill to be submitted to Parliament in the course of the subsequent session. The nation, more immediately interested in it, were persuaded, that the fullest opportunity would be afforded, of canvassing the provisions of a bill intended to alter, in any essential respect, their ancient judicial establishments; which, being called for by no sudden and unforeseen emergency, did not require any extraordinary dispatch; and they waited with exemplary, and praise worthy patience, till the picture, of which the outlines merely were presented to them, was completed, and delayed hazarding an opinion until the materials were laid before them, on which alone an opinion could safely be formed.

On the motion of Lord Grenville, the bill was read for the first time, in the House of Lords, on the 16th of February, 1807; and we shall now give a summary of its more important provisions.

The Court was to be divided into three Chambers, each consisting of five Judges; and these Chambers were to sit on successive days. To the summons, or writ, by which the cause is brought into Court, the defender was bound to give in written defences, which were to be followed by written answers; and these were to pave the way for another written pleading for each party, at the discretion of the Court or the Lord Ordinary. Trial by Jury was introduced into a very comprehensive description of cases. It was provided, that in all actions, or obligations, or other rights of a moveable nature, concluding for the payment of money, or the recovery of goods and effects, or the performance of facts; in all actions concluding for reparation of damages; in all actions of reduction, or reduction improbation, on the head of forgery or falsehood; in all actions of reduction on the head of force or fear, or on the heads of fraud, circumvention, lesion, facility, or other mental incapacity; in all actions of reduction on the heads

of minority and lesion, and on that of death-bed; and in all
actions of reduction on the acts of the Scots Parliament, 1621,
c. 18, and 1696, c. 5, the first entitled, *Act against unlawful
Alienations made by Bankrupts,* and the second, *Act for declaring notour Bankrupts;* the Court, on the requisition of either
party, or at their own discretion, shall order the issue to be tried
by a Jury, who were farther empowered to assess damages, in all
cases where a decree for damages has passed in absence against
the defender. Many enactments followed, for still farther extending the trial by Jury. Civil causes were to be tried at circuit
courts, to be held by the Lord President of the Court of Session,
or by one of the presiding Judges of the *second* and *third* Chambers. All actions competent to be tried by a Jury in the Supreme
Court were to be subject to the same mode of trial before any
of the Inferior Courts. And it was especially provided, that the
Jury shall deliberate upon the issue before them, till they are all
of one mind upon the verdict which they have to return.

As the court was constituted when this bill was prepared, the
party aggrieved had his remedy in the form of an immediate
appeal to the house of lords. The journey, previously felt to be
abundantly tedious, was now to be lengthened by the creation
of a Court of Review.

By an act passed in the reign of James V., the king was authorised, in addition to the ordinary judges of this court, to appoint
three or four persons of his Great Council to be extraordinary
Lords of Session, "who, according to the practice which followed,
have no salary, and are not obliged to attendance; but when they
come they have a vote."* In process of time, the evil of this institution, which might, from its origin, have been sufficiently
apparent, came to be perceived; and a statute, formerly mentioned, passed in the reign of George I., declaring, that, when
the places of the extraordinary Lords then alive shall be vacant,
no nomination shall be made to supply such vacancy. The bill
we are now examining provided, that it should be lawful to his
majesty to appoint an extraordinary Lord of Session, agreeably
to the constitution of the Court, as established in the reign of
James V., the act of the last century being repealed. This personage was to preside in the Chamber of Review, in the same
way and manner as the Chancellor of Scotland did preside in the

---

*Supplement to Spottiswood's History, p. 35.

Court of Session, by the ancient law of Scotland; and to him were to be added the Presidents of the three Chambers, and the Chief Baron of the Court of Exchequer, who was declared, by statute, an extraordinary Lord of Session. To this tribunal it was competent to appeal against every judgment of the Court of Session, within a year from the date of the judgment; and no sentence of any Scottish court could be brought under the cognizance of the House of Lords unless it was first submitted to this new judicature. The bill was concluded with certain minute regulations, of comparatively subordinate interest and importance.

It cannot be fairly alleged, we conceive, that the germ and first principles of this most comprehensive bill were not contained in Lord Grenville's resolutions; although its more material provisions were inveloped in language so general and ambiguous, as to convey to the people of Scotland no accurate notion of the changes intended to be made in their ancient code of law. The resolutions bore, on the contrary, so distinct an allusion to its enactments, and in the order they held, that it is difficult to avoid suspecting the bill had been prepared before the resolutions were drawn; and if this was the fact, the manly course of procedure would have been, to lay the bill on the table of the House in summer 1806, that its whole bearings might have been maturely considered by the country to which it related, before the next Session of Parliament. But these resolutions were exhibited as the outlines of a picture to be afterwards finished, as the basis of a measure of which a correct estimate could not be formed till its architecture was completed: they were so described by the official friends, and probably the real authors, of the measure in this country, for the avowed purpose of avoiding a premature discussion of its merits; and, for the reasons we have assigned, a respectful reserve was observed by all classes of the people. If, however, the bill was not to be communicated to the public in 1806, either because, contrary to our conjecture, it was not then prepared, or for some other reason which its authors considered to be sufficient, opportunity ought to have been afforded for that full and free enquiry which was so anxiously coveted; the more intelligent of the community ought to have been allowed to form and express a deliberate opinion on a project so varied, extensive, and important; every circumstance which could be construed into precipitation, which could be supposed, even by the most prejudiced, to indicate a desire of stifling the detailed examination of a measure deeply affecting the rights of an independent nation; every semblance of undue influence, or of mystery and concealment, ought, both in Parliament and out of doors, to have been most sedulously avoided.*

The bill, we have said, was read for the first time, and ordered to be printed, on the 16th of February, 1807. The 7th of March was fixed for the second reading, and the 16th for its commitment. Of the general nature of its provisions some idea may be formed from the summary we have given above. Their importance we shall not at present dwell upon; but, confining ourselves to an humbler view of the subject, we would shortly state, that, in the original, the bill extended to forty folios; that it could not be sent to the press till after the 16th of February; and that the intention was, to obtain the sanction of the House of Lords to its principle, on Monday, the 7th of March. If the discussion of it was to be confined within the walls of that house, the members could not fully understand a new and complicated subject in so short a period; but when it is recollected that the nation had a right to be made acquainted with it; that, from respect to the legislature; from a reluctance to hazard an opinion on a great project, of which only the embryo was exposed to their view; and in compliance with the wishes of those, who, with the approbation of his majesty's government, assumed the superintendance of the plan in this country,—the

---

*Extract from the Edinburgh Courant of 12th March, 1807. The paper gives an account of certain proceedings of the Faculty of Advocates relative to this bill, and goes on in these words: "It was our intention to have delayed any notice of the proceedings on the foregoing interesting subject till they had finally closed; but we find that this tardy mode of information is not suited to the anxiety of the public. The prevailing opinion seems to be, that too early, or too general, a publicity cannot be given to the progress of a measure in which all ranks of the community are so deeply interested.

"We have always understood that the freedom of the press, whether derived from the rights of the subject, or the tacit forbearance of government, is the same in this country as in England. That the exercise of this freedom with us has been more moderate and circumscribed, is owing to the habits and manners of the country, and not to any servile compliance on the part of those who have the management of it. There is a point, however, beyond which moderation degenerates into tameness. We are perfectly satisfied that there is no serious intention of hampering the press in this country; but we must deprecate every interference that has a tendency to it. For our parts, we shall persevere in that line of conduct we have hitherto pursued, viz. to avoid wounding the feelings of individuals, but, on no consideration, to withhold that information from the public which the public have a right to receive."

whole kingdom, and particularly several of its bodies the best
qualified to judge of its consequences, had waited with laudable
patience for its completion; we assert, without hazard of contradiction, that a much longer period ought to have been allowed
for the examination of a measure calculated to vary the law by
which they and their posterity were to be governed. In this way,
and in this way alone, could it be decisively ascertained whether
the silence of the people proceeded from their approbation of
the entire measure. If they were satisfied with the very general
reference to the provisions contained in the resolutions, they
would persevere in their approbatory silence: if that silence
arose from the causes *we* have assigned;—if they declined to
judge of the *principle* of the measure till they saw in what manner it was to be carried practically into effect, and of its *details,*
till they were laid before them in the bill, where alone they
could be found;—a period for deliberation ought to have been
granted, suitable to the difficulty and importance of the subject
presented to their attention. We have no hesitation in again af-
firming, that, in the period actually granted, all deliberation was
not only useless, but absolutely impracticable.

Nor ought it to be forgotten, that, from the whole process,
preparatory to the introduction of the bill into Parliament, the
Judges of the Supreme court were carefully excluded. We are by
no means of opinion, that to them every scheme for altering the
law, in any of its departments, ought to be communicated; or
that, if their approbation was withheld, the bill we are now
examining, ought, on that single ground, to have been abandoned;
but, recollecting the avowed objects of it, that it was described
in its title to be a Bill, "for better regulating the Courts in Scotland, and Administration of Justice therein, and establishing
Trial by Jury in certain civil Causes," it was due to them, and the
country whose laws they administered, to request their sentiments on a measure in which, it is to be presumed, they were
peculiarly versant; because, to use the words of Lord Hale, "no
persons are so fit to be employed in the first digestion of such a
business, but such as know best what belongs unto it, and how
far may be gone with safety and convenience: and as it were an
unworthy thing, especially in a judge, to prefer his own interest
or profit, or the interest of courts, or officers of courts, above
the public benefit; so it were an unworthy thing to suspect such
a business in those who are entrusted with the lives, liberties,

and estates of the people, in their judicial employments."

This course, which respect to the judges themselves might have dictated, is indispensably necessary in every extensive reform in the law of Scotland. Several of the English judges have seats in the House of Lords; by the constitution, they are all assistants to that House in their judicial capacity; and many of the most eminent of the profession are members of the other House of Parliament. These advantages, which have conduced so decisively to the amelioration of the law of England, have been denied to Scotland since the Union. None of her judges has a seat in either of the great councils of the empire. Unless, therefore, their assistance is required when important changes of the law are in contemplation, the kingdom is deprived of the advice of those best acquainted with its interests, at the period when that advice is most valuable: and accordingly, in the year 1747, in the course of which was projected the most extensive alteration in the law of Scotland, next to the present, ever submitted to the consideration of the British Parliament, the House of Lords directed *the Judges of the Court of Session,* "to prepare the draught of a bill for remedying the inconveniences arising from the several kinds of heritable jurisdictions, in that part of Great Britain called Scotland; and for making more effectual provision for the regular administration of justice throughout that part of the united kingdom, by the king's courts and judges there; and to cause such draught of a bill be laid before the House, at the beginning of next Session of Parliament." Yet this bill, calculated, in the opinion of many, to subvert several fundamental principles of our law, intended, by the confession of those who framed it, to regulate the courts, and their administration of justice, was prepared, and brought into Parliament, without the slightest communication with the oracles of that law it was meant to reform.

Although the real practical merits of the bill are to be estimated only from a careful examination of its provisions, we must be permitted to think, that, even on a general view, the innovations it sanctioned were much too vapid and extensive; that too little attention was given to the genius and characteristics of the law of Scotland; and too little deference paid to the unalterable habits of the people. An established system is not to be tried by those tests which may, with perfect correctness, be applied to a new theory. A civilized nation, long in possession of a code of

law, under which, with all its inconveniencies, they have found
means to flourish, is not to be regarded as an infant colony, on
which experiments in legislation may, without much charge of
presumption, be hazarded. A philosopher is not entitled to investigate such a system by those ideas which he has fixed in his
own mind as the standard of possible excellence. The only unerring test of every old establishment is the *effect* it has actually
produced; for that must be held to be good from whence good
is derived. The people have, by degrees, moulded their habits
to the law they are compelled to obey: for some of its imperfections, remedies have been found; to others they have reconciled themselves; till, at last, they have, from various causes,
attained the object which the most sanguine visionary could
promise to himself from his own perfect *unembodied* system.
Let us not be understood to mean, that a superstitious regard
for antiquity ought to stay the hand of a temperate reform. But
the task is delicate, and full of danger; perilous in its execution,
and extremely doubtful in its issue. Is there not rational ground
to apprehend, that, in attempting to eradicate the disease, the
sound part of the constitution may be essentially injured? Can
we be quite certain that less inconvenience will result from that
newly-discovered and unknown remedy than from the evil,
which the juices and humours with which it has long been in-
corporated may have neutralized? That, after a thorough reformation has been achieved, it may not be found necessary to
counter-work the antidote itself, by having recourse to the very
error we have incautiously abjured? We are taught, by great
authority, that "possibly they may espy something that may in
truth be mischievous in some particular case, but weigh not how
many inconveniences are, on the other side, prevented or remedied by that which is the supposed vicious strictness of the law;
and he that purchases a reformation of a law with the introduction of greater inconveniencies, by the amotion of a mischief,
makes an ill bargain. As I have before said, no human law can
be absolutely perfect. It is sufficient that it be best *ut plurimum;*
and as to the mischiefs that it occasions, as they are accidental
and casual, so they may be oftentimes, by due care, prevented,
without an alteration of the main."*

Every great reform, we farther conceive, ought to be taken at

---

*Lord Hale on the Amendment of the Laws.

a point somewhat lower than the necessity seems to require. Montesquieu has a chapter, of which the title is, *Qu'il ne faut pas tout corriger.* Our improvement ought to contain within itself a principle of progressive improvement. We are thus enabled to see our way distinctly before us; we have, at the same time, under our eyes, the ancient malady, with the palliatives by which the hand of time has controlled its natural symptoms, and the effects arising from the process intended to remove it; and our course, whether we advance or recede, will be safe, and confident, and honourable: whereas, by taking our reform at the utmost possible stretch of the wrong complained of, we cannot fail to bring into disrepute the order of things, as established, without any corresponding certainty that our innovations will produce the result which our sanguine hopes have anticipated; and we thus deprive ourselves of the chance of a secure retreat, in the event of our failure.

There are many obvious considerations, too, which merit our attention, when examining the expediency of transferring to one part of our island the rules which have been found beneficial in the other. For the reasons we have briefly hinted at, a legislator will, in the *first* place, be disposed to eradicate, with a diffident hand, usages that have struck their roots deep and wide,—which have grown up and mixed themselves with some of the most important concerns in life,—and of which the evil, whatever it be, has been lessened, by circumstances that frequently escape the eye of a careless observer. In legislating for an ancient people, the question is not, what is the best possible system of law, but what is the best they can bear. Their habitudes and prejudices must always be respected; and, whenever it is practicable, those prejudices, instead of being destroyed, ought to be taken as the basis of the new regulations. It is manifest, in the *second* place, that, to justify a legislator in imposing on one nation the code of law, and especially the forms and procedure in the administration of justice, that prevail in another, it is not enough that they have been found practically good in the country from which they are proposed to be transplanted. The adoption even of an untried system is not to be determined by its abstract perfection; but no system of great antiquity is ever theoretically perfect. The greater part of its excellencies have been produced by circumstances, some of them altogether accidental, others arising from causes which

cannot be traced, and many of them incapable of being distinctly perceived. Its defects have been remedied, and its vices and
errors removed, by a variety of correctives produced by the immediate necessity of the case, which, gradually increasing in
number, and improving in quality, imperceptibly ameliorate the
original design. An establishment like this, it is obviously not
easy to borrow. It is only in its natural soil, where it has long
been planted, that the tree can be expected to flourish: there
only are to be found those peculiarities which have contributed
to its beauty and vigour. In every transfer of the kind we are
now contemplating, there is danger that many of the circumstances to which the practical excellence of the system is to be
ascribed may be left behind; nor ought it to be forgotten, that
to such deviations as have been found unavoidable, the people,
in the lapse of ages, have gradually accommodated themselves,
and *that their ancient laws and customs have been twisted and
woven into them as a part of their nature.* *

Without dwelling longer on these general remarks, naturally
suggested by the whole general tenour of this bill, we shall now
proceed to examine its more material enactments.

The first of these, as they stand in the bill, though certainly
not the first in point of importance, is that by which the court
was to be divided into three chambers. Five of the judges, of
whom two were to be Lords of Justiciary, were to form a
Chamber, three to be the quorum; and the Chambers were
directed to sit during the Session, (or in term-time,) on successive days.

The chief reason assigned for the introduction of a Chamber
of Review, the nature and merits of which we shall bring fully
before our readers, was, the necessity of preserving uniformity
in the decisions of three separate and independent courts; and
were the expediency of so many judicatories first established, it
might be competent to enquire, whether any contrivance for
securing uniformity of decision was necessary, in addition to
the supreme appellate tribunal, and whether that provided by
the bill was the best that could be devised for that purpose. We
do not admit that the evil thus anticipated sanctioned the cure
meant to eradicate it. In our humble opinion, the three Chambers, with all their crossings and jostlings, would have proved

*Hale.

less grievous than the coarse and inconvenient machine by which they were to be pressed down into a semblance of uniformity; and, consequently, we deny both the premises and the conclusion of the argument. But the bare statement of that argument naturally suggests a preliminary enquiry. In so far as the Chamber of Review is rested on three courts, it must be shewn, in the first instance, that their establishment is necessary, or at least positively advantageous, otherwise the tortoise, on which the elephant stands, is itself without support; and nothing to us can be clearer, than that these projected by the bill would have proved highly injurious.

The corrective, as it appears to us, went far beyond the mischief proposed to be redressed. The undivided court, it is agreed by all, did not, and could not execute with sufficient dispatch, the business with which it was entrusted, partly owing to its standing alone, and partly to the vices in its constitution, especially the number of persons who composed it. The arrears, however, though incapable of being discharged by itself, were not very large. Contemplating the measure as it was brought before Parliament, we are not, perhaps, entitled to avail ourselves of subsequent experience acquired from the bill since passed into a law; but, without the benefit of that experiment, which has set the question for ever at rest, the conclusion was precisely the same. Could it have been made out that the number of undecided causes exceeded those which were decided, in the proportion of three to one, the proposed regulation would not even then have been justifiable on the score of necessity; for, it must be evident, that a court, consisting of three, or at most, of five Judges, is capable of executing much more than three times the quantity of business that could be performed by one court of fifteen. But the former court was, by no means, reduced to so hopeless a state of bankruptcy. It is notorious, that the annual arrear was not equal to one-twentieth part of the annual dispatch; and, if any intermediate measure between the erection of one court and of two had been practicable, that would have met all the exigencies of the case. This being unattainable, the obvious expedient remained of a division into two, unless some positive clear advantage can be said to have resulted from that which actually was adopted. But it was meant, by the confession of its most ardent admirers, to avoid or cure an *evil*, and not to acquire a *benefit*.

Let us remember, however, in what manner the jurisdiction of the three courts was to be carried on. Dispatch being the object, the plain and direct course was to have authorised them to proceed at the same period; but, by that provision, which directed them to sit on successive days, the functions of one only were in exercise at the same time; those of the remaining two being completely spellbound during two-thirds of the term.

We have already said, that the creation of two courts, whatever might be their constitution, was unnecessary. As they were constituted, several serious inconveniences would inevitably have resulted from them.

There was reason to anticipate from them consequences decidedly injurious to the judicial character. It is doubtful, in the *first* place, whether the Scottish bar could have afforded fifteen men possessed of qualifications adequate to the duties with which, by the new distribution, the courts were to be charged. The number of the court, as formerly established, does not solve this difficulty; for each individual judge was now to be brought more prominently under the eye of the public; his employments were to be more various and important; and the motives which are thought to have sometimes influenced the party in power to advert, in the disposal of seats on the bench, to other considerations than that of professional eminence, must have, in a great measure, ceased with the old court. Admitting, as we do, the benefit of this consequence, we would, on the other hand, avoid a system requiring from its nature a more abundant supply than is to be found in the market. If we are right in supposing, that, under the new arrangement, the time of the courts would not be sufficiently occupied, we need scarcely remark, secondly, that the judges would be degraded from their natural rank and order, and would be regarded as the possessors of sinecures at once burthensome and useless.—And it is implied in the proposal to erect a Court of Review, that much mischief would arise from the inconsistent judgements of three independent tribunals, because it was to *remedy* that mischief, that this measure was contrived, instead of *preventing* it, which the framers of the bill had it in their power to do, simply by declining to create that multiplicity of judicatories to which the evil was indebted for its birth.

But the merits of this branch of the enactment would be imperfectly understood if we did not take into our view that astonishing part of it which enjoined the courts to meet alternately. To whatever side we look, whether we regard the independence of the profession of the law, the dignity of the judges, or the interest of the country, the object of this provision is equally inexplicable. It defeated one benefit likely to arise from a number of courts, by continuing an undivided bar. The judges, feeling their time not sufficiently occupied, must have contracted habits of indolence, and would have been presented to the public as mere pensionaries, deprived of that respect and worship which the mind naturally pays to their high and honourable functions. The progress of the machine was stopped during two-thirds of the short season allotted for its activity. The sittings of each court would not have amounted to six weeks in the year; and, by the cessation of two days, which must have occasioned repeated adjournments in the discussion of a single cause, the whole procedure would have been disjointed and torn in pieces, the judges and counsel must have been loaded with labour of the most irksome description, and parties subjected to the penalties of unnecessary delay, anxiety, and expense. If three courts had been a part of our ancient juridical establishment, which it was impossible or inexpedient entirely to remove, and they had outworked (as they speedily must) the materials with which they were supplied, this contrivance for impeding the celerity of their motion, and producing an artificial inertness, would have been intelligible; but we are unable to devise the reason for parcelling the old court into three separate tribunals, and for suspending the energies of two of these by the very same bill.

The next great department of the plan was the Court of Review, proposed to be interjected betwixt the three chambers of the Court of Session, and the court of ultimate jurisdiction. We have already explained briefly the nature of its constitution; but the measure requires a more detailed examination.

We have said, that this formidable tribunal was to consist of five persons: the Presidents of the three chambers, the Chief Baron of the Court of Exchequer, and another high officer, who was to preside in the Chamber of Review, in the same manner as the Lord Chancellor did preside in the Court of Session prior to the Union; his majesty being authorised to appoint the two persons last mentioned, extraordinary Lords of Session, agreeably, as was said, to the constitution of that court, as enacted by the statute of the fifth parliament of King James V. Here every case was to be tried before it could be submitted to the House of Lords. After the appeals from judgements of the Court of Session, as formerly constituted, were discussed, the presidents of the chambers were incapacitated from sitting and voting in appeals from the judgements of the chambers to which they belonged. The Lord Chancellor (for so we may term him) had one vote, but no casting vote. In case of an equality of opinions, the judgement appealed from remained unaltered. The Chamber of Review was empowered, in any case of extraordinary difficulty, to state general questions of law upon which the opinions of the judges of all the chambers might be required; and those judges, it was provided, shall be *bound* to *attend* the Chamber of Review, in order to deliver their opinions accordingly.

There is room here for much and various meditation; and we must, in the *first* place, take leave to say a few words on an enquiry much agitated at the time, whether the arrangement was reconcilable to the fair construction of the act of Union between the two kingdoms.

By that solemn treaty, it was provided, that no alteration shall be made in laws which concern private right, except for evident utility of the subjects within Scotland; and further, that the College of Justice shall, after the Union, remain in all time coming as it is now constituted by the laws of Scotland, and with the same authority and privileges as before the Union, with a proviso, however, that such regulations for the better administration of justice, are still competent, as may be made by the Parliament of Great Britain. To those who agree with us as to the nature and probable effects of this part of the bill more immediately under our contemplation, a very anxious discussion of the question we have alluded to above, may seem rather curious than practically necessary; since, on our hypothesis, the whole plan ought to be rejected on the broad and satisfactory ground, that, so far from tending to the evident utility of the subjects in this kingdom, it was greatly inexpedient, or rather positively and extensively pernicious. In that view, it falls within the *exception* of the compact, and, independently of the compact, it did not merit the sanction of the legislature. The other branch of the question cannot, however, be overlooked. It is our duty to advert to it as forming a part of the history of the bill, and as being in itself extremely important. We shall, therefore, venture to offer our sentiments, under an unfeigned conviction of the difficulties which attend it, and of our inability to throw any additional light on a subject, of which opposite opinions have been entertained by eminent statesmen and lawyers.

It must be admitted, we think, that a legislative measure, of which the conformity to the Articles of Union, and the expediency to the subjects in Scotland, are both liable to rational *doubt,* ought not to pass into a law. No Scotsman who understands and values the true interests of his country, will be disposed to scrutinize a proposal substantially beneficial, by a strict and captious reference to that sacred compact; the end to be attained will induce him to turn his eyes away from a speculation not tending to any tangible good; he will be averse from pleading against himself the stipulations of an agreement framed for his own advantage. But, if the consequences likely to result from the measure in contemplation are of an ambiguous description, he is then justified in betaking himself to that enquiry; and, if that shall likewise appear to be involved in obscurity, the prudent and honourable course is to reject the innovation.

We are not of that description of persons who think that injustice was done to Scotland at the period of the Union, by unduly limiting the quantity of her representation, or that it is clear there was any just ground for that cry once so popular among our ancestors, that "the laws, liberties, estates, and whatever was near and dear to them, were left entirely to the determination and absolute disposal of the British Parliament; in which they being but to have but a small representation, supposing their own members to be always unbiassed and impartial, they should always be overruled, outvoted, oppressed, and subjected; that now they were to be slaves, and must run to Westminster to vote with a handful of members, who would never be able to carry a question, or to make any weight there, but just, for form's sake, to sit in the House, and be laughed at."* Whatever principle was adopted as the basis of legislative representation, whether the number of the people was to be taken, the proportion of taxes paid, or an estimate from both, (each of which theories had its partizans) it must not be forgotten, that the share allotted to Scotland must have been lower than that

*De Foe's History of the Union, pp. 222, 225.

granted to the other contracting party; and, in the event of any jealousy emerging between the two countries, the English members would be more disposed to avail themselves of their superiority, had the numbers been nearly equal, than they possibly could on the principle that was actually adopted. Such is human nature. In the one case, a contest might be provoked and exasperated by the mere doubtfulness of its issue; in the other, there is no motive to a contest of which a victory, unhonoured with triumph, cannot fail to be the result. The real interests of Scotland, it may be thought, will be more securely guarded, by an implicit reliance on the generous feelings of our generous brethren of the south, who have ever repaid confidence with kindness, than by establishing an order of things calculated to excite rivalry, and all those feelings which hold no affinity with generosity.

If we are right in this, Scotland ought to be patiently heard when she pleads, that, in violation of the Articles of the Union, the code of her ancient laws is brought into danger, and more especially ought she to be listened to with attention, when she maintains that regulations confessedly English, and of which, perhaps, the chief merit is that they are English, are against the meaning of that treaty to be impressed into the heart of her law, at the hazard of displacing the whole, or an essential branch of it. A plea like this merits the most serious investigation, and ought not, but on due consideration, to be repelled. It is the voice of the weak against the strong, of the few against the many, of a party entitled to protection, though unable to protect herself, imploring the mercy of a power capable of affording that aid she solicits. Every plan, in a word, ought to be avoided, that may seem calculated to make Scotland feel her own inferiority, and to give to her sister kingdom, united with her in a voluntary association, the insolent air of a conqueror, imposing his laws and customs on a colony which the fate of battles has laid at his feet.

These remarks are not altogether unworthy of our remembrance, when we are enquiring if the bill now under our consideration, abstracted from its utility, is agreeable to the Treaty of Union, and are entitled to some degree of weight, if that question shall, on its own merits, seem to be involved in doubt and difficulty, which we fairly acknowledge it to be.

We are aware that the Court of Session, while it is declared to remain as constituted, and with all its existing authority and priviledges, was, nevertheless, to be subject to such regulations as should be made by the British Parliament. Though the import of this provision is sufficiently intelligible, the extent and application of it are liable to much doubt. Nothing, however, can, in fair and honest construction, remain competent to the British Parliament, except matters of mere regulation in the Court of Session. The authority and priviledges of the court, as it existed in 1707, must be preserved inviolate; and, if the innovations sanctioned by this bill, did diminish that authority, or encroach on those priviledges, we do not see how they can be reconciled to the treaty between the two nations. For, to use the language of De Foe, "By the 19th article, the Court of Session, or, as it is called, the College of Justice, with the Court of Justiciary, are effectually established and confirmed; their being and *constitution* cannot be touched, *no, not by the Parliament;* they are indeed to submit to *regulations,* and it cannot but be reasonable it should be so; *but none of these regulations can affect them as a court.*"* Did these regulations affect them as a court? Under this bill, did the Court of Session enjoy the same authority and priviledges as it did before its introduction?

The Court was *supreme* within Scotland, in every sense of the word. In practice, there lay an appeal to the House of Lords, and that inestimable priviledge was granted by a special clause in the Claim of Right, an authority constitutionally as sacred as the Act of Union itself; but its decrees were reviewable in no other tribunal. This supremacy was now to be at an end. The Court of Session was rendered an inferior judicature; the value and importance of its judgements were lowered; its Judges were degraded in their rank; and another court, separate in its nature, vested with higher authority, and uniting in itself all the exterior circumstances by which the people are apt to be captivated and awed, was placed over their heads. We do not at present examine the policy, or even the constitutional legality of that part of the bill which gave to the embryo Chancellor, and the Chief Baron of Exchequer, the title of Extraordinary Lords of Session. To this we shall briefly allude afterwards. It must be acknowledged, first, That the court was distinct from the three chambers of the old Court of Session; and, secondly, That it was superior to all

*De Foe's History of the Union, p. 449.

of them, having authority to reverse their sentences, and to
summon the Judges, as the House of Lords summons the Judges
of England, whenever they deemed their attendance necessary.
By whatever colouring the project might be disguised, of whatever materials this new creation was formed, it cannot be denied,
that this is another tribunal interposed betwixt the House of
Lords and the Court of Session; and consequently, there is
strong ground for doubting whether it can honestly be regarded
as one of those our forefathers had in view, one requisite of
which was, that the authority and priviledges of the Court of
Session were to remain unimpaired.

If the addition of the two Extraordinary Lords did not
strengthen, it certainly did not weaken, or remove, the objection founded on the articles of the Union; and let us consider
for a moment, what would be thought of a court similar to that
provided by the bill, in every particular, except that it did not
contain an appointment of those exalted personages. A certain
proportion of the judges, as has been well observed, for example,
the six Lords of Justiciary, five of whom, *ex officio,* are Lords
of Session, might have been declared a Chamber of Review.
They might have been termed a chamber, or division of the
court, merely. If, however, these judges could reverse the inter-
locutors of their brethren, sitting in each of the chambers, who
had no right to communicate with them except when their
attendance was *required;* if they could adopt, for the regulation
of their proceedings, the standing orders of the House of Lords,
in regard to appeals, rejecting the forms prescribed by our own
acts of parliament, and acts of sederunt; and if every case submitted to that house, must first be heard and decided by them;
it will be difficult seriously to deny that they, in common sense,
would form a Chamber of Review, to which the Court of Session is subordinate. Under such a system, what would become of
the articles of the Union? The Court of Session could not then,
in any reasonable interpretation, be regarded as the Supreme
Civil Court; and it cannot be maintained, that it was changed,
as to its supremacy, by the ambidextrous expedient of bestowing
the title of Extraordinary Lords of Session, on two members of
this new tribunal.

It was separately urged, that the appointment of a Lord Chancellor for Scotland, different from the Lord Chancellor of Great
Britain, was illegal and unconstitutional; and by some, it was

thought, that the creation of extraordinary lords, amounted, in truth, to another violation of the Union, inasmuch, as in their description, power, and number, they differed essentially from those recognized by law, before the act of Geo. I. The objection to the constitution of the court itself, both in the view we have just now stated, and in the still more interesting view we have still to consider, that of utility, appear to us so very strong, that we are not inclined to discuss, with much labour, either of these considerations. The first is of little general importance.* The second is, perhaps, not altogether free from doubt. On one hand, it is true, that betwixt the year 1554, when Sir Richard Maitland, of Lethington, the head of a family well known in the history of the times, was appointed an extraordinary lord, to the æra of the restoration, many persons obtained that office who were not lords of parliament; and, in point of law, we think that the statute of George I., abolishing the office, may be repealed without infringing the Act of Union. It is equally true on the other, that no person, without a title of dignity, was appointed from the institution of the College of Justice, to 1554, or from the restoration, till the dangerous power of creating extraordinary lords was taken from the crown early in the last century; and that the contrary practice prevailed during a time in which no man will be desirous to look for precedents, and originated from causes not highly honourable to the country. The precise merits of these arguments, we deem it unnecessary to investigate. We have laid before our readers the reasons that incline us, upon the whole, to think that this bill was, in more serious respects, inconsistent with the Union Treaty; and when, to these, we add the pernicious effects it could not have failed to produce, we think the nomination of two officers, made to suit an emergency, and bearing names of portentous sound to every Scotsman who values the independence of his country, and the purity of her laws, important though it be, still is a matter of subordinate interest.

We hasten, therefore, to consider these effects; and by offering

---

*It would be easy to show, that the office of Lord Chancellor of Scotland was for ever abolished by the Act of Union, and that it cannot be revived without a violation of that Act. It might farther be shown that the appointment of Lord Sealfield to that honour, in 1713, and his protest against President Dalrymple, in the following year, arose from circumstances that do not affect the soundness of our general proposition; but the enquiry would neither be very entertaining or useful.

a summary of the views entertained on a subject that, from its
nature, was fully canvassed, we shall make our readers acquainted
with the reasons which convince us, that the inconveniences of
this branch of the plan were various, great, and unavoidable,
burthensome to the people, and injurious to the law, while its
advantages were altogether false and delusive.

If we have explained, intelligibly, the progress of a cause, from
its commencement, till its fate is unchangeably fixed in the
House of Lords, very strong reasons will be required for any addition to the length and expence of the journey; and a serious
increase of both was produced by the Court of Review. Had its
constitution been perfect, it was still a new inner-house, with a
strange name; enlarging the labours of litigation, degrading the
three chambers, and metamorphosing them from courts, who
judge of causes ripe for their decision, into little clusters of ordi-
naries, of no real utility, either in the preparation or determination of causes, since the causes depending before them were
previously *prepared* in their transit through the outer-house,
and were to be *judged* by that supereminent tribunal to which
they were hastening.

But the workmanship of this new inner-house was extremely
defective, neither calculated to settle doubtful points in law, nor
to obtain the confidence of the people. When the appeals from
the undivided court were discussed, the Chamber of Review
could consist only of four persons, the Lord Chancellor, the
Chief Baron, and the Presidents of the two chambers, from
which the appeal did not originate. These four judges might be
unanimous; and when they unanimously *affirmed* the interlocu-
tor of the inferior chamber, we do not deny that its authority,
as a legal precedent, was strengthened; but they might unanimously *reverse* an unanimous judgment of the inferior judicature; and in that event, we doubt extremely, whether the mere
superiority of rank, would have counteracted the deference
justly due to the opinion of the Chamber of Session. By a
change in the Court of Review, one of two judgments, precisely
similar, might be affirmed, and the other reversed. These, however, are suppositions too favourable to be regarded as tests of
the difficulty we are now examining. Three of these eminent
persons, the Chancellor, the Chief Baron, and one of the Presidents, were empowered to overturn the most deliberate judgments pronounced by any of the chambers. Would the unsuccess-

ful party be deterred, by that reversal, from seeking his remedy
in the House of Lords? Would the country have been disposed
to acquiesce in the judgment, as decisive of the law of the case?
According to the provisions of the bill, two of these persons
might have been entirely ignorant of the law of Scotland;* and
to them was committed the power of controuling the whole
judicial proceedings of the kingdom. The people of this country
are less likely than those of any other to be captivated by the
empty splendour of a name. A judgment, overturning the deliberate opinion of four or five professional men, compelled, by
their daily practice, to acquire skill in the science of law, required another recommendation than that it was pronounced
by an officer with an imposing title, since they are not ignorant,
that "no name, no power, no function, no artificial institution
whatever, can make the men of whom any system of authority
is composed, any other than God, and nature, and education,
and their habits of life, have made them."

In examining the probable consequences of the Review Chamber, we ought, further, to take into our contemplation, the
nature of the duties imposed on its members. The Chief Baron
was still to have his share of those of the Court of Exchequer.
The three presidents of the chambers were bound to execute
their several inferior departments, to go the circuits, and if the
Lord Justice Clerk was one of them, the chief burthen of the
criminal business of the kingdom rested on him. From this arrangement, several disadvantages might be apprehended. The
industry of these four judges could not be equal to the discharge
of their multifarious duties. The causes must be determined by
a fluctuating, and ever varying tribunal, or the pleadings must
be suspended for intervals, to the great delay of decision, and
the infinite embarrassment both of the judges and the counsel.
From the same circumstances, an undue influence would speedily be acquired by the chancellor. Not to mention the offensive
superiority of his rank, he was the only member of the court
who was never withdrawn by other avocations from its peculiar
duties; and, in this way, if the whole judicial authority did not
gradually centre in him, he must unavoidably have acquired a
more powerful preponderance, than ought ever, except in the

*It was generally understood that this defect was to be remedied: but our objec-
tion, even with that alteration, would not have been removed, though it would have
been weakened.

court of the last resort, where the anomaly is only justified by its necessity, to be enjoyed by one man.

And we think ourselves particularly bound to state, that the bill did most clearly violate that regard to individual justice, which ought to distinguish every act of the British Legislature. The Chief Baron, in addition to the appropriate duties of his office, as the head of the Revenue Court, was to be burthened with the labours of an ordinary judge in a new judicature; thus, at once subjecting him to services for which he did not stipulate, and lowering his rank and public estimation. The President of the College of Justice was to be so no longer but in name. He was to be placed at the head of one of the three chambers of co-ordinate jurisdiction, all equally inferior to the new court created by the bill; in the chair of which, an officer was to be placed, who must soon have monopolized a dangerous degree of power; and, by his rank, and other adventitious circumstances, must have overshadowed those degraded persons who were preposterously termed his colleagues. His labours were to be increased by those of the Court of Review, and, as we shall see, from the remaining parts of the bill, he was to be still farther tasked, and his official dignity still more lowered, by sending him to try civil causes at a circuit. These considerations, though affecting individuals alone, are not to be overlooked. The eminent persons we speak of were entitled to the undisturbed possession of all the rights and immunities attached to their franchise, as when they agreed to accept of it; and of all these, they were to be deprived, without their knowledge, when the bill was brought in, and against their declared opinion, after its contents were communicated to them as a part of the public. If this objection shall appear to be affected, or fantastic, we request those who differ from us, to consider what would be thought by the English bench, and English bar, of a proposition producing the same consequences to the chief justices of any of *their* courts.

But it is fair to turn the other end of the glass, and enquire what were the advantages anticipated from this part of the system. We have adverted to two of them, the uniformity of decisions among the different Chambers, and the establishment of the law of the country fixed on principle, and independent of minute circumstances. Both these, it is obvious, could be produced only by a well-constituted court, and our observations on the constitution of this court apply with equal force to the

advantages expected from it. The third advantage was the diminution of Appeals to the House of Lords. In this Court, it was said,
exempted from the labour of jury-trials, a greater degree of attention cannot fail to be bestowed, and the necessity and temptation to appeal will be diminished.

In this doctrine it is assumed, that the frequency of appeals, a
great and growing evil, is to be ascribed entirely to something in
the form or proceedings of the Court of Session; a proposition
we do, in the most unqualified manner, deny. Some appeals the
faulty constitution of the undivided Court may have produced;
but the far greater number now remaining undiscussed, are to be
ascribed alone to the manner in which judicial business is, and,
without a great change of system, must be, conducted in the
House of Lords. To look for a remedy for these in the Court of
Session, is to mistake the cause and seat of the distemper. Other
appeals are taken merely for the purpose of delay; and this
motive must continue to operate while two hundred causes
remain on the list of the House of Lords, of which a very small
number is annually decided. There is another class of judgments
complained of, in the hope that they may be tried by the principles of the law of England, rather than by those of that code by
which alone they ought to be governed. In questions involving
doubtful points of law, which it is of importance to set if possible at rest, the parties, as has been observed, might have been
deterred from appealing, unless the patrimonial interest be considerable, by the additional expence to which this new tribunal
would involve them;—but in none other could it produce that
effect, because it could not have attracted a greater degree of
confidence, and because the propensity to litigation is increased
by the succession of courts, to which, from one to one, the
litigant has access.

Another great department of this most comprehensive plan
still remains for our consideration. The Bill was entitled, "An
Act for establishing Trial by Jury in certain Civil Causes;" and
we have laid before our readers the formidable enumeration to
which this species of trial was to be extended. By far the larger
proportion of the enactments were intended to bring into operation, and subject to controul, the delicate and hazardous
machinery of the new engine, which, in a great class of cases,
was at once to supersede the forms by which the national
judicatories had long regulated their proceedings. Such particulars

of the plan as are suitable to a work like the present, we shall afterwards examine. We shall only at present repeat, that, besides the causes which were to be tried by a Jury in the Court of Session, it was provided, that Circuit Courts were to be tried twice a-year by the Presidents of the three Chambers, and that trial by jury was introduced into all the inferior courts in Scotland.

In canvassing the expediency of an individual measure, we may well spare our readers the fatigue of discussing the general merits of this mode of trial;—a speculation extremely difficult to those who, like us, have not known it by intimate experience, and long since exhausted. In Criminal and Revenue questions, tried between the Crown and the Subject, it merits every eulogium which can be bestowed on it. In the latter the Scottish system is as complete as that of England, the law as to these being the same in both parts of the island; in causes properly criminal it has attained the same point of perfection; and there almost is but one opinion, we believe, as to the expediency of supplying its deficiencies by bringing every case of the same description under the operation of the same admirable institution. For our own parts, we are disposed, for a variety of reasons, to attempt the same experiment on a scale considerably broader, and to try, by means of a jury, certain issues that are purely civil. With all these concessions, however, and under all these explanations, we must still doubt whether the jury-provisions *in this bill* were not liable to formidable and unsurmountable objections.

We throw out of our view, as foreign to the discussion, a topic to which some influence was attached,—that in establishing Trial by Jury in civil causes, nothing was aimed at but the revival of an usage familiar to the practice of our ancestors. In the sense which the remark implies, the fact is not historically correct. The inquests known in Scotland prior to the creation of the Court of Session, had no resemblance but in name to that institution to which it is assimilated; they were a coarse and imperfect machine, suited to the times when it had its origin, destitute of most, if not all, of those peculiarities on which the admirers of this mode of trial found their panegyric; and it has been unknown in Scotland for nearly 300 years. To consider the jury-establishment proposed in this Bill, or any other jury-establishment which, in these enlightened days, any legislator would suggest, as the enactment of an ancient law, as the re-animation of a form which has slept for upwards of two centuries, is a palpable fallacy;—the measure may be productive of good, but still it is undeniably an *innovation.*

We would farther submit, whether the fact, supposing it historically true, warrants the remark for which it is cited. The policy adopted in this Bill did not present to the people of Scotland an usage in favour of which any prejudice existed, independent of its intrinsic merits. The generation, which is supposed to have been acquainted with this institution, had long since gone by; the habits connected with it were forgotten as completely as if they had never been; and a Tribunal, framed on a quite different model, had centuries ago superseded those simple Courts, in whose proceedings something which bore the name of an Inquest participated. The prejudices in favour of jury-trial *in civilibus,* which may be conjectured to have prevailed before the establishment of the Court of Session, were lost in the lapse of ages; and therefore, in every intelligible acceptation of the term, the projected experiment was *new.* Nor ought it to be overlooked, that great circumspection was necessary in any attempt to engraft jury-trial on the form of a court made after a different frame, judicial forms being so interwoven with the system of rights and the essential rules of law, that any alteration in the one is extremely apt to extend itself to the other.

We feel it very difficult to associate with this subject any idea of political or personal liberty; both of which have been supposed to be secured, and even to be rendered more valuable, by means of the trial by jury in questions of private right. It is perhaps owing to our want of information, or to the phlegm and frigidity of our national character, that we cannot participate in that enthusiasm which the very name of this institution is said to excite in many a patriotic bosom. We can listen to the cabalistic sound of *Trial by Jury,* which has produced effects only to be paralleled by those of the mysterious words uttered by the Queen of the City of Enchantments, in the Arabian Tale, and retain the entire possession of our form and senses. We understand that sentiment of a celebrated author, that this barrier against the usurpation of power, in matters where *power* has any concern, may probably avert from our island the fate of many states that now exist but in history; and we think this great possession is peculiarly valuable in Scotland, where the privileges of the Public Prosecutor are not controuled by those of a Grand Jury. The merits of the establishment we are now examining are to be ascertained by a different test. It is merely a contrivance for attaining the ends of private justice, for developing the merits of a civil question in which individuals are interested; and that contrivance is the best which most speedily and effectually serves the purpose for which it was framed. In causes of that description no shield is necessary against the invasion of power; the issue is to be investigated without leaning or partiality, for whatever is unduly given to one party is unduly wrested from the other; and unless we take under our consideration those advantages which time or accident may have introduced, we see not what superiority can in the abstract be supposed to belong to this as a judicature for the determination of all or the greater number of civil actions. We discover no ground for suspecting that the judgments of a few well-educated and upright men may be influenced by any undue bias; that an interest merely patrimonial is more safely lodged in an obscure and evanescent body than in a dignified, independent, and permanent Tribunal, versed in the science to be administered, and responsible for the decisions they pronounce;—and we suspect that a philosopher, contemplating both in his closet, will augur more danger from a system which devolves on one set of men the responsibility of doctrines taught them by another, than from that system which attaches to the Judges all the consequences of the law they deliver. That by means of the Trial by Jury, there is preserved to the people that share which they ought to have in the administration of civil justice, is a topic we may forbear to discuss, until the right so to be preserved is made manifest to our comprehension. In courts of civil authority, we seek for nothing more than a fair and equal application of the immutable rules of justice; and in an enquiry regarding the establishment of such a court, we must dismiss from our attention many topics, to which, in their proper place, we should be among the readiest to defer.

When we turn to the legislative proposal that has suggested these remarks, too obvious to be of any utility, and too often repeated to be liable to question, we find that, with the whole of its accompanying forms, it is altogether English. An exact copy of a model had been taken, which, after being smoothed and decorated by English artists, after the English manner, was to be forced down into the heart of a machine, the movement of which was governed by powers and principles altogether dissimilar. We shall not repeat the general observations we have already submitted on the great hazard of this species of reform, by which the law of one civilized and independent country is made to bow the knee to that of another; and an alliance was to be formed betwixt two systems, proceeding from different sources, guided by different rules, and in which uniformity, if at all attainable, must be attended with those inconveniences which happen "in the interval between the promulgation of the new law, and the full and perfect knowledge thereof in those who are concerned in that law."* We are more disposed to illustrate the truth of them by noticing some of the provisions to be found in the Bill itself.

The enumeration of causes to be tried by a jury was highly exceptionable.

The first thing that must strike the most careless observer, is the *extent* of that enumeration. This may have been deemed necessary by those who have identified in their minds the liberty of the subject with trial by jury, in matters of private right; but they who consider it merely as an establishment for attaining the ends of justice, and who value it precisely as it is calculated to secure that object, would adopt the precautions under which all new experiments are introduced; and to these we have already had an opportunity of adverting. The constant and universal operation of jury trial was the *rule,* and the cases to be decided in the ancient mode were the *exceptions,* and within the rule it required little subtilty to bring almost every possible subject of litigation; that sort of trial was to be granted on the application of either party; and it was extended, as we have already mentioned, to all the inferior courts in Scotland, which are numerous.

The consequences of this were evil and various. The experiment itself could not be fairly so tried. Its extent must have proved fatal to it; for, no opportunity being afforded of attempting it in detail, that part of the measure which certainly was practicable, and probably would have been found expedient, would have been immediately condemned, by being coupled with the branch which must inevitably have failed. Another difficulty must have arisen from the dispositions and qualifications of those to whom the management of the machine was unavoidably committed. Many of the Judges were averse to jury trial; few, if any of them,

*Hale.

approved of that sanctioned by the Bill; and as the success of a new measure frequently depends as much on the operator as on its own merits, a favourable issue could not be anticipated to an attempt commenced with a preconceived expectation of its total failure, by those in whom such an opinion must have led to the failure. When we advert to those provisions which leave the species of trial in the option of the party, and to those extending it to the inferior courts; and when we remember that the ex- pence of summoning a jury, being pretty much the same in all cases, must be a grievous burthen in those involving a small patrimonial interest; we must be sensible that this became a most formidable engine of oppression to the poor in the hands of the rich. The same provisions, as they enabled a litigant in the inferior courts to bring a cause, at any stage of it, before the Court of Session, to be tried by a jury, must have had the double effect of superseding, or of rendering nearly useless, the jurisdic- tion of the Sheriffs in their several counties, and of overwhelm- ing the Supreme Court with numerous and petty disputes. There are other difficulties arising from the constitution of the Scots Court of Admiralty, which do not seem to have attracted the notice of those who framed the Bill; but these, with other mat- ters of detail, we think it unnecessary to dwell upon.

The *selection* of causes, we humbly think, was likewise in- judicious. No attempt was made to distinguish the cases cogniza- ble by the Court of Session as a Court of Equity, from those to which it was competent as a Court of Law, although they were necessarily governed by dissimilar modes of procedure. In those subject to the equitable jurisdiction of the Court, it was indis- pensible that the facts to be tried should be ascertained by the Court itself, and remedies and modes of discovery must be resorted to, quite unsuitable to a trial with the aid of a jury. Actions were to be tried by a jury, in which the evidence of wit- nesses was inadmissible by the law of Scotland, and yet the rule excluding that species of testimony was left untouched. There is another class, in which, for the most cogent reasons, execu- tion is allowed to take place in the face of averments, which, if proved, have the effect of establishing clearly the injustice of the decree so allowed to be carried into execution. We allude to those important questions that take their rise from the extended commerce and improved agriculture of this flourishing country. Under this Bill the whole of these questions were submitted to

the decision of a jury; and as by the simple expedient of putting
together a plausible story, a debtor was enabled to retain his
money, and a tenant to continue his possession, we may easily
conceive the extent of idle litigation which this branch of the
Bill would produce, and the hardship to which it would subject
the creditor and the landlord.

Connected with the first topic to which we have adverted,—
the number of cases in which jury-trial was introduced,—was the
establishment of Circuits. This might be advantageous after the
benefit of the hazarded experiment had been *proved;* attempted
in its infancy, this project could scarcely have failed to overlay
and extinguish it.

Throughout the whole of this enquiry we should bear in mind,
that in many respects, and in those more especially deserving our
present attention, the national character of the two kingdoms is
radically different. In England, the province of a jury, limiting
them to the consideration of the *fact* as distinguished from the
law, has long been understood; and it is seldom that they think
themselves warranted to disregard the charge of the Judge who
presides at the trial. In this country it is doubtful if a jury would
be found so passive an instrument. The middling classes are
better educated than those of the same description in England;
they are more sagacious, conceited, disputatious, and irritable;
much fonder of the exercise of power, and infinitely less disposed to bend to the authority of their superiors. We shall not
take upon us to conjecture whether time and experience would
have discovered antidotes to these dispositions. It is clear that
at first they must have produced much inconvenience, absurdity
and injustice; and we think it probable that the machine must
have stopt, and that the Bill would have been repealed, before
the means of carrying it into execution had been matured.

The proposed regulation, that the juries shall be unanimous in
their verdict, the only other provision in the Bill, which we think
it necessary particularly to notice, was suggested by views of
policy which we do not profess to understand. It is hardly con-
ceivable, that the unanimity of a Court, especially consisting of
so large a number as twelve persons, should ever form part of a
speculation on the best possible system of law; a requisite, which
seemed either to prevent the possibility of giving judgment on
the case, or to compel some of the Judges to acquiesce in a
result of which their consciences disapproved. It is peculiar to

the constitution of England, into which it found its way from
the operation of circumstances impossible to be traced, more
interesting to the antiquarian than to the philosopher; and accidental circumstances may very possibly have disarmed it of all
the inconvenience and absurdity, which in its own nature it
seems calculated to produce, and have rendered this apparent
anomaly positively beneficial. It is not without much consideration, that a contrivance, deriving its existence and value from
no principle in our common nature, produced by causes to be
found in the history of an individual country, ought to be given
to a nation which can only appretiate it from its abstract merits,
and which is imbued with prejudices tending to exaggerate all
its imperfections, and to neutralize whatever of beneficial it
may chance to contain.*

Its chief recommendation, that it would secure from every
juryman an attentive consideration of the cause at issue, would
not, we are afraid, overbalance the obstacles created by the
deep-rooted dislike of the people to an innovation inexplicable
to their understanding, and adverse to their religious opinions.
Their national character would prevent them from acquiescing,
through mere indolence, in the views entertained by others, and
sufficiently prompt them to investigate before they decided. Of
all this, the experience of juries in criminal cases, where a majority determines, affords satisfactory proof.

The other arguments adduced in support of this measure are
still less convincing. The practical benefit of an absurd theory
may deter a wise and cautious reformer from *abating* an *ancient*
anomaly, the good effects of which have been known; but it is
scarcely a decisive reason for introducing an anomaly; for on
such a scheme the absurdity is certain, and you take your chance
of its practical advantage. This is one of the reasons urged in support of the unanimity of juries.

This establishment, it was likewise supposed, would prevent an
invidious discovery of the names and votes of the jurors, and
exempt them from the resentment of the party against whom
their verdict is given; and would operate as a check on the
litigiousness of parties who may be encouraged to move for a

---

*"The unanimity of twelve men, so repugnant to all experience of their conduct,
passions and understandings, *could hardly in any age have been introduced into
practice by the deliberate act of the Legislature.*"—Christian's *Notes to Blackstone's
Commentaries,* Part III, c. 23.

new trial, on knowing that a verdict prejudicial to their interests was carried by a narrow majority.

We question the correctness of the first remark. We do not see for what reason the unanimity of the verdict should prevent a disclosure of the proceedings of the jury while they are inclosed; and we believe it will be found, that, in causes before the Court of Exchequer, the opinions of individual jurors may be learned with as little difficulty as in verdicts on criminal cases, returned by a majority of voices. Supposing, however, the remark to be true, we ought, before attaching any great importance to it, to ascertain, whether a Scots jury would not be disposed to brave all the consequences of the discovery of their votes, rather than be compelled to surrender their freedom of opinion, and to concur in a verdict contrary to their sense of the truth of the case.

The soundness of the second position is at least equally doubtful. It may be thought, that, in a mere question of private right, the parties ought to be afforded an opportunity of distinguishing a verdict that is really unanimous, from a verdict which, though carried solely by one vote, is declared to be unanimous by the force of the statute in that case made and provided. The costs of failure are the only legitimate check to intemperate litigation; and, in involving the whole proceedings in mystery, we resort to an expedient more suited to the personal convenience and indolence of the judge, than to the ends of substantial justice.

If these views, or any considerable part of them, be correct, much benefit could not be anticipated from the project sanctioned by the bill. It set afloat a spirit of change that must speedily have extended itself to every branch of the law of Scotland. The system of jury trial, in particular, settled on so broad a basis, must have occasioned great individual injustice, and incalculable perplexity to the whole profession of the law, judges, counsel, and solicitors. The bill did not, and could not, contain a detail of all the collateral aids requisite for the effectual operation of so vast a machine. Every instant new cases and new combinations of circumstances must have emerged, for which it was necessary immediately to provide; and, as no part of the scheme bore any congeniality with the ancient body of the law, the judges were deprived of the great benefit arising from analogy, and would have been compelled to solve the difficulty by the first scrambling expedient that suggested itself, deduced from no preconceived opinion, and moulded by no principle drawn from the stores of their professional experience. That very experience would have proved the source of embarrassment. The attempt was more likely to have proved successful, if committed to men of respectable talents, less versant in the peculiarities of the law of Scotland, than it would have been in the hands of judges, decidedly inimical to it, whose minds were imbued with doctrines, that, instead of lighting them on their journey, served only to bewilder and lead them astray. The probability is, as we have already hinted, that the measure would soon have been abandoned, as impracticable, and the bill repealed. But the waters would not have quietly returned to their former channel. Not to mention the mischief which in the *interim* many individuals must have suffered, the foundation of ancient establishments would have been broken up; principles, hitherto venerated as sacred, would have been violated; while a precedent was given to injudicious and intemperate tampering, that, at some future period, might have led to novelties equally great, and equally hazardous. In other respects, too, the country must have been injured. A number of offices were to be erected, some of them offensive from their splendour, and all of them united together, productive of great public expence; the holders of which, though the duties to be performed came to an end, had a right to expect indemnification from the state.

We have mentioned, that the bill was brought into the House of Lords on the 16th of February, 1807, by Lord Grenville, who was then prime minister; to the purity of whose motives, we join our feeble voice to that of the country, in yielding our most unqualified assent. In the course of the following month, from circumstances into which it would be preposterous here to enter, a complete change took place in his majesty's councils; in May the parliament was dissolved; and no serious attempt was made to revive a discussion that must have proved fruitless.

Soon after the new parliament met, the Lord Chancellor Eldon laid before the House of Lords a new plan for attaining the same desirable end, under the form of a bill, entitled, "An Act touching the Administration of Justice in Scotland, and touching appeals to the House of Lords." The progress of this bill, it is now unnecessary to trace. It was introduced into the House on the 10th of August, 1807, and immediately printed and circulated;

the consideration of it was reassumed during the next session of parliament, in the beginning of 1808; and, after some slight opposition in both Houses, it finally passed into a law in the month of July, 1808.

We must preface our examination of this statute, by offering our tribute of praise to the spirit in which it was framed. The object of its author plainly was to avoid the danger of precipitate and extensive change in an established system of law, and to obtain the sanction of the legislature to a reform, which, if it failed in the trial, might be abandoned without inconvenience, or, in the event of a more favourable result, might be adopted as the basis of farther improvement.

As a reason for making some new arrangements in the Court of Session, and to facilitate the dispatch of business, the act assigns the great extension of commerce, manufactories, and population, and the great multiplication of transactions in Scotland, which have greatly increased the number of law-suits brought into that court. It provides, that, in future, the Court shall sit in two divisions; one consisting of the Lord President of the College of Justice, and seven of the Ordinary Lords of Session; and the other, of the Lord Justice Clerk, and six of the Ordinary Lords. One judge of each division is directed to officiate weekly, as Ordinary, in the Outer-House and Bill-Chamber.—The Judges, in their respective divisions, or their quorum, which is four, possess the same power that formerly belonged to the whole Court. The Presidents have one voice, but not a casting voice: in case of an equality, the cause remains for subsequent discussion; and, if the voices shall again be equal, one of the Lords Ordinary, of the same division, in the order of seniority as Judges, is to be called in, to be at the discussion, and to have a vote. In cases of importance and difficulty, it is declared lawful for either Division to state questions of law arising on such cases, for the opinion of the Judges of the other; and all causes may, at the option of the party instituting them, be brought before either of the Courts. These are the most material provisions in the first part of the bill.

The second respected appeals to the House of Lords. No appeal was allowed against judgments of a Lord Ordinary, or interlocutory judgments, as distinguished from judgments on the whole merits of the cause, except by permission of the Division. On lodging an appeal, a copy of the petition of appeal is directed to be laid before the Division to which the cause belongs; and authority is given to them to regulate all matters relative to interim possession, or execution, and payment of costs; such regulations or orders not being competent to be appealed from.

These enactments, important as they are, did not provide an effectual remedy to all the evils experienced in the administration of justice, and still less did they afford an opportunity of realizing those views which speculative men had entertained for improving the whole system. The bill, therefore, farther empowered his majesty to issue a commission in favour of persons who shall make enquiry into the forms of the courts, the fees of clerks, the proceedings of inferior courts, and other matters. They were likewise appointed to make enquiry how far it might be of evident utility to introduce into the proceedings of the Court of Session, or any other court in Scotland, trial by jury, in any and what cases of a civil nature, and in what manner and form that mode of trial could be most usefully established:—The report to be made to his majesty, and afterwards to be laid before both Houses of Parliament.

We regret, that, in one important particular, this statute is equally deficient with Lord Grenville's bill, no provision being made for diminishing the number of judges. It may be still competent, under the commission, to establish constantly, in the Outer-House, a certain number of the judges to be hereafter appointed to try causes individually; but, tho' we are aware of the benefit of this arrangement, we think that a diminution in the number of judges is an essential part of any plan of radical and complete reform. The objections formerly urged to the separation into three chambers, render it unnecessary for us to state our entire approbation of the arrangement made by this act: and the experience that has ensued, completely demonstrates that this arrangement is right; for the arrears left by the undivided court, were exhausted within a year after the statute passed, and the whole judicial business is now conducted without fatigue to the judges, and to the satisfaction of the country.

The branch of the bill respecting appeals, seems as well calculated to prevent frivolous appeals, and to secure the rights of parties presenting appeals, as any regulation affecting the Court of Session that can be devised. The complete remedy is to be sought elsewhere.

It is farther proper to mention, that, by an act which passed during the same session of parliament, it was provided, that no stipend of any clergyman, which had been augmented prior to its date, should be again augmented until the expiration of 15 years from the date of the decree granting him the augmentation; and that such stipends as should be augmented after the bill received the royal assent, should not be increased for 20 years subsequent to the decree of augmentation.

Although it would be presumptuous to offer any opinion on the matters remitted to the commissioners, who have not yet made their report, we cannot conclude without expressing an earnest hope, that the trial by jury will be extended to some cases which at present are decided by the Court of Session. The prevailing sentiment undoubtedly is, that this mode of procedure is of evident utility in certain descriptions of causes; and, in deference to the public opinion, the experiment ought to be tried. In the cases to which it is suited, and we are persuaded there are such, it would serve the ends of justice, with little delay or expence to the parties, and it would most certainly tend to liberalize the profession of the law. We would extend it to all criminal actions; to all actions founded on delinquency; and other questions, depending on an issue in fact, might be settled by the verdict of a jury, provided the court shall, in its discretion, deem that mode of investigation practicable.

We shall offer no apology for the freedom with which we have investigated both these legislative measures. We have been actuated by no motive we are ashamed to avow. We are unalterably attached to that system of jurisprudence, under the protection of which, our native country has advanced from poverty and rudeness, to prosperity and civilization; and, if we cannot improve, we would at least preserve, our undoubted and invaluable inheritance, without waste or dilapidation.

Index

213